Collins

SCRABBLE
BRAND Crossword Game

HINTS & TIPS

Published by Collins
An imprint of HarperCollins Publishers
Westerhill Road
Bishopbriggs
Glasgow G64 2QT

Second Edition 2016

10 9 8 7 6 5 4 3 2 1

ISBN 978-0-00-758911-1

Collins® is a registered trademark of
HarperCollins Publishers Limited

SCRABBLE™ and associated trademarks and
trade dress are owned by, and used under
licence from, J. W. Spear & Sons Limited,
a subsidiary of Mattel, Inc. © 2016 Mattel,
Inc. All Rights Reserved.

www.harpercollins.co.uk/scrabble

Typeset by Davidson Publishing Solutions,
Glasgow

Printed in Great Britain by Clays Ltd,
St Ives plc

A catalogue record for this book is available
from the British Library.

If you would like to comment on any aspect
of this book, please contact us at the given
address or online.
E-mail: puzzles@harpercollins.co.uk
facebook.com/collinsdictionary
@collinsdict

CONTRIBUTORS
Barry Grossman
Allan Simmons

FOR THE PUBLISHER
Gerry Breslin
Kerry Ferguson

MIX
Paper from
responsible sources
FSC™ C007454

Contents

Introduction

Collins Scrabble Hints and Tips is aimed at casual Scrabble
enthusiasts, or those who like to Scrabble dabble. It deals
with each letter of the alphabet in turn, covering brief
advantages and disadvantages of each letter, followed by
a selection of useful and manageable wordlists of words
beginning with that letter. Sprinkled throughout the book
are various hints related to word learning or general advice
to improve your game.

    For the most part the wordlists are not intended to be
thorough and complete because that would make them too
unwieldy and cluttered with words which may not actually
be that useful for Scrabble. They are designed to serve as an
introduction to useful words that you might be unfamiliar
with and to inspire you to increase your Scrabble vocabulary.
For example, the lists of three-letter words exclude very
common words and those that cannot be formed from
two-letter words (unless they are worth eight points face-
value or more). Any words that might be deemed offensive
are also excluded. Having said that, because of their
importance in the game, the lists of two-letter words are
complete, as too are the lists showing how those two-letter
words can be extended into three-letter words. There is also
a complete dictionary of all of the two- and three-letter words
and definitions at the end of the book for added interest.

The basics

What is Scrabble?

Scrabble is a game for two to four players or, occasionally, teams. Each player draws seven tiles at the start of the game and takes it in turns to form words on the board. After the first word is played, every word formed must touch or intersect a word already on the board, incorporating the tile at the crossover point in the new word. When letters have been played, they are replaced at each turn by drawing tiles from a bag to make up a full rack of seven. High scores may be achieved by using the rarer, high-value letters, by forming words on premium squares on the board, and by playing all seven letters at once to achieve a 50-point bonus.

The Scrabble set

The full list of letters and their values in the Scrabble set is as follows:

Letter (Vowel)	Number in set	Value
A	9	1
E	12	1
I	9	1
O	8	1
U	4	1
BLANK	2	0

Letter (Consonant)	Number in set	Value
B	2	3
C	2	3
D	4	2
F	2	4
G	3	2

H	2	4
J	1	8
K	1	5
L	4	1
M	2	3
N	6	1
P	2	3
Q	1	10
R	6	1
S	4	1
T	6	1
V	2	4
W	2	4
X	1	8
Y	2	4
Z	1	10

Origins

Scrabble was invented by an American: Alfred Butts.
It was originally called Lexico when it was invented in
the 1930s but became successful in its current form in
the 1960s.

Gameplay tips

Use a dictionary when you play to check which words
are eligible when challenged and to avoid any arguments.
We suggest *Collins Scrabble Dictionary*, where you will find the
meanings for all of the words used in this book.

Shuffle the tiles on your rack: rearrange them, jiggle them
around, and place them in alphabetical order. Also try to form
prefixes or suffixes, and verb inflections (-ED, -ING, etc) as
this can help to form words in your mind.

Play longer words early on in a game if you can to get the board open to reach those elusive triple-word squares. The more places there are to make plays the more you can make wise choices and avoid getting a clogged up board and be forced just to play one or two letters at a time.

The challenge rule: you may challenge a word your opponent plays. If your challenge is successful, i.e. the disputed word is not in the *Collins Scrabble Dictionary*, or the dictionary you are using, your opponent takes back his or her tiles and loses their turn.

> **Note on diagrams:** Diagrams in this section depicting word plays, for aesthetics, don't necessarily show words covering the centre square. In actual games the first move must cover the centre square.

Forming words

Scrabble words can be formed in several ways other than by simply playing a new word to intersect with a word already on the board through a common letter, or by adding letters to an existing word. The key to successful Scrabble is constant awareness of the various opportunities for forming words on the board.

When words are formed in ways other than simple intersection or expansion, more than one new word is created in the process, potentially giving a higher score. The main ways of doing this are 'hooking' and 'parallel play'.

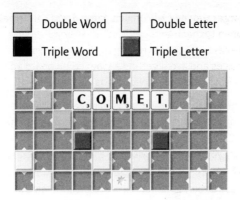

Hooking

This is the term for the act of 'hanging' one word on another – the word already on the board acts as a 'hook' on which the other word can be hung – changing the first word in the process. The player adds a letter to the beginning or end of a word already on the board in the process, transforming it into a longer word, as in the following example:

Player A has played COMET. Player B then plays HOUSE on the end of COMET, forming COMETH and HOUSE, and scoring 13 for COMETH plus 16 for HOUSE. COMET is an 'end-hook'; any word ending in H or S can be 'hung' on it.

S is a particularly useful letter when hooking, as most nouns have a plural formed by adding it to the end of the singular.

The following example shows how to add a 'front hook' to the word OX:

Here the player gets the 17 points for FOX as well as those for FICKLE. Thus hooking is generally a more profitable method of word formation than simply playing a word through, or adjacent to, one that is already on the board. In particular, hooking allows players the chance to benefit from high-scoring power tiles played by an opponent, as with the X in FOX in the above example. It is important to note that, when scoring double words like this, only the face value of tiles already played is counted and if the original word had been played on a premium square its bonus value would not count.

Blocking

Words that cannot form other words by having a letter added to their front or back are known as blockers, as they prevent other players from adding words by hooking.

Blockers are useful for preventing your opponent from capitalizing on words that you have played, and for blocking off sections of the board. If you are ahead on the scoreboard in the latter part of a game, you may wish to play tactically by concentrating on blockers, and thereby prevent your opponent from getting further opportunities to play high-scoring words.

Some examples of blocker words are as follows:

Parallel play

A word can be played parallel to one already on the board, so that one or more tiles are in contact, forming secondary words. Such plays can be more difficult than hooking because you need to form one additional word for each tile in contact with the word already on the board. These will usually be two-letter words, which is why these short words are so vital to the game. The more two-letter words you know, the greater your opportunities for fitting words onto the board through parallel plays – and of running up some impressive scores!

Player A has played:

Player B now 'tags' TROLL, also forming ET, AR and NO (all valid two-letter words). This play scores ten for TROLL, two each for ET and AR, and four for NO, so a total of 18.

Short words are obviously very handy for parallel plays, as seen in the following example:

Power tiles

It is important to use the 'power tiles' (J, Q, X and Z) wisely when they land on your rack. Learning some of the words that contain these letters will help you to employ the power tiles to maximum effect when they appear on your rack. Of special interest are words that use Q but not U, as these allow you to avoid the problem of needing to find a U to play your high-scoring Q tile. In the average two-player Scrabble game, you are likely to have two of the power tiles on your rack at some point during play and learning some words using these letters will help you to manoeuvre them onto premium squares for really high scores.

Two- and three-letter words

Two-letter words are essential for parallel plays: generally, you need one two-letter word for every point of contact. Three-letter words are also very useful in Scrabble, as a crowded board will often prevent you from playing longer words late in the game. While many two- and three-letter words will be familiar, it's a good idea to learn the less common ones, as knowing whether a given combination of two or three letters is a valid word can be vital when you are trying to get a high-scoring set of tiles onto the board through parallel plays or hooking.

The appendices starting on page 365 list all of the two- and three-letter words that are valid for Scrabble.

Using the S and blank tiles

S

The S tile is very useful as it can be placed at the end of many words (nearly every noun and verb, in fact) thus making it the ideal tile for end-hooking. This quality also makes S very handy for bonus words, as the odds of making a bonus word from six tiles plus an S are greatly improved from making a bonus from seven letters. However, a player can often get a good score without trying for a bonus by simply hooking an existing word, and scoring for both. S is also well suited for use as a front hook, particularly alongside words starting with H, L, P or T. Also watch out for hooking an S onto a Q word.

Blank

A blank tile has no value but may be used in the place of any letter, thus making it extremely useful, especially when it comes to forming bonus words. It is very important to use the blank tile wisely and not to waste it on a low-scoring word. Look at the letters on your rack and when considering the blank tile, run through the alphabet in your mind when thinking of the letter value to assign to it. Remember, it is much easier to form a bonus word from six letters plus one which you can choose than by using seven letters over which you have no control, so save the blank for a bonus word if you can. Finally, never ever change a blank tile!

Bonus words

Always remember that no matter how many words you form,
you are likely to achieve a higher score by playing all seven of
your letters in one go, as this earns you a 50-point bonus.
It takes a lot of power tiles or bonus squares to achieve
50 points, so playing a bonus word (bingo in the US) is the
most reliable method of getting an impressive score.

A bonus play generally involves a word of seven or eight
letters – either by attaching a complete seven-letter word
parallel to, or hooking a word already on the board, or by
forming an eight-letter word intersecting an existing word
by playing all seven tiles.

Words ineligible for Scrabble

There are several categories of ineligible words:
• Hyphenated words
• Words from multiple-word foreign phrases
• Capitalized words
• Abbreviations
• Words over 15 letters in length

Scrabble glossary

BLOCKER a word which cannot have a letter added to its beginning or end to form another valid word.

BONUS WORD a word that uses all seven of a player's tiles, earning a 50-point bonus.

END-HOOK a word that can form another valid word by having a letter added to its end.

FRONT-HOOK a word that can form another valid word by having a letter added to its front.

HEAVY WORDS words that have many consonants in relation to vowels.

HOOKING playing a word perpendicular to and in contact with another word, so that the first played word (the hook) has a letter added to it.

LIGHT WORDS words that have many vowels in relation to consonants.

PARALLEL PLAY playing a word parallel to, and in contact with, another word so that a valid word is formed at each point of contact.

POWER TILES (J, Q, X or Z) the tiles that score eight (J and X) or ten (Q and Z) points.

PREMIUM SQUARE one of the squares on the board that provides extra points: double letter, double word, triple letter or triple word.

RACK the small plastic shelf that holds a player's tiles; the combination of letters on the tiles currently held.

TILE one of the small plaques bearing letters that are used to form words on the board.

Essential info
Value: 1 point
Number in set: 9

A is a common tile and is very useful for forming short words to squeeze into tight corners, as it can be added easily to the majority of other tiles to form two-letter words. Even AA is a word, a Hawaiian word for rough volcanic rock, 2 points. A is also very helpful for short, high-scoring words such as AXE (10 points, or 9 points with its US variant AX). Some more unusual examples of three-letter words include AAL (an Asian shrub, 3 points), APO (a type of protein, 5 points) and the high-scoring ADZ (a tool for cutting roof tiles, 13 points). A is one of the letters of the RETAIN set and is therefore a good letter to keep if trying to get a bonus word.

Two-letter words beginning with A

AA	AI	AT
AB	AL	AW
AD	AM	AX
AE	AN	AY
AG	AR	
AH	AS	

Some three-letter words beginning with A

AAH	AJI	APO
AAL	AKA	ARB
ABA	ALA	ARD
ABB	ALB	ARF
ABO	ALF	ARY
ABY	ALP	ASP
ACH	ALT	ASS
ADO	ALU	ATT
ADZ	AMA	AWA
AFF	AME	AWK
AGA	AMI	AWL
AGO	AMP	AWN
AHA	AMU	AYE
AHI	ANA	AYU
AIA	ANE	AZO
AIN	ANI	
AIT	ANN	

HOOKS

Hooking requires a player to look at words already on the board without being distracted by their pronunciation. This can lead to simple hooking solutions being overlooked. Fortunately, A is one of the easier tiles to play as a hook or a tag and it can be front-hooked to many words as their negating form (e.g. MORAL can be changed to AMORAL).

Some front-hooks
Two letters to three

A-AH	A-ID	A-NE
A-AL	A-IN	A-NY
A-AS	A-IS	A-PE
A-BA	A-IT	A-PO
A-BO	A-KA	A-RE
A-BY	A-LA	A-SH
A-CH	A-MA	A-TE
A-DO	A-ME	A-WE
A-GO	A-MI	A-YE
A-HA	A-MU	A-YU
A-HI	A-NA	A-ZO

Three letters to four

A-BED	A-JAR	A-NON
A-BET	A-KIN	A-NOW
A-BID	A-LAP	A-PAY
A-BUT	A-LAY	A-POD
A-BYE	A-LEE	A-RED
A-DRY	A-LIT	A-RID
A-FAR	A-LOO	A-ROW
A-GAS	A-LOW	A-RUM
A-GIN	A-MEN	A-SEA
A-HEM	A-MID	A-SHY
A-HIS	A-NAN	A-TAP
A-HOY	A-NEW	A-TOP
A-IDE	A-NIL	A-UGH

| A-VOW | A-WED | A-WRY |
| A-WAY | A-WEE | A-YES |

Four letters to five

A-BACK	A-GAPE	A-LINE
A-BAND	A-GATE	A-LIST
A-BASE	A-GAVE	A-LIVE
A-BASH	A-GAZE	A-LOFT
A-BASK	A-GENE	A-LONE
A-BEAM	A-GENT	A-LONG
A-BEAR	A-GIST	A-LOUD
A-BIDE	A-GLEE	A-LURE
A-BLED	A-GLOW	A-MAIN
A-BLOW	A-GONE	A-MASS
A-BODE	A-GOOD	A-MATE
A-BOIL	A-GRIN	A-MAZE
A-BORE	A-HEAD	A-MEND
A-BOUT	A-HEAP	A-MICE
A-BRAY	A-HIGH	A-MINE
A-BRIM	A-HIND	A-MISS
A-BUZZ	A-HINT	A-MOLE
A-CHAR	A-HOLD	A-MOVE
A-COLD	A-HULL	A-MUCK
A-CORN	A-ISLE	A-MUSE
A-CUTE	A-ITCH	A-NEAR
A-DOWN	A-KING	A-NIGH
A-DOZE	A-LACK	A-NODE
A-DUST	A-LAND	A-PACE
A-FEAR	A-LANE	A-PAGE
A-FIRE	A-LANT	A-PAID
A-FOOT	A-LATE	A-PART
A-FORE	A-LEFT	A-PEAK
A-FOUL	A-LIEN	A-PEEK
A-GAIN	A-LIKE	A-PERT

A-PING   A-STUN   A-WAIT
A-PORT   A-SWAY   A-WAKE
A-READ   A-SWIM   A-WARD
A-REAL   A-TILT   A-WARE
A-REAR   A-TOLL   A-WARN
A-RISE   A-TONE   A-WASH
A-ROSE   A-TRIP   A-WAVE
A-SCOT   A-VAIL   A-WING
A-SHED   A-VALE   A-WOKE
A-SIDE   A-VAST   A-WORK
A-SKEW   A-VINE   A-YELP
A-STIR   A-VOID

Five letters to six

A-BASED   A-CRAWL   A-GUISE
A-BASER   A-CROSS   A-HORSE
A-BATED   A-CUTER   A-LIGHT
A-BIDED   A-DREAD   A-LINED
A-BIDER   A-DRIFT   A-LINER
A-BLATE   A-DROIT   A-MATED
A-BLAZE   A-ETHER   A-MAZED
A-BLING   A-FIELD   A-MIDST
A-BLOOM   A-FLAME   A-MORAL
A-BLUSH   A-FLOAT   A-MOUNT
A-BOARD   A-FOCAL   A-MOVED
A-BODED   A-FRESH   A-MUSED
A-BORNE   A-FRONT   A-MUSER
A-BOUND   A-GAZED   A-MUSIC
A-BRAID   A-GEIST   A-NEATH
A-BROAD   A-GHAST   A-NIGHT
A-BURST   A-GLARE   A-PIECE
A-BUSED   A-GLEAM   A-RAISE
A-CATER   A-GOING   A-REACH
A-CIDER   A-GREED   A-RIDER

A-RIGHT	A-STARE	A-UNTIE
A-RILED	A-START	A-VAUNT
A-RISEN	A-STERN	A-VENGE
A-ROUND	A-STONE	A-VENUE
A-ROUSE	A-STONY	A-VERSE
A-SCEND	A-STOOP	A-VISED
A-SCENT	A-STRAY	A-VITAL
A-SHAKE	A-STRUT	A-VOUCH
A-SHAME	A-SWARM	A-VOWED
A-SHIER	A-SWING	A-VOWER
A-SHINE	A-SWIRL	A-WAKED
A-SHORE	A-SWOON	A-WAKEN
A-SLAKE	A-TONAL	A-WATCH
A-SLANT	A-TONED	A-WEARY
A-SLEEP	A-TONER	A-WEIGH
A-SLOPE	A-TONIC	A-WHEEL
A-SLOSH	A-TOPIC	A-WHILE
A-SMEAR	A-TRIAL	A-WHIRL
A-SPINE	A-TWAIN	A-WOKEN
A-SPIRE	A-TWEEL	A-WRACK
A-SPORT	A-TWEEN	A-WRONG
A-SPOUT	A-TWIXT	A-ZONAL
A-SQUAT	A-TYPIC	

Six letters to seven

A-BANDED	A-BOUGHT	A-CUTELY
A-BASHED	A-BRAYED	A-CUTEST
A-BASING	A-BRIDGE	A-CYCLIC
A-BATING	A-BROACH	A-DEEMED
A-BETTED	A-BUBBLE	A-DUSTED
A-BETTER	A-BUTTED	A-FEARED
A-BIDING	A-BUTTER	A-GENTRY
A-BIOTIC	A-CLINIC	A-GROUND
A-BODING	A-CORNED	A-LAYING

6

A-LENGTH
A-LINING
A-LONELY
A-MASSED
A-MAZING
A-MENDED
A-MENDER
A-MENTAL
A-MOTION
A-MOVING
A-MUSING
A-NEARED
A-NOTHER
A-PAYING
A-PLENTY
A-QUIVER
A-RAISED
A-REALLY
A-RIPPLE
A-RISING

A-SCARED
A-SCONCE
A-SCRIBE
A-SEPTIC
A-SHAMED
A-SHIEST
A-SHIVER
A-SOCIAL
A-SPIRED
A-SPRAWL
A-SPREAD
A-SPROUT
A-SQUINT
A-STABLE
A-STATIC
A-STONED
A-STOUND
A-STRAND
A-STRICT
A-STRIDE

A-SUDDEN
A-SUNDER
A-THIRST
A-THRILL
A-TINGLE
A-TONING
A-TROPHY
A-VAILED
A-VENGED
A-VENGER
A-VERTED
A-VOIDED
A-VOIDER
A-VOWING
A-WAITED
A-WAITER
A-WAKING
A-WARDED
A-WARDER
A-WARNED

Seven letters to eight

A-BANDING
A-BASHING
A-BATABLE
A-BEARING
A-BEGGING
A-BETTING
A-BOUNDED
A-BRAIDED
A-BRAYING
A-BRIDGED
A-BROOKED
A-BUTTING

A-CENTRIC
A-CERATED
A-CHROMIC
A-COSMISM
A-COSMIST
A-DEEMING
A-DREADED
A-DUSTING
A-DYNAMIC
A-ESTHETE
A-ESTIVAL
A-ETHERIC

A-FEARING
A-FEBRILE
A-FLUTTER
A-GENESIS
A-GENETIC
A-GLIMMER
A-GLITTER
A-GNOSTIC
A-GRAPHIC
A-GREEING
A-GRISING
A-GUISING

A-KINESES
A-KINESIS
A-KINETIC
A-LEGGING
A-LIGHTED
A-LOGICAL
A-MASSING
A-MAZEDLY
A-MEIOSIS
A-MENAGED
A-MENDING
A-MIDMOST
A-MIDSHIP
A-MISSING
A-MITOSIS
A-MITOTIC
A-MORALLY
A-MORTISE
A-MOUNTED
A-NEARING
A-NEURISM
A-NODALLY
A-NOINTED
A-NOINTER
A-PIARIST
A-PLASTIC
A-PRACTIC

A-PYRETIC
A-PYREXIA
A-RAISING
A-REACHED
A-READING
A-RETTING
A-SCENDED
A-SCRIBED
A-SEISMIC
A-SEPTATE
A-SHAMING
A-SHINESS
A-SLAKING
A-SOCIALS
A-SPARKLE
A-SPERSED
A-SPHERIC
A-SPIRANT
A-SPIRING
A-SPORTED
A-STARTED
A-STERNAL
A-STEROID
A-STONIED
A-STONING
A-STONISH
A-STUNNED

A-SYNERGY
A-SYSTOLE
A-TECHNIC
A-TONALLY
A-TREMBLE
A-TROPHIC
A-TROPINE
A-TROPISM
A-TWITTER
A-TYPICAL
A-VAILING
A-VAUNTED
A-VENGING
A-VENTURE
A-VERSION
A-VERTING
A-VOIDING
A-VOUCHED
A-VOUCHER
A-WAITING
A-WAKENED
A-WAKENER
A-WANTING
A-WARDING
A-WARNING
A-WEARIED
A-WEATHER

Handy Hint: Challenge!

Never be afraid to challenge a word which looks unusual, misspelled or which you do not recognise. Many an invalid word has slipped through the net this way. Unless you are playing at a tournament with a penalty for invalid challenges, you have nothing to lose by challenging your opponent. Occasionally, some gamesmanship occurs in Scrabble too and your opponent may be hoping you will let their mistakes or guesses go unnoticed or unchallenged.

Some end-hooks

Two letters to three

AB-A	ER-A	OM-A
AG-A	ET-A	OP-A
AH-A	FA-A	OR-A
AI-A	GO-A	PE-A
AL-A	HO-A	PI-A
AM-A	IT-A	PO-A
AN-A	KO-A	SH-A
AW-A	MA-A	TE-A
BA-A	MO-A	UT-A
BO-A	OB-A	YE-A
CH-A	OD-A	ZO-A

Three letters to four

AID-A	GAL-A	MES-A
ALB-A	GAM-A	MON-A
ARE-A	GIG-A	NAN-A
BET-A	HAH-A	OFF-A
BON-A	IDE-A	ORC-A
COD-A	KAT-A	PAP-A
COL-A	KOR-A	PIC-A
DAD-A	LAM-A	PIN-A
DIV-A	LAV-A	PIT-A
DOP-A	MAL-A	PUP-A
FET-A	MAM-A	RAJ-A
FIL-A	MAY-A	RAT-A
GAG-A	MEG-A	ROM-A

ROT-A	TIN-A	VEG-A
SAG-A	TOG-A	VIN-A
SOD-A	TOR-A	VIS-A
SOM-A	TUB-A	WET-A
SOY-A	TUN-A	ZED-A

Four letters to five

BALS-A	GUAN-A	PRIM-A
BURK-A	HOND-A	PUCK-A
CHIN-A	HYEN-A	PUFF-A
COCO-A	KANG-A	PUNK-A
COMM-A	LAIK-A	RAGG-A
COST-A	LOOF-A	RAIT-A
DELT-A	MANG-A	RAST-A
DERM-A	MANI-A	RUED-A
DICT-A	MOCH-A	SALS-A
DOON-A	MOOL-A	SUNN-A
DRAM-A	MULL-A	TAIG-A
FACT-A	MURR-A	TIAR-A
FAUN-A	PAND-A	TONK-A
FELL-A	PARK-A	VEST-A
FETT-A	PASH-A	VILL-A
FLOR-A	PAST-A	VIOL-A
GAMB-A	POLK-A	VOLT-A

Five letters to six

BROTH-A	MAXIM-A	PLASM-A
CREST-A	MIASM-A	QUANT-A
FASCI-A	MINIM-A	RHUMB-A
FAVEL-A	NYMPH-A	SATYR-A
FIEST-A	ORBIT-A	SCARP-A
GRAMP-A	ORGAN-A	SENOR-A
KORUN-A	PAGOD-A	SHISH-A
LORIC-A	PATIN-A	SPIRE-A

STELL-A   TAPET-A   VALET-A
STERN-A   TARSI-A   WATCH-A
TALUK-A   TUNIC-A

Six letters to seven

ADDEND-A   DRACHM-A   PROPYL-A
ALUMIN-A   EMBLEM-A   QUININ-A
ANALOG-A   EXOTIC-A   ROBUST-A
ANONYM-A   FAVELL-A   ROSACE-A
ARABIC-A   FORMIC-A   ROTUND-A
ASHRAM-A   GALLET-A   SCHISM-A
BUZUKI-A   GALLIC-A   SECRET-A
CANDID-A   GUNNER-A   SELECT-A
CANTAL-A   INFANT-A   SEQUEL-A
CEMENT-A   INGEST-A   SERING-A
CHIASM-A   KHALIF-A   SHEIKH-A
CHIMER-A   LAVOLT-A   SIGNOR-A
CHOLER-A   LOCUST-A   SULTAN-A
CODEIN-A   MADRAS-A   TAMBUR-A
CORTIN-A   MOMENT-A   TARTAN-A
CURIOS-A   PAISAN-A   TAVERN-A
CYATHI-A   PERSON-A   TEMPER-A
DEJECT-A   PLACIT-A
DEODAR-A   POTASS-A

Seven letters to eight

ANGELIC-A   CHAMPAC-A   EXCERPT-A
ANTEFIX-A   CHARISM-A   FASCIST-A
ARBORET-A   CISTERN-A   HEPATIC-A
AUTOMAT-A   CONSULT-A   JAVELIN-A
BASILIC-A   DEMENTI-A   MANDIOC-A
BOTANIC-A   DIASTEM-A   MARCHES-A
BRONCHI-A   DULCIAN-A   MARINER-A
BROUGHT-A   EPITHEM-A   MATADOR-A

MELODIC-A	RAKSHAS-A	SYNTAGM-A
MOLLUSC-A	RANCHER-A	TAMANDU-A
MONSTER-A	SALICET-A	TAMBOUR-A
NYMPHAE-A	SARMENT-A	THERIAC-A
PERFECT-A	SCIATIC-A	TORMENT-A
PIGNOLI-A	SIGNORI-A	TOURIST-A
QUILLAI-A	STROBIL-A	UNGUENT-A

Handy Hint: Say AA

If you have too many vowels on your rack, some useful short words beginning with A and using no consonants are: AA, AE and AI (2 points each). It is also worthwhile remembering common words which feature many vowels, including an A, such as ADIEU (6 points), AURA (4 points) and AERIAL (6 points).

BLOCKERS

It is useful to know which words are blockers and can't therefore be extended before or after. You may want to play a blocker that your opponent can't extend, or you may want to avoid playing a blocker because you want to keep the board open.

Three-letter blocker beginning with A

AUE

Some four-letter blockers beginning with A

ABLY	AGLY	AJEE
ACHY	AHEM	ALAE
ADRY	AHOY	ALEE
AESC	AJAR	ALIT

ALSO	AREW	AWRY
ANEW	AROW	AXAL
ANOW	ASEA	
AREG	AWFY	

Some five-letter blockers beginning with A (except words ending in '-ED', '-J', '-S', '-X', '-Y' or '-Z')

AARGH	AGOOD	APACE
ABACK	AHEAD	APAGE
ABASH	AHEAP	APAID
ABASK	AHIGH	APART
ABEAM	AIGHT	APIAN
ABLOW	AITCH	APPLY
ABOIL	ALACK	AROSE
ABORE	ALGAE	ASKEW
ABRIM	ALGAL	ASTIR
ACERB	ALGID	ASWIM
ACRID	ALIKE	ATILT
ADOZE	ALIVE	AURAL
AFIRE	ALOFT	AVAST
AFOOT	ALONE	AWASH
AFORE	ALOOF	AWAVE
AFOUL	ALOUD	AWORK
AGAIN	ALTHO	AXIAL
AGLEE	AMAIN	AXILE
AGLOW	ANILE	

Some six-letter blockers beginning with A (except words ending in '-ED', '-J', '-S', '-X', '-Y' or '-Z')

ABLAZE	ABORNE	ACIDIC
ABLEST	ABURST	ACRAWL
ABLOOM	ACETIC	ACUTER
ABLUSH	ACHIER	ADNATE
ABOARD	ACIDER	ADRIFT

ADROIT	ANEMIC	ASWING
AFIELD	ANGOLA	ASWIRL
AFLAME	ANOXIC	ATONAL
AFLOAT	ANYHOW	ATOPIC
AFRAID	AORTAL	ATWIXT
AFRESH	AORTIC	AUDIAL
AFRONT	APIECE	AVERSE
AGHAST	APTEST	AVIDER
AGILER	APTING	AVITAL
AGLARE	ARCANE	AVOUCH
AGLEAM	ARDENT	AWARER
AIMFUL	AREACH	AWATCH
AKIMBO	ARISEN	AWEIGH
ALBEIT	AROUND	AWEING
ALMOST	ASHAKE	AWHILE
ALUMNI	ASHINE	AWHIRL
AMBERY	ASHORE	AWOKEN
AMBUSH	ASLANT	AWRACK
AMEBIC	ASLEEP	AWRONG
AMIDST	ASLOPE	AWSOME
AMMINO	ASTOOP	AXONIC
AMORAL	ASTRUT	AZONAL
ANEATH	ASWARM	

BONUS WORDS

Bonus words on your rack can be hard to spot, especially for the less experienced player. One way to help find them is by using prefixes and suffixes.

Many longer words include a common prefix or suffix – remembering these and using them where you can is a good way to discover any longer words on your rack, including any potential bonus words. The key prefixes to remember beginning with A are AB-, AD-, AIR- and the key suffixes are -ABLE, -AGE, -ANCE, -ANCY and -ARCH.

Some words beginning with AB-

Seven-letter words

AB-DUCTS	AB-SOLVE	AB-USAGE
AB-JOINT	AB-SORBS	AB-USERS
AB-REACT	AB-STAIN	AB-USING
AB-SEILS	AB-SURDS	
AB-SENTS	AB-THANE	

Eight-letter words

AB-DUCTED	AB-ORALLY	AB-SOLVER
AB-ERRANT	AB-ORIGIN	AB-SOLVES
AB-ESSIVE	AB-SEILED	AB-SONANT
AB-LEGATE	AB-SENTED	AB-SORBED
AB-NEGATE	AB-SOLUTE	AB-STRICT
AB-NORMAL	AB-SOLVED	AB-USABLE

Some words beginning with AD-

Seven-letter words

AD-APTED	AD-JOINT	AD-OPTED
AD-APTER	AD-JUDGE	AD-OPTER
AD-DICTS	AD-JUROR	AD-PRESS
AD-DRESS	AD-JUSTS	AD-RENAL
AD-DUCES	AD-MIRED	AD-SORBS
AD-DUCTS	AD-MIRES	AD-VENTS
AD-HERES	AD-MIXED	AD-VERBS
AD-JOINS	AD-MIXES	AD-VERSE

AD-VERTS	AD-VISED	AD-VISOR
AD-VICES	AD-VISES	

Eight-letter words

AD-APTING	AD-JOINED	AD-OPTING
AD-DEBTED	AD-JUDGED	AD-OPTION
AD-DEEMED	AD-JUSTED	AD-SCRIPT
AD-DICTED	AD-JUSTER	AD-SORBED
AD-DOOMED	AD-MASSES	AD-UMBRAL
AD-DUCTED	AD-MIRING	AD-UNCATE
AD-EQUATE	AD-MIXING	AD-VERSER
AD-ESSIVE	AD-MONISH	AD-VERTED
AD-JACENT	AD-NATION	AD-VISING

Some words beginning with AIR-

Seven-letter words

AIR-BAGS	AIR-HOLE	AIR-SHIP
AIR-BASE	AIR-LESS	AIR-SHOT
AIR-BOAT	AIR-LIFT	AIR-SHOW
AIR-CREW	AIR-LIKE	AIR-SICK
AIR-DATE	AIR-LINE	AIR-SIDE
AIR-DROP	AIR-LOCK	AIR-STOP
AIR-FARE	AIR-MAIL	AIR-TIME
AIR-FLOW	AIR-PARK	AIR-TING
AIR-FOIL	AIR-PLAY	AIR-WARD
AIR-GAPS	AIR-PORT	AIR-WAVE
AIR-GLOW	AIR-POST	AIR-WAYS
AIR-HEAD	AIR-SHED	AIR-WISE

Eight-letter words

AIR-BASES	AIR-BOUND	AIR-BURST
AIR-BOATS	AIR-BRICK	AIR-BUSES
AIR-BORNE	AIR-BRUSH	AIR-CHECK

16

AIR-COACH   AIR-GRAPH   AIR-SHAFT   **A**
AIR-CRAFT   AIR-HOLES   AIR-SPACE
AIR-DRAWN   AIR-LIFTS   AIR-SPEED
AIR-DROME   AIR-LINER   AIR-STRIP
AIR-DROPS   AIR-PLANE   AIR-THING
AIR-FARES   AIR-POWER   AIR-TIGHT
AIR-FIELD   AIR-PROOF   AIR-WAVES
AIR-FRAME   AIR-SCAPE   AIR-WOMAN
AIR-GLOWS   AIR-SCREW   AIR-WOMEN

Some words ending with -ABLE
Seven-letter words

ACT-ABLE   FLY-ABLE   NAM-ABLE
ADD-ABLE   FRI-ABLE   NOT-ABLE
AFF-ABLE   FRY-ABLE   OWN-ABLE
AMI-ABLE   GEL-ABLE   PAR-ABLE
BAT-ABLE   GET-ABLE   PAY-ABLE
BUY-ABLE   GIV-ABLE   PLI-ABLE
CAP-ABLE   HAT-ABLE   POK-ABLE
CIT-ABLE   HEW-ABLE   POS-ABLE
COD-ABLE   HID-ABLE   POT-ABLE
CUR-ABLE   HIR-ABLE   RAT-ABLE
DAT-ABLE   LIK-ABLE   ROW-ABLE
DIS-ABLE   LIN-ABLE   SAL-ABLE
DRY-ABLE   LIV-ABLE   SAV-ABLE
DUP-ABLE   LOS-ABLE   SAY-ABLE
DUR-ABLE   LOV-ABLE   SEE-ABLE
DYE-ABLE   MAK-ABLE   SEW-ABLE
EAT-ABLE   MIN-ABLE   SIZ-ABLE
EQU-ABLE   MIR-ABLE   SKI-ABLE
EYE-ABLE   MIX-ABLE   SOW-ABLE
FAX-ABLE   MOV-ABLE   SUE-ABLE
FIX-ABLE   MUT-ABLE   TAK-ABLE

17

TAM-ABLE	TUN-ABLE	VOL-ABLE
TAX-ABLE	TYP-ABLE	VOT-ABLE
TEN-ABLE	UNH-ABLE	WAD-ABLE
TOT-ABLE	USE-ABLE	WAX-ABLE
TOW-ABLE	VAT-ABLE	WOO-ABLE
TRI-ABLE	VOC-ABLE	

Eight-letter words

ADOR-ABLE	CUTT-ABLE	HOLD-ABLE
AGIT-ABLE	DENI-ABLE	HUNT-ABLE
AMEN-ABLE	DRAW-ABLE	IMIT-ABLE
AMIC-ABLE	DRIV-ABLE	INVI-ABLE
ARGU-ABLE	EDIT-ABLE	JOIN-ABLE
ATON-ABLE	EDUC-ABLE	JUMP-ABLE
BAIL-ABLE	ENVI-ABLE	KICK-ABLE
BANK-ABLE	ERAS-ABLE	KILL-ABLE
BEAR-ABLE	EROD-ABLE	KISS-ABLE
BEAT-ABLE	EVAD-ABLE	KNOW-ABLE
BEND-ABLE	FACE-ABLE	LAUD-ABLE
BILL-ABLE	FARM-ABLE	LEAD-ABLE
BITE-ABLE	FEED-ABLE	LEAS-ABLE
BLAM-ABLE	FILE-ABLE	LEND-ABLE
BRIB-ABLE	FILM-ABLE	LIKE-ABLE
CASH-ABLE	FLOW-ABLE	LIVE-ABLE
CAUS-ABLE	FOLD-ABLE	LOAD-ABLE
CHEW-ABLE	FUND-ABLE	LOCK-ABLE
CITE-ABLE	GAIN-ABLE	LOVE-ABLE
CLOS-ABLE	GETT-ABLE	MAIL-ABLE
COIN-ABLE	GIVE-ABLE	MEND-ABLE
COOK-ABLE	GRAD-ABLE	MISS-ABLE
COPI-ABLE	GROW-ABLE	MOVE-ABLE
COPY-ABLE	GUID-ABLE	NAME-ABLE
CUFF-ABLE	HEAR-ABLE	OPEN-ABLE
CULP-ABLE	HEAT-ABLE	OPER-ABLE

PALP-ABLE   SACK-ABLE   TAKE-ABLE
PASS-ABLE   SALE-ABLE   TALK-ABLE
PICK-ABLE   SAVE-ABLE   TAME-ABLE
PITI-ABLE   SEAL-ABLE   TEAR-ABLE
PLAY-ABLE   SEIZ-ABLE   TEAS-ABLE
PORT-ABLE   SELL-ABLE   TRAD-ABLE
POSE-ABLE   SEND-ABLE   TURN-ABLE
POTT-ABLE   SERV-ABLE   UNST-ABLE
POUR-ABLE   SHAK-ABLE   VALU-ABLE
PROB-ABLE   SHAM-ABLE   VARI-ABLE
PROV-ABLE   SHOW-ABLE   VIEW-ABLE
PUMP-ABLE   SING-ABLE   VIOL-ABLE
QUOT-ABLE   SINK-ABLE   VOID-ABLE
RACE-ABLE   SIPP-ABLE   VOTE-ABLE
RATE-ABLE   SIZE-ABLE   WALK-ABLE
READ-ABLE   SMOK-ABLE   WASH-ABLE
REAP-ABLE   SOCI-ABLE   WEAR-ABLE
RELI-ABLE   SOLV-ABLE   WINN-ABLE
RENT-ABLE   SORT-ABLE   WIPE-ABLE
REUS-ABLE   SUIT-ABLE   WORK-ABLE
RINS-ABLE   SURF-ABLE   WRIT-ABLE
RIPP-ABLE   SWAY-ABLE   ZOOM-ABLE
ROUS-ABLE   SYLL-ABLE

Some words ending with -AGE

Seven-letter words

ACRE-AGE   BREW-AGE   COLL-AGE
ASSU-AGE   BULK-AGE   CORS-AGE
AVER-AGE   BUOY-AGE   COTT-AGE
BAGG-AGE   CABB-AGE   COUR-AGE
BAND-AGE   CAKE-AGE   FLOW-AGE
BARR-AGE   CARN-AGE   FOLI-AGE
BEER-AGE   COIN-AGE   FOOT-AGE

GARB-AGE
HAUL-AGE
HERB-AGE
HOST-AGE
LEAK-AGE
LINE-AGE
LINK-AGE
LUGG-AGE
MASS-AGE
MESS-AGE
MILE-AGE
MONT-AGE
PACK-AGE

PASS-AGE
PEER-AGE
PLUM-AGE
POST-AGE
POTT-AGE
PRES-AGE
RAMP-AGE
RIFF-AGE
RUMM-AGE
SALV-AGE
SAUS-AGE
SEEP-AGE
SIGN-AGE

SOIL-AGE
STOR-AGE
TONN-AGE
UMBR-AGE
VANT-AGE
VILL-AGE
VINT-AGE
VOLT-AGE
WARP-AGE
WAST-AGE
WATT-AGE
YARD-AGE

Eight-letter words

AMPER-AGE
BARON-AGE
BEVER-AGE
BLOCK-AGE
BREAK-AGE
CARRI-AGE
CLEAR-AGE
COVER-AGE
CREEP-AGE
CRIBB-AGE
DRAIN-AGE
DRESS-AGE
ENVIS-AGE
FRAPE-AGE
FRONT-AGE

FUSEL-AGE
GRAIN-AGE
GROUP-AGE
HERIT-AGE
LANGU-AGE
LEVER-AGE
LITRE-AGE
MARRI-AGE
METER-AGE
MISUS-AGE
PILOT-AGE
PLANT-AGE
PUPIL-AGE
ROUGH-AGE
SABOT-AGE

SEWER-AGE
SHORT-AGE
SLIPP-AGE
SPILL-AGE
SPOIL-AGE
STEER-AGE
STOPP-AGE
SUFFR-AGE
TRACK-AGE
TUTEL-AGE
TUTOR-AGE
VAUNT-AGE
VERBI-AGE
VICAR-AGE

Some words ending with -ANCE

Seven-letter words

AID-ANCE	FIN-ANCE	SON-ANCE
ASK-ANCE	JOY-ANCE	SUR-ANCE
BAL-ANCE	PEN-ANCE	VAC-ANCE
DUR-ANCE	ROM-ANCE	VAL-ANCE

Eight-letter words

ABEY-ANCE	DIST-ANCE	PIQU-ANCE
ABID-ANCE	ELEG-ANCE	PITT-ANCE
ACUT-ANCE	ENTR-ANCE	PORT-ANCE
ADAM-ANCE	EXIT-ANCE	RADI-ANCE
AFFI-ANCE	FEAS-ANCE	RELI-ANCE
ALLI-ANCE	GUID-ANCE	RESI-ANCE
AMBI-ANCE	INST-ANCE	RIDD-ANCE
AMOR-ANCE	ISSU-ANCE	SORT-ANCE
BECH-ANCE	ITER-ANCE	TEND-ANCE
BRIS-ANCE	LAIT-ANCE	VALI-ANCE
BRO-MANCE	NOND-ANCE	VARI-ANCE
BUOY-ANCE	NUIS-ANCE	VIBR-ANCE
CREP-ANCE	ORDN-ANCE	VOID-ANCE
DEFI-ANCE	PARL-ANCE	
DEVI-ANCE	PAST-ANCE	

Some words ending with -ANCY

Seven-letter words

ERR-ANCY	TEN-ANCY
INF-ANCY	TRU-ANCY
PLI-ANCY	UNF-ANCY
SON-ANCY	VAC-ANCY

Eight-letter words

ABEY-ANCY	GEOM-ANCY	RAMP-ANCY
ADAM-ANCY	IMIT-ANCY	REGN-ANCY
BLAT-ANCY	INST-ANCY	VAGR-ANCY
BUOY-ANCY	MORD-ANCY	VALI-ANCY
CLAM-ANCY	PECC-ANCY	VERD-ANCY
DEVI-ANCY	PERN-ANCY	VIBR-ANCY
DORM-ANCY	PIQU-ANCY	
ELEG-ANCY	RADI-ANCY	

Some words ending with -ARCH

Seven-letter words

AUT-ARCH	MON-ARCH	TRI-ARCH
END-ARCH	NAV-ARCH	XER-ARCH
HEX-ARCH	NOM-ARCH	
MES-ARCH	TOP-ARCH	

Eight-letter words

ETHN-ARCH	OLIG-ARCH	PHYL-ARCH
HEPT-ARCH	OMNI-ARCH	POLY-ARCH
HIER-ARCH	OVER-ARCH	TAXI-ARCH
HIPP-ARCH	PENT-ARCH	TETR-ARCH

UNUSUAL WORDS FROM OVERSEAS ENGLISH

If you have an awkward combination of letters on your rack then words from overseas English may come in handy. Here are some beginning with A.

Australian words

ADJIGO	yam plant
ARVO	afternoon
ASPRO	associate professor

Canadian words

AGLOO	breathing hole made in ice by a seal
AMAUT	hood on an Inuit woman's parka for carrying a child
ATIGI	Inuit parka

Hindi words

AKHARA	gymnasium
ALAP	vocal music without words
AMBARY	tropical plant
ANKUS	elephant goad
ANNA	old copper coin
ARTI	Hindu ritual
ASURA	a Hindu demon
AYAH	maidservant or nursemaid

New Zealand words

New Zealand English features a great variety of words adopted from the Maori language. Many of these words use two (and sometimes three) As but are often also dependent on a consonant such as K or T.

HAKA	war dance
KAUPAPA	strategy, policy or cause
TAIAHA	ceremonial fighting staff
WAKA	Maori canoe

South African words

South African English is fed into by various different languages, including Afrikaans and Nguni languages such as Zulu and Xhosa. Afrikaans-derived words often feature a double A and Nguni words frequently contain two or three.

AMADODA	grown men
AMANDLA	political slogan calling for power to the Black population
BABALAS	drunk or hungover
KRAAL	stockaded village
PLAAS	farm

B

3

Essential info
Value: 3 points
Number in set: 2

B can form a two-letter word with every vowel except for U. If you have a letter B you can form various short everyday words, some of which can be high-scoring such as BOX (12 points), BAY (8 points), BOW (8 points), BUY (8 points) and BYE (also 8). Some more unusual three-letter words beginning with B are BEY (an official in the Ottoman Empire, 8 points) and BEZ (the second spike of a deer's antler, 14 points).

Two-letter words beginning with B

BA	BI	BY
BE	BO	

Some three-letter words beginning with B

BAA	BEY	BOK
BAC	BEZ	BON
BAH	BIO	BOP
BAL	BIZ	BOR
BAM	BOA	BOT
BAP	BOD	BUR
BEL	BOH	
BEN	BOI	

HOOKS

Hooking requires a subtle change in a player's thought process, in that they must look at words already on the board without becoming distracted by their pronunciation.

Some front-hooks
Two letters to three

B-AA	B-AY	B-IS
B-AD	B-ED	B-IT
B-AG	B-EE	B-OB
B-AH	B-EL	B-OD
B-AL	B-EN	B-OH
B-AM	B-ES	B-OI
B-AN	B-ET	B-ON
B-AR	B-ID	B-OO
B-AS	B-IN	B-OP
B-AT	B-IO	B-OR

B-OS	B-UG	B-US
B-OW	B-UM	B-UT
B-OX	B-UN	B-YE
B-OY	B-UR	

Three letters to four

B-AFT	B-ILK	B-OLD
B-AIL	B-ILL	B-ONE
B-ALE	B-INK	B-OOH
B-ALL	B-IRK	B-ORE
B-AND	B-ISH	B-OUT
B-ANT	B-LAB	B-OWL
B-ARE	B-LAD	B-OXY
B-ARK	B-LAG	B-RAG
B-ARM	B-LAW	B-RAN
B-ASH	B-LAY	B-RAP
B-ASK	B-LED	B-RAT
B-ATE	B-LET	B-RAW
B-AUK	B-LEY	B-RAY
B-AYE	B-LIP	B-RED
B-EAR	B-LIT	B-RIG
B-EAT	B-LOB	B-RIM
B-EAU	B-LOG	B-ROD
B-EGO	B-LOT	B-ROO
B-END	B-LOW	B-ROW
B-EST	B-OAR	B-RUT
B-HAT	B-OAT	B-URN
B-HUT	B-ODE	B-YES
B-ICE	B-OFF	
B-IDE	B-OIL	

Four letters to five

B-ALAS	B-ALMS	B-EARD
B-ALKY	B-ARMY	B-EAST
B-ALLY	B-EACH	B-EAUX

27

B-EGAD
B-EVER
B-HAJI
B-HANG
B-HOOT
B-IFFY
B-IGGS
B-IOTA
B-LACK
B-LADE
B-LADY
B-LAME
B-LAND
B-LANK
B-LARE
B-LASH
B-LAST
B-LATE
B-LAUD
B-LAWN
B-LAZE
B-LEAK
B-LECH
B-LEND
B-LENT
B-LESS
B-LEST

B-LIMP
B-LIMY
B-LINK
B-LIST
B-LITE
B-LIVE
B-LOCK
B-LOOM
B-LOOP
B-LORE
B-LUSH
B-OGLE
B-OINK
B-ONCE
B-ONUS
B-OOZE
B-ORAL
B-OWED
B-OWER
B-OXEN
B-RACE
B-RAID
B-RAIL
B-RAIN
B-RAKE
B-RANK
B-RANT

B-RASH
B-RAVE
B-RAZE
B-READ
B-REAM
B-REED
B-RENT
B-RICK
B-RIDE
B-RING
B-RINK
B-RISE
B-RISK
B-ROAD
B-ROCK
B-ROOK
B-ROOM
B-ROSE
B-ROSY
B-RUIN
B-RULE
B-RUNG
B-RUNT
B-RUSH
B-RUSK
B-RUST
B-USED

Five letters to six

B-ACHED
B-ADDER
B-ADMAN
B-AILED
B-ALLOT
B-ALLOW

B-ANGER
B-ANGLE
B-ARROW
B-ASHED
B-ASKED
B-ASSET

B-EAGLE
B-EARED
B-EATEN
B-EATER
B-EGGED
B-ELATE

B-ENDED
B-ENDER
B-IONIC
B-LAMER
B-LANKY
B-LATER
B-LAWED
B-LAZED
B-LEACH
B-LEAKY
B-LEARY
B-LIGHT
B-LIMEY
B-LITHE
B-LOBBY
B-LOTTO
B-LOUSE
B-LOUSY
B-LOWED
B-LOWER
B-LUNGE
B-OAKED
B-OATER

B-OFFED
B-OILED
B-OILER
B-OLDEN
B-OLDER
B-ORATE
B-ORDER
B-OTHER
B-OUGHT
B-OUNCE
B-OVATE
B-OWING
B-OWNED
B-RACED
B-RACER
B-RAGGY
B-RAINY
B-RAISE
B-RAKED
B-RANCH
B-RANDY
B-RATTY
B-RAVED

B-RAVER
B-RAWER
B-RAWLY
B-RAYED
B-RAZED
B-RAZER
B-REACH
B-READY
B-RIDGE
B-RIGHT
B-RISKY
B-ROACH
B-ROGUE
B-ROOMY
B-ROUGH
B-ROWED
B-UDDER
B-UNION
B-URNED
B-USHER
B-UTTER

Six letters to seven

B-ABACUS
B-ACHING
B-AILING
B-ANGLED
B-ASHING
B-ASKING
B-ASSIST
B-ATONED
B-EAGLED
B-EATING

B-EERIER
B-EERILY
B-EGGING
B-ELATED
B-ENDING
B-INNING
B-LACKED
B-LADDER
B-LADING
B-LAGGED

B-LANDED
B-LANDER
B-LASTED
B-LASTER
B-LATEST
B-LATHER
B-LATTER
B-LAUDED
B-LAZING
B-LEAKER

B-LENDER
B-LESSER
B-LETTED
B-LIMPED
B-LINGER
B-LINKED
B-LINKER
B-LISTER
B-LITTER
B-LOBBED
B-LOCKED
B-LOCKER
B-LOGGED
B-LOGGER
B-LOOMED
B-LOOPED
B-LOOPER
B-LOUSED
B-LOWING
B-LOWSED
B-LUBBER
B-LUNGED

B-LUNGER
B-LUSTER
B-OFFING
B-OILING
B-OINKED
B-OLDEST
B-OOZILY
B-OOZING
B-ORATED
B-OWNING
B-OXLIKE
B-RABBLE
B-RACING
B-RACKET
B-RAGGED
B-RAIDED
B-RAIDER
B-RAILED
B-RAINED
B-RAISED
B-RAKING
B-RAMBLE

B-RANKED
B-RASHER
B-RASHLY
B-RATTLE
B-RAUNCH
B-RAVING
B-RAWEST
B-RAYING
B-RAZING
B-REAMED
B-RIDGED
B-RIDING
B-RINGER
B-RISKED
B-RISKER
B-ROCKED
B-ROCKET
B-ROOKIE
B-ROOMED
B-ROSIER
B-RUSHED
B-RUSHER

Seven letters to eight

B-ACRONYM
B-AILMENT
B-ARTISAN
B-ASHLESS
B-ATONING
B-EAGLING
B-EARDING
B-EARLIKE
B-EATABLE
B-EERIEST
B-ELATING

B-ENDWISE
B-ESPOUSE
B-INGOING
B-LACKING
B-LAGGING
B-LANDING
B-LASHING
B-LASTING
B-LAUDING
B-LEACHED
B-LEACHER

B-LENDING
B-LETTING
B-LIGHTED
B-LIGHTER
B-LIMPING
B-LINKING
B-LITHELY
B-LOGGING
B-LOGROLL
B-LOOMING
B-LOOPIER

B-LOOPING	B-RAMBLED	B-RIGHTER
B-LOUSIER	B-RANCHED	B-RIGHTLY
B-LOUSILY	B-RANCHER	B-RIMLESS
B-LOWDOWN	B-RANDING	B-RINGING
B-LUNGING	B-RANKING	B-RISKIER
B-OLDNESS	B-RASHEST	B-RISKING
B-ORATING	B-RATPACK	B-ROACHED
B-ORDERED	B-RATTIER	B-ROADWAY
B-ORDERER	B-RATTISH	B-ROASTED
B-RABBLER	B-RATTLED	B-ROGUISH
B-RAGGIER	B-REACHED	B-ROILING
B-RAGGING	B-REACHER	B-ROMANCE
B-RAIDING	B-REACHES	B-ROOMING
B-RAILING	B-READIER	B-ROSIEST
B-RAINIER	B-READING	B-RUSHIER
B-RAINILY	B-REEDING	B-RUSHING
B-RAINING	B-RIDGING	B-UTTERED
B-RAISING	B-RIGHTEN	

Handy Hint: Seek out the unusual

The more difficult or uncommon words you remember, the easier it is to sort out your rack and to keep scoring well. You could even be lucky enough to have two power tiles at your disposal to be able to play some rare high-scoring gems. Some excellent examples beginning with B are BANJAX (to ruin something, 22 points) and BEZIQUE (a card game, 27 points).

Some end-hooks
Two letters to three

AB-B	BI-B	DE-B
AL-B	BO-B	DI-B
AR-B	DA-B	DO-B

B

FA-B	LA-B	OR-B
GI-B	LI-B	RE-B
GO-B	LO-B	SI-B
GU-B	MI-B	SO-B
HO-B	MO-B	TA-B
JA-B	NA-B	UR-B
JO-B	NE-B	WE-B
KA-B	NO-B	YO-B
KO-B	NU-B	

Three letters to four

BAR-B	DOR-B	LAM-B
BIB-B	FEE-B	NEW-B
BOA-B	FLU-B	NIM-B
BUR-B	FOR-B	NOO-B
CAR-B	GAM-B	PRO-B
CHI-B	GAR-B	TOM-B
COB-B	HER-B	WAR-B
CUR-B	JAM-B	
DIE-B	JIB-B	

Four letters to five

ACER-B	DEMO-B	SLUR-B
BLUR-B	MANE-B	THRO-B
CUBE-B	PLUM-B	ZEBU-B

Five letters to six

SCRAM-B	SUPER-B

Six letters to seven

POTHER-B	PROVER-B	REPLUM-B

BLOCKERS

It is useful to know which words are blockers and can't therefore be extended before or after. You may want to play a blocker that your opponent can't extend, or you may want to avoid playing a blocker because you want to keep the board open.

Three-letter blocker beginning with B

BEZ

Some four-letter blockers beginning with B

BABY	BEVY	BRAP
BADE	BHAT	BUBO
BEDU	BLEW	BURY
BEEN	BODY	BUSY

Some five-letter blockers beginning with B
(except words ending in '-ED', '-J', '-S', '-X', '-Y' or '-Z')

BAITH	BELCH	BONZA
BANAL	BIRCH	BOWIE
BARER	BITOU	BOXEN
BASHO	BIVIA	BRUNG
BATCH	BLASÉ	BUILT
BEGAN	BLIVE	BURNT
BEGAT	BLOWN	BUTCH
BEGOT	BLUER	BUXOM

Some six-letter blockers beginning with B
(except words ending in '-ED', '-J', '-S', '-X', '-Y' or '-Z')

BADDER	BARBAL	BARING
BALDER	BAREST	BARISH
BANISH	BARFUL	BASEST

BEATEN	BLAISE	BOXIER
BECAME	BLAIZE	BOYING
BEFORE	BLANCH	BOYISH
BEGONE	BLEACH	BREACH
BEHALF	BLUEST	BREECH
BEHELD	BLUIER	BRICHT
BENIGN	BLUISH	BROKEN
BEREFT	BOLDER	BROOCH
BIFORM	BONIER	BRUNCH
BIGGER	BONSAI	BRUTAL
BIMBLE	BONZER	BUMALO
BINATE	BOSKER	BUSIER
BITTEN	BOSSER	BYPAST

BONUS WORDS

Bonus words on your rack can be hard to spot, especially for the less experienced player. One way to help find them is by using prefixes and suffixes.

Many larger words include a common prefix or suffix – remembering these and using them where you can is a good way to discover any longer words on your rack, including any potential bonus words. The key prefixes to remember beginning with B are BE- and BI- and the key suffixes are -BACK, -BALL, -BAND and -BIRD.

Some words beginning with BE-

Seven-letter words

BE-CAUSE	BE-FALLS	BE-HEADS
BE-COMES	BE-FOULS	BE-HINDS
BE-DECKS	BE-GUILE	BE-HOLDS
BE-DEVIL	BE-HAVER	BE-HOOFS

BE-JEWEL	BE-MUSED	BE-SPOKE
BE-LATED	BE-NEATH	BE-STOWS
BE-LAYED	BE-QUEST	BE-TIDES
BE-LIEFS	BE-RATED	BE-TRAYS
BE-LONGS	BE-REAVE	BE-TWEEN
BE-LOVED	BE-SIDES	BE-TWIXT
BE-MOANS	BE-SIEGE	BE-WITCH

Eight-letter words

BE-BOPPED	BE-HAVING	BE-REAVED
BE-CALMED	BE-HAVIOR	BE-REAVER
BE-CHANCE	BE-HEADED	BE-SIEGED
BE-COMING	BE-HEADER	BE-SIEGER
BE-CURSED	BE-HOLDEN	BE-SMIRCH
BE-DAUBED	BE-HOLDER	BE-SPOKEN
BE-DAZZLE	BE-HOOVED	BE-STOWED
BE-DECKED	BE-HOVING	BE-STREWN
BE-FOULED	BE-KNIGHT	BE-SUITED
BE-FRIEND	BE-LAYING	BE-TIDING
BE-FUDDLE	BE-LIEVER	BE-TITLED
BE-GETTER	BE-LITTLE	BE-WARING
BE-GINNER	BE-LONGED	BE-WIGGED
BE-GOTTEN	BE-LONGER	BE-WILDER
BE-GRUDGE	BE-MUSING	
BE-GUILED	BE-RATING	

Some words beginning with BI-

Seven-letter words

BI-AXIAL	BI-LEVEL	BI-POLAR
BI-CARBS	BI-MODAL	BI-SECTS
BI-CYCLE	BI-OPTIC	BI-TONAL
BI-FOCAL	BI-PARTY	BI-VALVE
BI-FOLDS	BI-PEDAL	BI-VINYL
BI-JURAL	BI-PLANE	BI-ZONAL

Eight-letter words

B

BI-ANNUAL
BI-CHROME
BI-COLOUR
BI-CONVEX
BI-CUSPID
BI-CYCLED
BI-CYCLER
BI-CYCLIC

BI-FACIAL
BI-FORMED
BI-HOURLY
BI-LINEAR
BI-MANUAL
BI-METHYL
BI-PARTED
BI-PHASIC

BI-RADIAL
BI-STABLE
BI-UNIQUE
BI-VALVED
BI-WEEKLY
BI-YEARLY

Some words ending with -BACK

Seven-letter words

BUY-BACK
CUT-BACK
DIE-BACK
FAT-BACK
FIN-BACK

FLY-BACK
LAY-BACK
OUT-BACK
PAY-BACK
RED-BACK

SET-BACK
SUN-BACK
TIE-BACK

Eight-letter words

BARE-BACK
BLOW-BACK
BLUE-BACK
CALL-BACK
CASH-BACK
CLAW-BACK
COME-BACK
DRAW-BACK
FALL-BACK
FAST-BACK
FEED-BACK

FLAT-BACK
FULL-BACK
GREY-BACK
HALF-BACK
HAUL-BACK
HOLD-BACK
HUMP-BACK
KICK-BACK
LIFT-BACK
LOAN-BACK
PLAY-BACK

PUFF-BACK
PULL-BACK
PUSH-BACK
ROLL-BACK
SEAT-BACK
SNAP-BACK
TAIL-BACK
TALK-BACK
TURN-BACK
WING-BACK

Some words ending with -BALL
Seven-letter words

AIR-BALL	GUM-BALL	ODD-BALL
EYE-BALL	LOW-BALL	PIN-BALL
FUR-BALL	NET-BALL	

Eight-letter words

BASE-BALL	FOOT-BALL	MOTH-BALL
BLUE-BALL	GLUE-BALL	PALM-BALL
CORN-BALL	GOOF-BALL	PUFF-BALL
DIRT-BALL	HAIR-BALL	ROOT-BALL
DUST-BALL	HAND-BALL	SNOW-BALL
FAST-BALL	HARD-BALL	SOFT-BALL
FIRE-BALL	HIGH-BALL	SPIT-BALL
FISH-BALL	KICK-BALL	
FOOS-BALL	MEAT-BALL	

Some words ending with -BAND
Seven-letter words

ARM-BAND	HAT-BAND	MAN-BAND
DIS-BAND	HUS-BAND	MID-BAND

Eight-letter words

BACK-BAND	HEAD-BAND	SIDE-BAND
BASE-BAND	NECK-BAND	STOP-BAND
BROW-BAND	NOSE-BAND	WAVE-BAND
HAIR-BAND	RAIN-BAND	WIDE-BAND

Some words ending with -BIRD
Seven-letter words

ANT-BIRD	BOO-BIRD	COW-BIRD
AXE-BIRD	CAT-BIRD	FAT-BIRD

JAY-BIRD	RED-BIRD	WAR-BIRD
MAY-BIRD	SEA-BIRD	
OIL-BIRD	SUN-BIRD	

Eight-letter words

BELL-BIRD	JAIL-BIRD	RAIN-BIRD
BLUE-BIRD	KING-BIRD	REED-BIRD
CAGE-BIRD	LADY-BIRD	RICE-BIRD
FERN-BIRD	LOVE-BIRD	SNOW-BIRD
FIRE-BIRD	LYRE-BIRD	SONG-BIRD
GAOL-BIRD	OVEN-BIRD	SURF-BIRD
HANG-BIRD	PUFF-BIRD	WHIP-BIRD
HOME-BIRD	RAIL-BIRD	YARD-BIRD

Handy Hint: Use the blanks wisely

There are two blank tiles in the set. A blank tile is, by its nature, incredibly versatile as it can be substituted for any other letter. Although it scores no points in itself, the blank tile can make forming bonus words that much easier. Players should avoid using the blank for just a few extra points and they should certainly never, ever change one.

UNUSUAL WORDS FROM OVERSEAS ENGLISH

If you have an awkward combination of letters on your rack then words from overseas English may come in handy. Here are some beginning with B.

Australian words

BARRO	embarrassing
BAUERA	small evergreen shrub
BELAH	casuarina tree
BERKO	berserk
BIFFO	fighting or aggressive behaviour
BILBY	burrowing marsupial
BIZZO	empty and irrelevant talk
BOAB	baobab tree
BODGIE	unruly or uncouth man
BOGAN	youth who dresses and behaves rebelliously
BOOBOOK	small spotted brown owl
BOOFY	strong but stupid
BORA	native Australian coming-of-age ceremony
BORAK	rubbish or nonsense
BRASCO	lavatory
BROLGA	large grey crane with a trumpeting call
BRUMBY	wild horse
BUNYA	tall dome-shaped coniferous tree
BUNYIP	legendary monster

Canadian words

BABICHE	thongs or lacings of rawhide
BARACHOIS	shallow lagoon formed by a sand bar
BATEAU	light flat-bottomed boat
BEIGNET	deep-fried pastry
BREWIS	bread soaked in broth, gravy, etc
BUTTE	isolated steep-sided flat-topped hill

Hindi words

BABU	Mr
BAEL	spiny tree
BAHADUR	title for distinguished Indian during the Raj
BANDH	general strike
BANYAN	tree whose branches grow down into the soil
BHAJI	deep-fried vegetable savoury
BHANGRA	music combining traditional Punjabi music with Western pop
BHAVAN	large house or building
BHISHTI	water-carrier
BINDI	decorative dot in middle of forehead
BOBBERY	mixed pack of hunting dogs
BUND	embankment

New Zealand word

BOOHAI	thoroughly lost

South African words

BAAS	boss
BABALAS	drunk or hungover
BAKKIE	small truck
BRAAI	grill or roast meat
BRAAIVLEIS	barbecue
BUNDU	wild, remote region

Urdu words

BAGH	garden
BALTI	spicy Indian dish stewed until most liquid has evaporated
BASTI	slum
BEGUM	woman of high rank
BIRYANI	Indian dish of highly flavoured rice mixed with meat or fish

C₃

Essential info
Value: 3 points
Number in set: 2

C can be a difficult letter to play (for example, it only forms one two-letter word: CH, an old dialect word for I, 7 points). However, it does form some good three-letter words including CAW, COW and COY (all 8 points) and also CAZ (short form of casual, 14 points). Worth remembering also are the short words which don't use any vowels: CLY (a word for steal, 8 points) and CWM (a Welsh word for valley, 10 points).

Two-letter word beginning with C

CH

Some three-letter words beginning with C

CAA	CEL	COR
CAF	CHA	COS
CAG	CHE	COX
CAL	CHI	COZ
CAM	CID	CUM
CAW	CIS	CUR
CAY	CIT	CUZ
CAZ	CLY	CWM
CEE	COO	

HOOKS

Hooking requires a subtle change in a player's thought process, in that they must look at words already on the board without becoming distracted by their pronunciation.

Some front-hooks
Two letters to three

C-AA	C-AT	C-ID
C-AB	C-AW	C-IS
C-AD	C-AY	C-IT
C-AG	C-EE	C-OB
C-AL	C-EL	C-OD
C-AM	C-HA	C-ON
C-AN	C-HE	C-OO
C-AR	C-HI	C-OP

C-OR	C-OX	C-UP
C-OS	C-OY	C-UR
C-OW	C-UM	C-UT

Three letters to four

C-AGE	C-HOG	C-OCH
C-AID	C-HOP	C-ODA
C-AKE	C-HOW	C-ODE
C-ALF	C-HUB	C-OFF
C-ALL	C-HUG	C-OFT
C-ALP	C-HUM	C-OHO
C-AMP	C-HUT	C-OIL
C-ANT	C-IDE	C-OLD
C-ANY	C-ILL	C-ONE
C-APE	C-ION	C-ONS
C-ARE	C-IRE	C-ORE
C-ARK	C-LAD	C-OUR
C-ART	C-LAM	C-OWL
C-ASH	C-LAP	C-RAG
C-ASK	C-LAW	C-RAM
C-ATE	C-LAY	C-RAN
C-HAD	C-LEG	C-RAW
C-HAM	C-LIP	C-RAY
C-HAT	C-LOD	C-RED
C-HAY	C-LOG	C-RIB
C-HEM	C-LOP	C-RIM
C-HER	C-LOT	C-RIP
C-HEW	C-LOW	C-ROW
C-HID	C-LOY	C-RUE
C-HIP	C-OAT	C-URN
C-HIS	C-OBS	C-UTE
C-HIT	C-OCA	

Four letters to five

C

C-ABLE	C-HIVE	C-LOSE
C-ACHE	C-HOCK	C-LOUD
C-AGED	C-HOKE	C-LOUT
C-AGER	C-HOOF	C-LOVE
C-AIRN	C-HOOK	C-LOWN
C-AKED	C-HOPS	C-LUCK
C-ANON	C-HORE	C-LUMP
C-APED	C-HOSE	C-LUNG
C-APER	C-HOUT	C-OAST
C-APEX	C-HOWK	C-OMER
C-ARED	C-HUCK	C-OPED
C-AULD	C-HUFF	C-ORAL
C-AVER	C-HUMP	C-OUCH
C-AWED	C-HUNK	C-OVEN
C-EASE	C-HURL	C-OVER
C-HAFF	C-INCH	C-OWED
C-HAIN	C-LACK	C-RACK
C-HAIR	C-LAME	C-RAFT
C-HARM	C-LAMP	C-RAKE
C-HART	C-LAMS	C-RAMP
C-HATS	C-LANG	C-RANK
C-HAVE	C-LANK	C-RARE
C-HEAP	C-LASH	C-RASH
C-HEAT	C-LASS	C-RATE
C-HECK	C-LAST	C-RAVE
C-HELP	C-LEAN	C-RAZE
C-HERE	C-LEAR	C-REAM
C-HEST	C-LEFT	C-REDO
C-HICK	C-LICK	C-REED
C-HIDE	C-LIMB	C-REEK
C-HILD	C-LING	C-REEL
C-HILI	C-LOCK	C-REST
C-HILL	C-LONE	C-RIPE

44

C-RISE	C-RUCK	C-RUST
C-ROCK	C-RUDE	C-UNIT
C-ROOK	C-RUSH	

Five letters to six

C-ABLED	C-HIPPY	C-OVERT
C-ABLER	C-HOKEY	C-OVINE
C-ACHED	C-HOPPY	C-RAGGY
C-AGING	C-HUBBY	C-RATED
C-ALLOW	C-HUFFY	C-RATER
C-AMBER	C-HUNKY	C-RAVED
C-AMPED	C-LANKY	C-RAVEN
C-AMPLY	C-LEAVE	C-RAYON
C-ANKLE	C-LONER	C-RAZED
C-APING	C-LOSED	C-ROWED
C-ASKED	C-LOSER	C-RUDER
C-AUGHT	C-LOVER	C-RUMMY
C-EASED	C-LOWED	C-RUSTY
C-HAPPY	C-LUCKY	C-UMBER
C-HASTE	C-LUMPY	C-UPPED
C-HEWED	C-ODDER	C-UPPER
C-HIDER	C-OILED	C-UTTER
C-HILLY	C-OLDER	

Six letters to seven

C-ABLING	C-ASTRAL	C-HARING
C-ACHING	C-AULDER	C-HARKED
C-AMPING	C-EASING	C-HARMED
C-ANGLED	C-ENSURE	C-HARMER
C-AROUSE	C-HACKED	C-HASTEN
C-ARTFUL	C-HAIRED	C-HATTED
C-ASHIER	C-HAMPER	C-HATTER
C-ASHING	C-HANGED	C-HAWING
C-ASKING	C-HANGER	C-HEAPER

C-HEATED	C-LEANED	C-RABBIT
C-HEATER	C-LEANER	C-RACKED
C-HELPED	C-LEANLY	C-RACKER
C-HEWING	C-LEARED	C-RAFTED
C-HIDING	C-LEAVED	C-RAFTER
C-HILLED	C-LEAVER	C-RAGGED
C-HILLER	C-LICKED	C-RAMMED
C-HIPPED	C-LICKER	C-RAMPED
C-HIPPER	C-LIMBED	C-RANKED
C-HIPPIE	C-LIMBER	C-RASHED
C-HITTER	C-LINGER	C-RASHER
C-HOPPED	C-LINKED	C-RAVING
C-HOPPER	C-LINKER	C-REAKED
C-HUCKLE	C-LIPPED	C-REAMED
C-HUFFED	C-LIPPER	C-RESTED
C-HUFFER	C-LITTER	C-RIBBED
C-HUGGED	C-LOBBER	C-RIBBER
C-HUGGER	C-LOCKED	C-RICKED
C-HUMMED	C-LOCKER	C-RINGED
C-HUNTER	C-LOGGED	C-RINGER
C-INCHED	C-LOGGER	C-RIPPLE
C-LACKED	C-LOPPED	C-ROCKED
C-LACKER	C-LOSING	C-ROCKET
C-LAMBER	C-LOTTED	C-ROOKED
C-LAMMED	C-LOWING	C-ROSIER
C-LAMMER	C-LUBBER	C-ROWING
C-LAMPED	C-LUCKED	C-RUDELY
C-LAMPER	C-LUMPED	C-RUDEST
C-LANGER	C-LUMPER	C-RUMBLE
C-LANKED	C-LUNKER	C-RUMPLE
C-LAPPED	C-LUSTER	C-RUSHED
C-LAPPER	C-OILING	C-RUSHER
C-LASHED	C-OLDEST	C-RUSTED
C-LASHER	C-OLDISH	C-UPPING
C-LATTER	C-ORACLE	

46

HIGHEST WORD SCORE

The highest-scoring word ever played in a Scrabble game was CAZIQUES, which achieved an enormous total of 392 points. It was played by Karl Khoshnaw of Richmond, Surrey. There is one word that has potential to score more and that is QUINZHEE which could net 401 points across two triple word squares.

Seven letters to eight

C-AMBERED	C-HUMMING	C-LOCKING
C-ANGLING	C-HUMPING	C-LOGGING
C-ASHLESS	C-HUNKIER	C-LOPPING
C-ENSURED	C-INCHING	C-LOSABLE
C-ENTERED	C-LACKING	C-LOTTING
C-HAIRING	C-LAGGING	C-LOUTING
C-HANDLER	C-LAMMING	C-LUCKIER
C-HANGING	C-LAMPING	C-LUCKING
C-HANTING	C-LANKIER	C-LUMPIER
C-HAPLESS	C-LANKING	C-LUMPING
C-HAPPIER	C-LAPPING	C-LUMPISH
C-HARMFUL	C-LASHING	C-OFFERED
C-HARMING	C-LATCHED	C-OLDNESS
C-HATTING	C-LAWLESS	C-OTTERED
C-HEATING	C-LAWLIKE	C-OVERAGE
C-HELPING	C-LEANEST	C-OVERALL
C-HEWABLE	C-LEANING	C-OVERTLY
C-HICKORY	C-LEARING	C-RACKING
C-HILDING	C-LEAVING	C-RAFTING
C-HILLIER	C-LICKING	C-RAGGIER
C-HOPPING	C-LIMBING	C-RAMMING
C-HUFFING	C-LINGIER	C-RAMPING
C-HUGGERS	C-LINKING	C-RANKING
C-HUGGING	C-LIPPING	C-RASHING

C-REAMING	C-RIMPLED	C-RUMBLED
C-REELING	C-RINGING	C-RUMPLED
C-RESTING	C-RIPPLED	C-RUSHING
C-RIBBING	C-RIPPLER	C-RUSTIER
C-RICKING	C-ROCKERY	C-RUSTILY

Some end-hooks

Two letters to three

AR-C	MI-C	RE-C
BA-C	MO-C	SI-C
DO-C	MY-C	SO-C
HI-C	OR-C	TE-C
HO-C	PA-C	TI-C
LA-C	PE-C	TO-C
MA-C	PI-C	

Three letters to four

ABA-C	DIS-C	SAI-C
ALE-C	HUI-C	SYN-C
BAN-C	MAR-C	TOR-C
CHI-C	PER-C	ZIN-C

Four letters to five

ANTI-C	ILIA-C	SERA-C
ARTI-C	LOTI-C	TARO-C
CODE-C	MAGI-C	TOPI-C
CONI-C	MALI-C	TORI-C
DURO-C	MANI-C	TRON-C
ILEA-C	RABI-C	YOGI-C

Five letters to six

ACINI-C	CHOLI-C	FILMI-C
AGAMI-C	CULTI-C	FUNDI-C

| FUNGI-C | MANIA-C | PARSE-C |
| LIMBI-C | MYTHI-C | TRAGI-C |

Six letters to seven

ALKALI-C	EMBOLI-C	SCORIA-C
CARDIA-C	NUCLEI-C	THALLI-C
COLONI-C	RHOMBI-C	TROPHI-C

Seven letters to eight

AMMONIA-C	CHIASMI-C	SYLLABI-C
AMNESIA-C	DACTYLI-C	TSUNAMI-C
BULIMIA-C	RHYTHMI-C	TYMPANI-C

BLOCKERS

It is useful to know which words are blockers and can't therefore be extended before or after. You may want to play a blocker that your opponent can't extend, or you may want to avoid playing a blocker because you want to keep the board open.

The three-letter blockers beginning with C

| CAZ | CLY | CUZ |

Some four-letter blockers beginning with C

CASH	CITO	COSY
CAUF	CITY	COZY
CAVY	COAX	CRUX
CHEZ	COPY	CUED
CIAO	COSH	CURT

Some five-letter blockers beginning with C (except words ending in '-ED', '-J', '-S', '-X', '-Y' or '-Z')

C

CABRE	CLASH	CREPT
CACTI	CLOMB	CRONK
CAJON	CLUNG	CRUSH
CAJUN	CORAM	CUING
CHOTA	COULD	CYBER
CINCH	CRASH	

Some six-letter blockers beginning with C (except words ending in '-ED', '-J', '-S', '-X', '-Y' or '-Z')

CAGIER	CHEVAL	COMETH
CAGING	CHOSEN	CONING
CALCIC	CISTIC	COSMIC
CALMER	CITING	COXING
CANIER	CITRIC	COYEST
CANNOT	CLENCH	CROUCH
CARTOP	CLINCH	CRUDER
CATTLE	CLONAL	CRUTCH
CAUGHT	CLOVEN	CURIAL
CAUSEN	CLUING	CURING
CEDARN	COGENT	CURTER
CEDING	COINOP	CYANIC
CERTIE	COITAL	CYSTIC

BONUS WORDS

Bonus words on your rack can be hard to spot, especially for the less experienced player. One way to help find them is by using prefixes and suffixes.

Many larger words include a common prefix or suffix – remembering these and using them where you can is a good way to discover any longer words on your rack, including any potential bonus words. The key prefixes to remember beginning with C are COM- and CON-.

Some words beginning with COM-

Seven-letter words

COM-BATS	COM-MODE	COM-PILE
COM-BINE	COM-MUTE	COM-PLEX
COM-BING	COM-PACT	COM-PORT
COM-BUST	COM-PARE	COM-POSE
COM-MAND	COM-PASS	COM-POST
COM-MEND	COM-PEND	COM-POTE
COM-MENT	COM-PERE	COM-RADE

Eight-letter words

COM-BATED	COM-PARED	COM-PLIER
COM-BINER	COM-PILED	COM-POSED
COM-BINES	COM-PILER	COM-POSER
COM-MUTED	COM-PLAIN	COM-POUND
COM-MUTER	COM-PLEAT	COM-PRESS
COM-PADRE	COM-PLIED	COM-PRISE

Some words beginning with CON-

Seven-letter words

CON-CAVE	CON-DONE	CON-FIRM
CON-CEDE	CON-DUCE	CON-FORM
CON-CERT	CON-DUCT	CON-FUSE
CON-CORD	CON-DUIT	CON-GEAL
CON-CUSS	CON-FESS	CON-GEST
CON-DOLE	CON-FINE	CON-JOIN

C

CON-JURE CON-SORT CON-TEXT
CON-JURY CON-SPUE CON-TORT
CON-NOTE CON-TACT CON-TOUR
CON-SENT CON-TAIN CON-VENT
CON-SIGN CON-TEND CON-VERT
CON-SIST CON-TENT
CON-SOLE CON-TEST

Eight-letter words

CON-CAVED CON-FUSED CON-SPIRE
CON-CEDED CON-GENIC CON-SPUED
CON-CEDER CON-JOINT CON-TEMPT
CON-CLAVE CON-JUGAL CON-TRACT
CON-DENSE CON-JUROR CON-TRITE
CON-DOLED CON-QUEST CON-VERGE
CON-DONER CON-SERVE CON-VERSE
CON-FINED CON-SIDER CON-VEXED
CON-FOUND CON-SOLED
CON-FRONT CON-SOLER

UNUSUAL WORDS FROM OVERSEAS ENGLISH

If you have an awkward combination of letters on your rack then words from overseas English may come in handy. Here are some beginning with C.

Australian words

CADAGI	tropical eucalyptus tree
CARBY	carburettor
CHEWI	chewing gum
CHIACK	tease or banter
CHOOK	hen or chicken
CHOOM	Englishman
COMPO	compensation
CORREA	evergreen shrub
COUCAL	long-legged bird
COUGAN	rowdy person
CRONK	unfit or unsound
CROOL	spoil
CROWEA	pink-flowered shrub

Canadian words

CABOOSE	mobile bunkhouse used by lumbermen
CANOLA	cooking oil extracted from a variety of rapeseed developed in Canada
CAYUSE	small Native American pony used by cowboys
CIPAILLE	type of meat pie
CUSK	gadoid food fish

Hindi words

CHAI	tea, especially with added spices
CHAMPAC	tree with fragrant yellow flowers

CHAPATI	flat coarse unleavened bread
CHAPPAL	sandal
CHARKHA	spinning wheel
CHEETAH	large swift feline mammal
CHELA	disciple of a religious teacher
CHINTZ	printed cotton with glazed finish
CHITAL	type of deer
CHOKEY	prison
CHOLI	short-sleeved bodice
CHOWK	marketplace
CHUDDAR	large shawl or veil
CHUDDIES	underpants
CHUKAR	Indian partridge
CHUKKA	period of play in polo
COWAGE	tropical climbing plant with stinging pods
CRORE	ten million
CUSHY	comfortable

New Zealand word

| COOTIE | body louse |

Urdu words

| CHARPAI | bedstead of woven webbing on a wooden frame |

Essential info
Value: 2 points
Number in set: 4

D can begin a two-letter word alongside every vowel except for U. It also forms many three-letter words, especially in combination with W or Y: DAY, DYE and DEW are all worth 7 points.

Two-letter words beginning with D

DA	DI
DE	DO

D

Some three-letter words beginning with D

DAE	DEP	DOL
DAG	DEV	DOM
DAH	DEX	DOO
DAK	DEY	DOP
DAL	DIB	DOR
DAN	DIF	DOW
DAP	DIS	DOY
DAW	DIT	DSO
DEB	DIV	DUH
DEE	DOB	DUM
DEF	DOC	DUN
DEG	DOD	DUP
DEI	DOF	DUX
DEL	DOH	DZO

HOOKS

Hooking requires a subtle change in a player's thought process, in that they must look at words already on the board without becoming distracted by their pronunciation. D benefits from the past participle form of many words, providing many options when it comes to end-hooking.

Some front-hooks

Two letters to three

D-AB	D-EN	D-OO
D-AD	D-EX	D-OP
D-AE	D-ID	D-OR
D-AG	D-IF	D-OS
D-AH	D-IN	D-OW
D-AL	D-IS	D-OY
D-AM	D-IT	D-SO
D-AN	D-OB	D-UG
D-AS	D-OD	D-UH
D-AW	D-OE	D-UM
D-AY	D-OF	D-UN
D-EE	D-OH	D-UP
D-EF	D-OM	D-YE
D-EL	D-ON	D-ZO

Three letters to four

D-AFT	D-HOW	D-RAG
D-ALE	D-ICE	D-RAM
D-AMP	D-ILL	D-RAT
D-ARE	D-IRE	D-RAW
D-ARK	D-IRK	D-RAY
D-ART	D-ISH	D-REW
D-ASH	D-OFF	D-RIP
D-ATE	D-OLE	D-ROW
D-AWN	D-ONE	D-RUB
D-EAN	D-OOR	D-RUG
D-EAR	D-OPE	D-RUM
D-ECO	D-OSE	D-ZHO
D-EFT	D-OUR	
D-ELL	D-OWL	
D-EMO	D-OWN	

D

Four letters to five

D-AIRY	D-OILY	D-REAM
D-ALLY	D-ONER	D-RIFT
D-AUNT	D-OOZY	D-RILL
D-EVIL	D-RAFT	D-RINK
D-ICED	D-RAIN	D-ROLL
D-ICKY	D-RAKE	D-WELL
D-INKY	D-RANK	D-WELT
D-ITCH	D-RAWN	
D-JINN	D-READ	

Five letters to six

D-AFTER	D-EJECT	D-OFFED
D-AMPLY	D-ELUDE	D-OFFER
D-ANGER	D-EMOTE	D-OWNED
D-ANGLE	D-ICIER	D-OWNER
D-APPLE	D-ICING	D-RAYED
D-ASHED	D-IMPLY	D-RIVEN
D-AWNED	D-INNER	D-ROGUE
D-EARLY	D-IVIED	D-ROVER
D-EARTH	D-OCKER	D-UMBER

Six letters to seven

D-ALLIED	D-INKIER	D-RILLED
D-AMPING	D-ITCHED	D-RIPPED
D-ANGLED	D-OFFING	D-RIPPER
D-ANGLER	D-OWNING	D-ROLLER
D-ASHING	D-RAFTED	D-RUBBED
D-AWNING	D-RAGGED	D-RUBBER
D-ELATED	D-RAINED	D-RUGGED
D-ELUDED	D-RAWING	D-RUMMER
D-EMOTED	D-REAMED	D-WELLED
D-EVOLVE	D-REAMER	
D-ICIEST	D-RIFTED	

Seven letters to eight

D-ALLYING	D-EMOTION	D-READING
D-ANGERED	D-ENOUNCE	D-REAMING
D-ANGLING	D-EVOLVED	D-RIFTING
D-EJECTED	D-INKIEST	D-RUBBING
D-ELUDING	D-ITCHING	D-RUGGING
D-ELUSION	D-RAFTING	D-WELLING
D-EMERGED	D-RAGGING	D-WINDLED
D-EMOTING	D-RAINING	

D

Some end-hooks

Two letters to three

AD-D	GO-D	OR-D
AI-D	HA-D	OU-D
AN-D	HI-D	PA-D
AR-D	HO-D	PE-D
BA-D	KI-D	PO-D
BE-D	LA-D	RE-D
BI-D	LI-D	SO-D
BO-D	LO-D	TA-D
DA-D	MA-D	TE-D
DI-D	ME-D	TI-D
DO-D	MI-D	TO-D
EL-D	MO-D	UR-D
EN-D	MU-D	WE-D
FA-D	NE-D	YA-D
FE-D	NO-D	YO-D
GI-D	OD-D	

Three letters to four

ACE-D	AMI-D	AWE-D
AGE-D	APE-D	AXE-D
AKE-D	ARE-D	BAL-D

BAN-D	FOU-D	MOL-D
BAR-D	FUN-D	MOO-D
BEN-D	GAE-D	NEE-D
BIN-D	GAU-D	OPE-D
BON-D	GEE-D	OWE-D
BOR-D	GEL-D	PAN-D
BRO-D	GIE-D	PAR-D
BUN-D	GOA-D	PEN-D
BUR-D	GOO-D	PIE-D
CAR-D	HAE-D	PRO-D
CHA-D	HAN-D	QUA-D
CHI-D	HEN-D	RAI-D
COL-D	HER-D	RAN-D
CON-D	HIE-D	RED-D
COR-D	HIN-D	REE-D
CRU-D	HOE-D	REN-D
CUE-D	HOO-D	RIA-D
CUR-D	HUE-D	RIN-D
DIE-D	ICE-D	ROE-D
DOW-D	IRE-D	RUE-D
DUE-D	KIN-D	RUN-D
DYE-D	KON-D	SAI-D
EAR-D	LAR-D	SAN-D
ECO-D	LEA-D	SAR-D
EKE-D	LEE-D	SEE-D
ERE-D	LEU-D	SEL-D
EYE-D	LEW-D	SEN-D
FAN-D	LIE-D	SHE-D
FAR-D	LIN-D	SIN-D
FEE-D	LOR-D	SKI-D
FEN-D	LOU-D	SOL-D
FEU-D	MAN-D	SUD-D
FIN-D	MEL-D	SUE-D
FON-D	MEN-D	SUR-D
FOR-D	MIL-D	TAE-D

TEA-D	TYE-D	WEN-D
TEE-D	USE-D	WIN-D
TEL-D	VIE-D	WOO-D
TEN-D	WAI-D	WYN-D
TIE-D	WAN-D	YAR-D
TIN-D	WAR-D	
TOE-D	WEE-D	

Four letters to five

ABLE-D	CAVE-D	DUKE-D
ACHE-D	CEDE-D	DUPE-D
ACNE-D	CITE-D	EASE-D
ACRE-D	CLUE-D	EDGE-D
AIDE-D	CODE-D	FACE-D
AMEN-D	COKE-D	FADE-D
AXLE-D	CONE-D	FAKE-D
BAKE-D	COPE-D	FAME-D
BALE-D	CORE-D	FARE-D
BARE-D	COVE-D	FATE-D
BASE-D	COZE-D	FAZE-D
BEAR-D	CROW-D	FETE-D
BIDE-D	CUBE-D	FILE-D
BIKE-D	CURE-D	FINE-D
BLUE-D	DARE-D	FIRE-D
BOAR-D	DATE-D	FRAU-D
BODE-D	DAZE-D	FREE-D
BONE-D	DICE-D	FUME-D
BORE-D	DINE-D	FUSE-D
BRAN-D	DIVE-D	GALE-D
CAGE-D	DOLE-D	GAME-D
CAKE-D	DOME-D	GAPE-D
CANE-D	DOPE-D	GATE-D
CAPE-D	DOSE-D	GAZE-D
CARE-D	DOTE-D	GLUE-D
CASE-D	DOZE-D	GORE-D

GRAN-D	LUXE-D	RABI-D
GRIN-D	MACE-D	RACE-D
GUAR-D	MATE-D	RAGE-D
HARE-D	MAZE-D	RAKE-D
HATE-D	METE-D	RARE-D
HAZE-D	MIKE-D	RATE-D
HEAR-D	MIME-D	RAVE-D
HIKE-D	MINE-D	RAZE-D
HIRE-D	MIRE-D	RILE-D
HOLE-D	MOLE-D	ROBE-D
HOME-D	MOPE-D	ROPE-D
HONE-D	MOVE-D	ROSE-D
HOPE-D	MUSE-D	ROVE-D
HOSE-D	MUTE-D	RULE-D
HYPE-D	NAME-D	RUNE-D
IDLE-D	NOSE-D	SATE-D
JADE-D	NOTE-D	SAVE-D
JAPE-D	NUKE-D	SHOE-D
JIBE-D	OGEE-D	SIDE-D
JIVE-D	OGLE-D	SIRE-D
JOKE-D	OOZE-D	SITE-D
KNEE-D	PACE-D	SIZE-D
LACE-D	PAGE-D	SPIE-D
LAIR-D	PALE-D	SURE-D
LAZE-D	PARE-D	TAME-D
LIKE-D	PAVE-D	TAPE-D
LIME-D	PIKE-D	TILE-D
LINE-D	PILE-D	TIME-D
LIVE-D	PINE-D	TIRE-D
LOPE-D	PIPE-D	TONE-D
LOVE-D	PLEA-D	TREE-D
LOWE-D	PLIE-D	TRIE-D
LUGE-D	POKE-D	TUNE-D
LURE-D	PORE-D	TWEE-D
LUTE-D	POSE-D	TYPE-D

URGE-D	WAVE-D	WIRE-D
VOTE-D	WEIR-D	YOKE-D
WADE-D	WINE-D	ZONE-D
WANE-D	WIPE-D	

Five letters to six

ABASE-D	CABLE-D	ENSUE-D
ABATE-D	CACHE-D	ERASE-D
ABIDE-D	CARTE-D	ERODE-D
ABUSE-D	CARVE-D	EVADE-D
ADDLE-D	CAUSE-D	EVOKE-D
ADORE-D	CEASE-D	EXILE-D
AGREE-D	CHASE-D	FABLE-D
AMAZE-D	CHIME-D	FENCE-D
AMBLE-D	CHOKE-D	FLAKE-D
AMUSE-D	CLONE-D	FLAME-D
ANGLE-D	CLOSE-D	FLARE-D
ANKLE-D	CRANE-D	FLUKE-D
ARGUE-D	CRAVE-D	FORCE-D
ATONE-D	CRAZE-D	FORGE-D
BARGE-D	CURSE-D	FRAME-D
BASTE-D	CURVE-D	GAUGE-D
BELIE-D	CYCLE-D	GLACE-D
BINGE-D	DANCE-D	GLARE-D
BLAME-D	DELVE-D	GLAZE-D
BLARE-D	DEUCE-D	GLIDE-D
BLAZE-D	DODGE-D	GLOVE-D
BOOZE-D	DOUSE-D	GORGE-D
BRACE-D	DOWSE-D	GOUGE-D
BRAKE-D	DRAPE-D	GRACE-D
BRAVE-D	DRONE-D	GRADE-D
BRIBE-D	ELATE-D	GRAPE-D
BUDGE-D	ELOPE-D	GRATE-D
BUGLE-D	ELUDE-D	GRAVE-D
BULGE-D	EMOTE-D	GRAZE-D

63

GRIPE-D	POISE-D	SHINE-D
GROPE-D	PRICE-D	SHORE-D
GROVE-D	PRIDE-D	SHOVE-D
GUIDE-D	PRIME-D	SHREW-D
HASTE-D	PRISE-D	SIDLE-D
HEAVE-D	PROBE-D	SIEGE-D
HEDGE-D	PROVE-D	SIEVE-D
HINGE-D	PRUNE-D	SINGE-D
HORSE-D	PULSE-D	SKATE-D
HOUSE-D	PURGE-D	SLATE-D
IMAGE-D	QUAKE-D	SLAVE-D
ISSUE-D	QUEUE-D	SLICE-D
JUDGE-D	QUOTE-D	SLIME-D
JUICE-D	RAISE-D	SLOPE-D
KNIFE-D	RANGE-D	SMILE-D
LADLE-D	REAVE-D	SMOKE-D
LANCE-D	RETRO-D	SNAKE-D
LAPSE-D	RHYME-D	SNARE-D
LEASE-D	RIDGE-D	SNIPE-D
LEAVE-D	RIFLE-D	SNORE-D
LEDGE-D	RINSE-D	SOLVE-D
LODGE-D	ROGUE-D	SPACE-D
LOOSE-D	ROUTE-D	SPARE-D
LUNGE-D	SALVE-D	SPICE-D
MERGE-D	SAUTE-D	SPIKE-D
MINCE-D	SCALE-D	STAGE-D
NUDGE-D	SCARE-D	STAKE-D
NURSE-D	SCOPE-D	STALE-D
PASTE-D	SCORE-D	STARE-D
PAUSE-D	SEIZE-D	STATE-D
PHASE-D	SENSE-D	STOKE-D
PHONE-D	SHADE-D	STONE-D
PIECE-D	SHAKE-D	STORE-D
PLACE-D	SHAPE-D	STYLE-D
PLANE-D	SHAVE-D	SURGE-D

SWIPE-D	TRADE-D	WAIVE-D
TABLE-D	TRUCE-D	WASTE-D
TASTE-D	TWINE-D	WEAVE-D
TEASE-D	UNITE-D	WEDGE-D
TENSE-D	UNTIE-D	WHALE-D
THEME-D	VALUE-D	WHINE-D
TINGE-D	VERGE-D	WHITE-D
TITLE-D	VERSE-D	WINCE-D
TRACE-D	VOICE-D	

D

Six letters to seven

ACCRUE-D	BREEZE-D	COUPLE-D
ACCUSE-D	BRIDGE-D	COURSE-D
ADHERE-D	BRIDLE-D	CRADLE-D
ADMIRE-D	BRONZE-D	CREASE-D
ADVISE-D	BROWSE-D	CREATE-D
ALLUDE-D	BRUISE-D	CRINGE-D
ALLURE-D	BUCKLE-D	CRUISE-D
ARRIVE-D	BUNDLE-D	CUDDLE-D
ASHAME-D	BUNGLE-D	CURDLE-D
ASSUME-D	BURBLE-D	DAMAGE-D
ASSURE-D	BURGLE-D	DANGLE-D
AVENGE-D	BUSTLE-D	DAPPLE-D
BABBLE-D	CACKLE-D	DAWDLE-D
BAFFLE-D	CASTLE-D	DAZZLE-D
BATTLE-D	CENTRE-D	DEBASE-D
BEETLE-D	CHANCE-D	DEBATE-D
BEHAVE-D	CHANGE-D	DECIDE-D
BELATE-D	CHARGE-D	DECODE-D
BELOVE-D	CHEESE-D	DECREE-D
BEMUSE-D	CIRCLE-D	DEDUCE-D
BERATE-D	CLEAVE-D	DEFACE-D
BOGGLE-D	CLICHE-D	DEFAME-D
BOTTLE-D	COERCE-D	DEFILE-D
BOUNCE-D	CORPSE-D	DEFINE-D

DEFUSE-D	ENDURE-D	GRIEVE-D
DEGREE-D	ENGAGE-D	GROOVE-D
DELATE-D	ENGINE-D	GRUDGE-D
DELETE-D	ENRAGE-D	GUZZLE-D
DELUDE-D	ENSURE-D	GYRATE-D
DELUGE-D	ENTICE-D	HANDLE-D
DEMISE-D	EQUATE-D	HECKLE-D
DEMODE-D	ESCAPE-D	HOMAGE-D
DEMOTE-D	ESTATE-D	HUDDLE-D
DEMURE-D	EVOLVE-D	HUMBLE-D
DENOTE-D	EXCISE-D	HURDLE-D
DENUDE-D	EXCITE-D	HURTLE-D
DEPOSE-D	EXCUSE-D	HUSTLE-D
DERIDE-D	EXHALE-D	ICICLE-D
DERIVE-D	EXHUME-D	IGNITE-D
DESIRE-D	EXPIRE-D	IGNORE-D
DETUNE-D	EXPOSE-D	IMPALE-D
DEVISE-D	FETTLE-D	IMPEDE-D
DEVOTE-D	FIDDLE-D	IMPOSE-D
DILATE-D	FIGURE-D	INCITE-D
DILUTE-D	FISSLE-D	INDUCE-D
DISUSE-D	FIZZLE-D	INFAME-D
DIVIDE-D	FLEDGE-D	INFUSE-D
DIVINE-D	FLEECE-D	INHALE-D
DONATE-D	FONDLE-D	INJURE-D
DOODLE-D	FORAGE-D	INVADE-D
DOUBLE-D	FRIDGE-D	INVITE-D
DREDGE-D	FUMBLE-D	INVOKE-D
DRUDGE-D	GARBLE-D	IONISE-D
ELAPSE-D	GARGLE-D	JANGLE-D
EMERGE-D	GENTLE-D	JIGGLE-D
ENABLE-D	GIGGLE-D	JINGLE-D
ENCASE-D	GLANCE-D	JOSTLE-D
ENCODE-D	GOBBLE-D	JUGGLE-D
ENCORE-D	GREASE-D	JUMBLE-D

LIAISE-D	PICKLE-D	RESIDE-D
LOATHE-D	PIERCE-D	RESIZE-D
LOCATE-D	PIRATE-D	RESUME-D
LOUNGE-D	PLAGUE-D	RETIRE-D
MANAGE-D	PLEASE-D	REVERE-D
MANGLE-D	PLEDGE-D	REVILE-D
MANURE-D	PLUNGE-D	REVISE-D
MARBLE-D	POLICE-D	REVIVE-D
MATURE-D	POOTLE-D	REVOKE-D
MENACE-D	POUNCE-D	RIDDLE-D
MINGLE-D	PRAISE-D	ROTATE-D
MINUTE-D	PRANCE-D	RUBBLE-D
MISUSE-D	PSYCHE-D	RUFFLE-D
MUDDLE-D	PUDDLE-D	RUMBLE-D
MUFFLE-D	PUPATE-D	RUSTLE-D
MUMBLE-D	PURSUE-D	SADDLE-D
MUSCLE-D	PUZZLE-D	SALUTE-D
MUTATE-D	RAFFLE-D	SAMPLE-D
MUZZLE-D	RAMBLE-D	SAVAGE-D
NEEDLE-D	RATTLE-D	SCHEME-D
NEGATE-D	RAVAGE-D	SCRAPE-D
NESTLE-D	REBUKE-D	SCYTHE-D
NIBBLE-D	RECEDE-D	SECEDE-D
NOTICE-D	RECITE-D	SECURE-D
NUANCE-D	REDUCE-D	SEDATE-D
OBLIGE-D	REFINE-D	SEDUCE-D
OPPOSE-D	REFUSE-D	SEETHE-D
PADDLE-D	REGALE-D	SEVERE-D
PALACE-D	REHIRE-D	SLEAZE-D
PARADE-D	RELATE-D	SNOOZE-D
PAROLE-D	RELINE-D	SOMBRE-D
PEDDLE-D	REMOVE-D	SOURCE-D
PEOPLE-D	RENEGE-D	SPONGE-D
PERUSE-D	REPUTE-D	SQUIRE-D
PHRASE-D	RESCUE-D	STABLE-D

D

STAPLE-D	TINGLE-D	TUMBLE-D
STARVE-D	TIPTOE-D	TUSSLE-D
STATUE-D	TITTLE-D	UMPIRE-D
STRIPE-D	TONGUE-D	UNDATE-D
STRIVE-D	TOPPLE-D	UNLIKE-D
STROBE-D	TORQUE-D	UNLOVE-D
STROKE-D	TOUCHE-D	UNSURE-D
SUBDUE-D	TOUPEE-D	UPDATE-D
SUCKLE-D	TOUSLE-D	VOYAGE-D
SUPPLE-D	TRANCE-D	WABBLE-D
SWATHE-D	TREBLE-D	WHINGE-D
SWERVE-D	TRIFLE-D	WIGGLE-D
TACKLE-D	TRIPLE-D	WINKLE-D
TICKLE-D	TRUDGE-D	WOBBLE-D

Seven letters to eight

ABRIDGE-D	BANDAGE-D	COMPILE-D
ABSOLVE-D	BARCODE-D	COMPOSE-D
ACCURSE-D	BEEHIVE-D	COMPUTE-D
ACHIEVE-D	BEGUILE-D	CONCEDE-D
ACQUIRE-D	BELIEVE-D	CONCISE-D
ADVANCE-D	BEREAVE-D	CONFIDE-D
AGITATE-D	BRIGADE-D	CONFUSE-D
AGONISE-D	CAPSIZE-D	CONJURE-D
ALLEDGE-D	CAPTURE-D	CONSOLE-D
ANALYSE-D	CHORTLE-D	CONSUME-D
ANIMATE-D	CHUCKLE-D	CONVENE-D
APPROVE-D	COLLATE-D	CORRODE-D
ARCHIVE-D	COLLIDE-D	COSTUME-D
ARRANGE-D	COLLUDE-D	CRACKLE-D
ARTICLE-D	COMBINE-D	CREMATE-D
ATOMISE-D	COMMUTE-D	CRINKLE-D
ATTACHE-D	COMPARE-D	CRIPPLE-D
AVERAGE-D	COMPERE-D	CRUMBLE-D
BALANCE-D	COMPETE-D	CRUMPLE-D

CRUSADE-D	ENLARGE-D	MESSAGE-D
CULTURE-D	ENTHUSE-D	MIGRATE-D
DECEASE-D	ENTITLE-D	MISTIME-D
DECEIVE-D	EXAMINE-D	OBSCURE-D
DECLARE-D	EXCLUDE-D	OBSERVE-D
DECLINE-D	EXECUTE-D	OPERATE-D
DEGRADE-D	EXPLODE-D	OUTLINE-D
DEPRAVE-D	EXPLORE-D	OUTRAGE-D
DEPRIVE-D	FATIGUE-D	OUTSIZE-D
DESERVE-D	FEATURE-D	OVERUSE-D
DESPISE-D	FINANCE-D	OZONIZE-D
DESTINE-D	FLOUNCE-D	PACKAGE-D
DEVALUE-D	GESTATE-D	PICTURE-D
DEVIATE-D	GESTURE-D	PILLAGE-D
DICTATE-D	GRUNTLE-D	PLACATE-D
DIFFUSE-D	HYDRATE-D	POLLUTE-D
DISABLE-D	IDOLISE-D	PRECEDE-D
DISEASE-D	IMAGINE-D	PREFACE-D
DISJUNE-D	IMITATE-D	PREPARE-D
DISLIKE-D	IMMERSE-D	PRESUME-D
DISPOSE-D	IMPLODE-D	PRODUCE-D
DISPUTE-D	IMPLORE-D	PROFILE-D
DIVERGE-D	IMPROVE-D	PROMISE-D
DIVORCE-D	INCLUDE-D	PROMOTE-D
DRIBBLE-D	INDULGE-D	PROPOSE-D
EDUCATE-D	INFLAME-D	PROVIDE-D
ELEVATE-D	INFLATE-D	RAMPAGE-D
EMANATE-D	INSPIRE-D	REALISE-D
EMBRACE-D	INVOLVE-D	REALIZE-D
EMULATE-D	LICENCE-D	RECEIVE-D
ENCLOSE-D	LICENSE-D	RECYCLE-D
ENDORSE-D	MANACLE-D	REJOICE-D
ENFORCE-D	MANDATE-D	RELAPSE-D
ENGRAVE-D	MASSAGE-D	RELEASE-D
ENHANCE-D	MEASURE-D	RELIEVE-D

D

REPLACE-D	SQUEEZE-D	UPGRADE-D
REPULSE-D	STUBBLE-D	UPSTAGE-D
REQUIRE-D	STUMBLE-D	VENTURE-D
RESERVE-D	SUBSIDE-D	VIBRATE-D
REVENGE-D	SUFFICE-D	VIOLATE-D
REVERSE-D	SUPPOSE-D	WARGAME-D
REVOLVE-D	SURFACE-D	WELCOME-D
SALVAGE-D	SURVIVE-D	WHISTLE-D
SCUFFLE-D	SUSPIRE-D	WHITTLE-D
SERVICE-D	TEXTURE-D	WREATHE-D
SHUFFLE-D	TRAMPLE-D	WRESTLE-D
SILENCE-D	TROUBLE-D	WRIGGLE-D
SMUGGLE-D	UNHINGE-D	
SPARKLE-D	UNNERVE-D	

Handy Hint: Desirable D words

Some unusual short words it is worth remembering
are DA (a Burmese knife, 3 points), DAW (a shortened
form of jackdaw, 7 points), DEY (an Ottoman governor,
7 points) and DOW (an Arab ship, also 7).

BLOCKERS

It is useful to know which words are blockers and can't
therefore be extended before or after. You may want to
play a blocker that your opponent can't extend, or you
may want to avoid playing a blocker because you want
to keep the board open.

The three-letter blockers beginning with D

DUH   DUX

Some four-letter blockers beginning with D

DAFT	DIPT	DOTY
DAVY	DISS	DOUN
DEAF	DIXY	DOUX
DEEK	DOBY	DOWF
DEFT	DOEN	DOXY
DEFY	DOGY	DOZY
DEMY	DOMY	DREW
DENY	DOPY	DUCI
DEUS	DORY	DUED
DEWY	DOSH	DULY
DEXY	DOSS	DUSH
DIDY	DOST	DUTY
DIED	DOTH	DYED

Some five-letter blockers beginning with D (except words ending in '-ED', '-J', '-S', '-X', '-Y' or '-Z')

DEALT	DOILT	DRAWN
DIANE	DOLIA	DRENT
DICTA	DONER	DREST
DIRER	DORIC	DRIPT
DITCH	DRACK	DUNNO
DIVNA	DRACO	DURST
DOCHT	DRANK	DUTCH
DOEST	DRAVE	DWELT

Some six-letter blockers beginning with D (except words ending in '-ED', '-J', '-S', '-X', '-Y' or '-Z')

DAFTER	DAZING	DEFTER
DAIMEN	DEAFER	DEGAGE
DANISH	DEARER	DELISH
DANKER	DEBILE	DELUXE
DARKER	DECENT	DENSER
DAYLIT	DEEPER	DERMAL

DETACH	DOMING	DROLER
DEVOID	DOPIER	DRYEST
DEVOUT	DOSING	DRYISH
DEWIER	DOURER	DUEFUL
DEWING	DOVING	DUKING
DEXTRO	DOZIER	DULLER
DICIER	DREAMT	DUMBER
DIREST	DREICH	DUMELA
DOABLE	DRENCH	DUPING
DOITIT	DRIEST	DURING
DOLING	DRIVEN	DYABLE

BONUS WORDS

Bonus words on your rack can be hard to spot, especially for the less experienced player. One way to help find them is by using prefixes and suffixes.

Many larger words include a common prefix or suffix – remembering these and using them where you can is a good way to discover any longer words on your rack, including any potential bonus words. The key prefixes to remember beginning with D are DE- and DIS- and the key suffix is -DOM.

Some words beginning with DE-
Seven-letter words

DE-ALIGN	DE-CODED	DE-FENCE
DE-BASED	DE-CREED	DE-FILED
DE-BASER	DE-CRIED	DE-FINED
DE-BATED	DE-CRYPT	DE-FORMS
DE-BONED	DE-FACED	DE-FRAUD
DE-BRIEF	DE-FAULT	DE-FROST

72

DE-FUSED	DE-MINER	DE-RAILS
DE-GRADE	DE-NOTED	DE-RIDER
DE-ICING	DE-PARTS	DE-SIGNS
DE-LAYED	DE-PLOYS	DE-SIRED
DE-LIGHT	DE-PORTS	DE-SPITE
DE-LIVER	DE-POSED	DE-TAILS
DE-LUGED	DE-POSIT	DE-TOURS
DE-MEANS	DE-PRESS	DE-TRACT
DE-MERIT	DE-QUEUE	DE-VALUE

D

Eight-letter words

DE-AERATE	DE-GRADED	DE-SCALER
DE-BASING	DE-HAIRED	DE-SCRIBE
DE-BUGGED	DE-LAYING	DE-SEEDED
DE-BUNKED	DE-LINKED	DE-SEEDER
DE-CANTER	DE-MINING	DE-SELECT
DE-CEASED	DE-MISTED	DE-SERVED
DE-CIPHER	DE-MOTION	DE-SIGNED
DE-CODING	DE-NOTING	DE-STREAM
DE-CRYING	DE-PARTED	DE-STRESS
DE-DUCTED	DE-PENDED	DE-TAILED
DE-FACING	DE-PORTED	DE-TANGLE
DE-FOREST	DE-RAILED	DE-VOLVED
DE-FORMED	DE-RANGED	
DE-FRIEND	DE-RIDING	

Some words beginning with DIS-
Seven-letter words

DIS-ABLE	DIS-GUST	DIS-POSE
DIS-ARMS	DIS-LIKE	DIS-SECT
DIS-BAND	DIS-MISS	DIS-SENT
DIS-CARD	DIS-OBEY	DIS-TILL
DIS-CUSS	DIS-OWNS	DIS-TORT
DIS-EASE	DIS-PLAY	DIS-USED

Eight-letter words

DIS-AGREE
DIS-ALLOW
DIS-APPLY
DIS-ARRAY
DIS-CLOSE
DIS-COLOR
DIS-COVER
DIS-FAMED
DIS-GORGE
DIS-GRACE

DIS-GUISE
DIS-HOARD
DIS-HONOR
DIS-JOINT
DIS-LOYAL
DIS-MOUNT
DIS-ORDER
DIS-OWNED
DIS-PATCH
DIS-PERSE

DIS-PLACE
DIS-PROVE
DIS-QUIET
DIS-SOLVE
DIS-TASTE
DIS-TRACT
DIS-TRUST
DIS-UNITY

Some words ending with -DOM

Seven-letter words

BORE-DOM
DUKE-DOM
EARL-DOM
FIEF-DOM

FREE-DOM
JOCK-DOM
KING-DOM
SERF-DOM

STAR-DOM
TEEN-DOM

Eight-letter words

CHIEF-DOM
CLERK-DOM
DEVIL-DOM
DUNCE-DOM
HOTEL-DOM

LIEGE-DOM
QUEEN-DOM
SAINT-DOM
SHEIK-DOM
THANE-DOM

THRAL-DOM
UNWIS-DOM
YUPPY-DOM

UNUSUAL WORDS FROM OVERSEAS ENGLISH

If you have an awkward combination of letters on your rack then words from overseas English may come in handy. Here are some beginning with D.

Australian words

DASYURE	small carnivorous marsupial
DELO	delegate
DERRO	vagrant
DINKUM	genuine or right
DOCO	documentary
DONGA	steep-sided gully
DORBA	stupid, inept, or clumsy person
DRACK	unattractive
DRONGO	slow-witted person
DROOB	pathetic person
DUBBO	stupid
DUGITE	venomous snake
DURRY	cigarette

Canadian word

DEKE	act or instance of feinting in ice hockey

Hindi words

DACOIT	member of a gang of armed robbers
DACOITY	robbery by an armed gang
DAK	system of mail delivery
DAL	split grain
DATURA	plant with trumpet-shaped flowers
DEKKO	look or glance
DEODAR	Himalayan cedar
DEWAN	chief minister of an Indian princedom

DHAK	tropical tree with red flowers
DHAL	curry made from lentils
DHARNA	method of obtaining justice by fasting
DHOBI	washerman
DHOTI	loincloth
DUPATTA	scarf
DURRIE	cotton carpet
DURZI	Indian tailor

D

South African word

DWAAL	state of befuddlement

Urdu words

DAROGHA	manager
DHANSAK	Indian dish of meat or vegetables braised with lentils

Essential info
Value: 1 point
Number in set: 12

E may be worth only one point, but it is extremely useful which is why it is the most common letter in the Scrabble set. Many words contain more than one E and it is worthwhile keeping these in mind, as there is a good chance you will find yourself with more than one E on your rack. Three-letter words formed by E on either side of a consonant include EYE, EWE, EVE (6 points) and EKE (7 points). E and K combine well to form a selection of other three-letter words, including ELK, EEK (7 points) and EWK (a dialect word for itch, 10 points). E is one of the letters of the RETAIN set and is therefore a good letter to keep if trying to get a bonus word.

Two-letter words beginning with E

EA	EH	ER
ED	EL	ES
EE	EM	ET
EF	EN	EX

Some three-letter words beginning with E

EAN	ELL	ERK
EAU	ELT	ERM
ECH	EME	ERN
EDH	EMO	ESS
EEK	EMU	EST
EEN	ENE	ETA
EEW	ENG	ETH
EFF	EON	EWK
EFT	ERE	EXO
EGO	ERF	
ELD	ERG	

HOOKS

Hooking requires a subtle change in a player's thought process, in that they must look at words already on the board without becoming distracted by their pronunciation.

Some front-hooks
Two letters to three

E-AN	E-AT	E-EN
E-AR	E-CH	E-GO
E-AS	E-EL	E-ME

E-MO   E-ON   E-TA
E-MU   E-RE   E-WE
E-NE   E-ST   E-YE

Three letters to four

E-ACH   E-NOW   E-THE
E-ARD   E-PIC   E-TIC
E-AVE   E-RED   E-TUI
E-DIT   E-RES   E-UGH
E-GAD   E-REV   E-VET
E-GAL   E-SKY   E-VOE
E-KED   E-SPY   E-YEN
E-MIR   E-TAT
E-NEW   E-TEN

Four letters to five

E-AGER   E-LITE   E-NORM
E-ARED   E-LOGE   E-PACT
E-BONY   E-LOGY   E-POXY
E-BOOK   E-LOIN   E-PROM
E-DICT   E-LOPE   E-QUID
E-DUCE   E-LUDE   E-QUIP
E-GEST   E-LUTE   E-RODE
E-HING   E-MAIL   E-STOP
E-IKON   E-MEER   E-TAPE
E-KING   E-MEND   E-VADE
E-LAIN   E-MOTE   E-VENT
E-LAND   E-MOVE   E-VERY
E-LATE   E-MULE   E-ZINE
E-LINT   E-NEWS

Five letters to six

E-ASTER
E-CARTE
E-CHARD
E-DITED
E-GALLY
E-ITHER
E-LAPSE
E-LATED
E-LATER
E-LEGIT
E-LICIT
E-LOPED

E-LOPER
E-MERGE
E-METIC
E-MOTED
E-NERVE
E-NEWED
E-PATER
E-PRISE
E-QUATE
E-QUINE
E-RASED
E-RASER

E-SCAPE
E-SCARP
E-SCROW
E-SPIED
E-SPIER
E-SPRIT
E-STATE
E-VADED
E-VILER
E-VOLVE

Six letters to seven

E-ASTERN
E-BAYING
E-BONIST
E-CLOSED
E-COTYPE
E-DITING
E-LANCED
E-LAPSED
E-LECTOR
E-LEGIST
E-LOPING

E-MAILED
E-MAILER
E-MERGED
E-MOTION
E-MOTIVE
E-MOVING
E-NERVED
E-RASING
E-RASURE
E-RODING
E-SCAPED

E-SPOUSE
E-SPYING
E-SQUIRE
E-STATED
E-TERNAL
E-VADING
E-VENTER
E-VILEST
E-VOLUTE
E-VOLVED

Seven letters to eight

E-LAPSING
E-LECTION
E-LEVATOR
E-MAILING
E-MENDING

E-MERGING
E-MERSION
E-MIGRANT
E-MIGRATE
E-MISSION

E-MISSIVE
E-NERVATE
E-NERVING
E-QUALITY
E-QUIPPED

E-QUIPPER	E-SPECIAL	E-TYPICAL
E-RADIATE	E-SPOUSAL	E-VACUATE
E-SCALADE	E-SQUIRED	E-VALUATE
E-SCAPING	E-STATING	E-VENTING
E-SCARPED	E-STOPPED	E-VERSION
E-SCRIBED	E-STRANGE	E-VOLVING

Handy Hint: Easy vowel dumps

If you find yourself with a vowel-heavy rack, handy short words to remember which use no consonants are EA and EE (both 2 points) or EAU (3 points). And there's always EUOUAE (a mnemonic used in Gregorian chant, 6 points) and EUOI (an interjection of Bacchic frenzy, 4 points).

Some end-hooks

Two letters to three

AG-E	DO-E	KY-E
AL-E	EM-E	LI-E
AM-E	EN-E	MA-E
AN-E	ER-E	ME-E
AR-E	FA-E	MO-E
AT-E	FE-E	NA-E
AW-E	GI-E	NE-E
AX-E	GO-E	NY-E
AY-E	GU-E	OB-E
BE-E	HA-E	OD-E
BY-E	HI-E	ON-E
CH-E	HO-E	OP-E
DA-E	ID-E	OR-E
DE-E	JO-E	OS-E
DI-E	KA-E	OW-E

OY-E   TA-E   US-E
PE-E   TE-E   UT-E
PI-E   TI-E   WE-E
RE-E   TO-E   WO-E
SH-E   UR-E   YA-E

E **Three letters to four**

ACH-E	CUR-E	FUM-E
ADZ-E	CUT-E	GAL-E
AID-E	DAL-E	GAM-E
ANT-E	DAM-E	GAP-E
BAL-E	DIM-E	GAT-E
BAN-E	DIN-E	GEN-E
BAR-E	DIV-E	GIB-E
BAS-E	DOL-E	GON-E
BAT-E	DOM-E	GOR-E
BIB-E	DON-E	HAT-E
BID-E	DOP-E	HER-E
BIT-E	DOS-E	HID-E
BON-E	DOT-E	HOM-E
BOR-E	DUD-E	HOP-E
BOT-E	DUN-E	HOS-E
BRA-E	DUP-E	HUG-E
CAG-E	EAS-E	HYP-E
CAM-E	ELS-E	JAP-E
CAN-E	FAD-E	JIB-E
CAP-E	FAR-E	JUT-E
CAR-E	FAT-E	KIT-E
CIT-E	FET-E	LAC-E
CON-E	FIL-E	LAM-E
COP-E	FIN-E	LAT-E
COR-E	FIR-E	LED-E
COS-E	FLU-E	LIN-E
CUB-E	FOR-E	LIT-E

LOB-E	NOT-E	SIT-E
LOD-E	OBO-E	SOL-E
LOP-E	OLD-E	SOM-E
LOR-E	PAC-E	SUR-E
LOS-E	PAL-E	TAK-E
LUD-E	PAN-E	TAM-E
LUG-E	PAR-E	TAP-E
LUR-E	PAT-E	THE-E
MAC-E	PAV-E	TID-E
MAD-E	PIN-E	TIL-E
MAG-E	PIP-E	TIN-E
MAK-E	POL-E	TOM-E
MAL-E	POP-E	TON-E
MAN-E	POS-E	TOP-E
MAR-E	PUR-E	TOT-E
MAT-E	RAG-E	TUB-E
MEM-E	RAT-E	TUN-E
MIC-E	RID-E	VAN-E
MIL-E	RIF-E	VAR-E
MIM-E	RIP-E	VAS-E
MIR-E	ROB-E	VIN-E
MOD-E	ROD-E	VIS-E
MOL-E	ROT-E	VOL-E
MOP-E	RUD-E	WAD-E
MOR-E	RUN-E	WAG-E
MUS-E	SAG-E	WAN-E
MUT-E	SAL-E	WAR-E
NAM-E	SAM-E	WIN-E
NAP-E	SAN-E	WIS-E
NIT-E	SAT-E	WOK-E
NOD-E	SAV-E	YOK-E
NON-E	SIN-E	
NOS-E	SIR-E	

E

Four letters to five

AMID-E
BATH-E
BING-E
BLAM-E
BOMB-E
BOOS-E
BRAN-E
BRUT-E
CART-E
CAST-E
CHIV-E
COPS-E
COUP-E
CREW-E
CRIM-E
CURS-E
DOWS-E
ERAS-E
FLAK-E
FLAN-E
FLIT-E
FORT-E
GEES-E
GLAD-E
GLOB-E
GRAD-E

GRIM-E
GRIP-E
HAST-E
HING-E
HIRE-E
LAPS-E
LENS-E
LOCH-E
LOOS-E
MANS-E
PASS-E
PAST-E
PEAS-E
PLAN-E
PLAT-E
PLOY-E
PLUM-E
PRIM-E
PROS-E
PURE-E
QUIT-E
RANG-E
SCAR-E
SHAM-E
SHIN-E
SING-E

SLAT-E
SLID-E
SLIM-E
SLOP-E
SNIP-E
SPAR-E
SPAT-E
SPIN-E
SPIT-E
STAG-E
STAR-E
STAT-E
STUD-E
SUED-E
SUET-E
SUIT-E
TEAS-E
TENS-E
THEM-E
TRAD-E
TRIP-E
TWIN-E
UNIT-E
WHIN-E
WHIT-E
WRIT-E

Five letters to six

BLOND-E
CHINS-E
CLOTH-E
EQUIP-E

FINAL-E
GOATS-E
GRAND-E
HEARS-E

HUMAN-E
IMPED-E
LOATH-E
LOCAL-E

LUPIN-E	REPOS-E	STING-E
MADAM-E	RESIT-E	STRIP-E
MORAL-E	SCRAP-E	STYLE-E
PETIT-E	SOOTH-E	SWATH-E
PLEAS-E	SPARS-E	TOUCH-E
REGAL-E	SPRIT-E	URBAN-E

Six letters to seven

ADVISE-E	DIVERS-E	OBLIGE-E
ARTIST-E	ESCAPE-E	REFUGE-E
ATTACH-E	FIANCE-E	RETIRE-E
AUGUST-E	FLAMBE-E	REVERS-E
BREATH-E	GERMAN-E	SECRET-E
CORNEA-E	HEROIN-E	SMOOTH-E
CRAVAT-E	IMPING-E	TARTAR-E
DEVOTE-E	IMPROV-E	WREATH-E

Seven letters to eight

ABSINTH-E	EMPLOYE-E	LICENCE-E
ALKALIS-E	ENDORSE-E	LICENSE-E
AMPHORA-E	ENVELOP-E	NOCTURN-E
BACKBIT-E	ESCALOP-E	OUTWRIT-E
DECLASS-E	GELATIN-E	PROTEGE-E
DIVORCE-E	INHUMAN-E	SILICON-E
DOMICIL-E	INTERNE-E	

Handy Hint: Strive for excellence

A good short word which uses the X and a couple of vowels is EXO (informal Australian term meaning excellent, 10 points). Note that the word could enable you to make a play that involves hooking your O onto an existing EX, and EXO itself can take an N hook for EXON.

BLOCKERS

It is useful to know which words are blockers and can't therefore be extended before or after. You may want to play a blocker that your opponent can't extend, or you may want to avoid playing a blocker because you want to keep the board open.

Some four-letter blockers beginning with E

EASY	ESPY	EYNE
EDDO	EUGE	EYRY
ELSE	EVOE	

Five-letter blockers beginning with E (except words ending in '-ED', '-J', '-S', '-X', '-Y' or '-Z')

ELMEN	ENLIT	EVHOE
ELVEN	ETYMA	EVOHE

Some six-letter blockers beginning with E (except words ending in '-ED', '-J', '-S', '-X', '-Y' or '-Z')

EASIER	ENCASH	ENRICH
EFFETE	ENDASH	ETERNE
EIDOLA	ENGIRT	EXUENT
ELVISH	ENMESH	EYEING
EMDASH	ENRAPT	

BONUS WORDS

Bonus words on your rack can be hard to spot, especially for the less experienced player. One way to help find them is by using prefixes and suffixes.

Many larger words include a common prefix or suffix – remembering these and using them where you can is a good way to discover any longer words on your rack, including any potential bonus words. The key prefixes to remember beginning with E are EM-, EN- and EX- and the key suffixes are -EAU, -ENCE, -ENCY, -EST, -ETTE and -EUR.

Some words beginning with EM-

Seven-letter words

EM-BARKS	EM-PANEL	EM-PLOYS
EM-BRACE	EM-PARTS	EM-POWER
EM-BROIL	EM-PEACH	

Eight-letter words

EM-BALMED	EM-BLAZED	EM-PALING
EM-BARKED	EM-BODIED	EM-PARTED
EM-BATTLE	EM-BOLDEN	EM-PATHIC
EM-BEDDED	EM-BOSSED	EM-PHATIC
EM-BITTER	EM-BRACED	EM-PLOYED

Some words beginning with EN-

Seven-letter words

EN-ABLED	EN-CRYPT	EN-SLAVE
EN-ACTED	EN-DEARS	EN-SNARE
EN-CAGED	EN-FORCE	EN-SUING
EN-CASED	EN-GORGE	EN-SURED
EN-CLOSE	EN-QUEUE	EN-TAILS
EN-CODED	EN-QUIRE	EN-TIRES
EN-CORED	EN-RAGED	EN-TITLE

EN-TRAIL   EN-TRIES   EN-VYING
EN-TREES   EN-URNED   EN-ZYMES

Eight-letter words

EN-ABLING   EN-DURING   EN-RICHED
EN-CAMPED   EN-FOLDED   EN-ROLLED
EN-CASING   EN-GENDER   EN-SHRINE
EN-CHANTS   EN-GORGED   EN-SIGNED
EN-CIPHER   EN-GRAVED   EN-SNARED
EN-CIRCLE   EN-GULFED   EN-SURING
EN-CLOSED   EN-JOYING   EN-TAILED
EN-CORING   EN-LISTED   EN-TITLED
EN-DANGER   EN-QUEUED   EN-TRENCH
EN-DEARED   EN-QUIRED   EN-URNING

Some words beginning with EX-

Seven-letter words

EX-ACTED   EX-PLAIN   EX-TENDS
EX-CITED   EX-PORTS   EX-TOLLS
EX-CLAIM   EX-POSED   EX-TRACT
EX-PENDS   EX-PRESS   EX-TROPY

Eight-letter words

EX-ACTING   EX-CITING   EX-PERTLY
EX-CELLED   EX-FILLED   EX-PLAINS
EX-CESSES   EX-PANDER   EX-PORTED

Some words ending with -EAU

Seven-letter words

BAND-EAU   JAMB-EAU   MOIN-EAU
CHAP-EAU   MANT-EAU   MORC-EAU

NOUV-EAU   ROND-EAU   TONN-EAU
PLAT-EAU   TABL-EAU

Eight-letter words

ABOID-EAU   FLAMB-EAU
ABOIT-EAU   ROUSS-EAU

Some words ending with -ENCE
Seven-letter words

ABS-ENCE   FLU-ENCE   SIL-ENCE
CAD-ENCE   LIC-ENCE   URG-ENCE
COG-ENCE   OFF-ENCE   VAL-ENCE
DEF-ENCE   POT-ENCE
ESS-ENCE   SCI-ENCE

Eight-letter words

AMBI-ENCE   LENI-ENCE   SALI-ENCE
AUDI-ENCE   NASC-ENCE   SAPI-ENCE
COMM-ENCE   OPUL-ENCE   SEQU-ENCE
CRED-ENCE   PATI-ENCE   SIXP-ENCE
DISP-ENCE   PRES-ENCE   TEND-ENCE
EMIN-ENCE   PRET-ENCE   VIOL-ENCE
EVID-ENCE   PRUD-ENCE

Some words ending with -ENCY
Seven-letter words

COG-ENCY   POT-ENCY   URG-ENCY
DEC-ENCY   REC-ENCY   VAL-ENCY
FLU-ENCY   REG-ENCY

Eight-letter words

CLEM-ENCY	LENI-ENCY	TEND-ENCY
CURR-ENCY	PUNG-ENCY	
FERV-ENCY	SOLV-ENCY	

E ## Some words ending with -EST

Seven-letter words

AIRI-EST	HARD-EST	POOR-EST
BALD-EST	KIND-EST	TALL-EST
BOLD-EST	LONG-EST	TENS-EST
DAMP-EST	MEEK-EST	WARM-EST
DARK-EST	NEAR-EST	WILD-EST
FULL-EST	OATI-EST	

Eight-letter words

ACRID-EST	FAIRI-EST	PEPPI-EST
BLACK-EST	FLASH-EST	QUICK-EST
BLOND-EST	GAUDI-EST	SIMPL-EST
BRIEF-EST	GLAMM-EST	SUNNI-EST
CLEAN-EST	GRAND-EST	TOUGH-EST
CLEAR-EST	GREEN-EST	URBAN-EST
DIVIN-EST	INERT-EST	WRONG-EST
EAGER-EST	MINUT-EST	
EXACT-EST	ORANG-EST	

Some words ending with -ETTE

Seven-letter words

BLU-ETTE	GAZ-ETTE	PIP-ETTE
CAS-ETTE	LAD-ETTE	POP-ETTE
DIN-ETTE	MIN-ETTE	ROS-ETTE
DUD-ETTE	OCT-ETTE	
FUM-ETTE	PAL-ETTE	

Eight-letter words

AMUS-ETTE

BAGU-ETTE

BRUN-ETTE

CASS-ETTE

COQU-ETTE

CORV-ETTE

CUTL-ETTE

DISK-ETTE

JEAN-ETTE

MAQU-ETTE

NOIS-ETTE

PALL-ETTE

PUNK-ETTE

RING-ETTE

ROOM-ETTE

ROQU-ETTE

ROUL-ETTE

SEPT-ETTE

STAG-ETTE

VIGN-ETTE

Some words ending with -EUR

Seven-letter words

AMAT-EUR

LIQU-EUR

MASS-EUR

PRIM-EUR

SABR-EUR

SIGN-EUR

TRAC-EUR

Eight-letter words

CHASS-EUR

COIFF-EUR

GRAND-EUR

JONGL-EUR

LONGU-EUR

MONSI-EUR

SABOT-EUR

SECAT-EUR

SEIGN-EUR

VOYAG-EUR

UNUSUAL WORDS FROM OVERSEAS ENGLISH

If you have an awkward combination of letters on your rack then words from overseas English may come in handy. Here are some beginning with E.

E

Australian words

EARBASH	talk incessantly
EUMUNG	type of acacia
EVO	evening
EXO	excellent

Essential info
Value: 4 points
Number in set: 2

F can be a useful letter for scoring with short words on premium squares. There are three two-letter words beginning with F (FA and FE, 5 points each, and FY, 8 points), complemented with EF, IF, and OF. There are also quite a few short, high-scoring words beginning with F which use X (FAX, FIX, FOX, 13 points each), Y (FAY, FEY, FOY, 9 points each) or Z (FEZ, FIZ, 15 points each).

Two-letter words beginning with F

| FA | FE | FY |

Some three-letter words beginning with F

FAA	FEN	FON
FAE	FER	FOO
FAH	FET	FOP
FAP	FEU	FOU
FAW	FEY	FOY
FAX	FEZ	FUB
FAY	FID	FUG
FEG	FIZ	FUM
FEH	FOB	
FEM	FOH	

HOOKS

Hooking requires a subtle change in a player's thought process, in that they must look at words already on the board without becoming distracted by their pronunciation.

Some front-hooks
Two letters to three

F-AA	F-AR	F-EE
F-AB	F-AS	F-EH
F-AD	F-AT	F-EM
F-AE	F-AW	F-EN
F-AG	F-AX	F-ER
F-AH	F-AY	F-ES
F-AN	F-ED	F-ET

F-ID	F-OH	F-OX
F-IN	F-ON	F-OY
F-IT	F-OO	F-UG
F-OB	F-OP	F-UM
F-OE	F-OR	F-UN
F-OG	F-OU	F-UR

Three letters to four

F-ACE	F-ETA	F-LOW
F-ACT	F-ILL	F-LOX
F-AFF	F-ILK	F-LUX
F-AIL	F-INK	F-OIL
F-AIR	F-IRE	F-OLD
F-AKE	F-ISH	F-OOT
F-ALL	F-LAB	F-ORD
F-ARE	F-LAG	F-ORE
F-ARM	F-LAP	F-ORT
F-ASH	F-LAT	F-OUR
F-ATE	F-LAW	F-OWL
F-AVA	F-LAX	F-OXY
F-AVE	F-LAY	F-RAG
F-AWN	F-LEA	F-RAT
F-EAR	F-LED	F-RAY
F-EAT	F-LEE	F-REE
F-EEL	F-LEW	F-RET
F-ELL	F-LEX	F-RIZ
F-ELT	F-LIP	F-ROM
F-END	F-LIT	F-RUG
F-ERN	F-LOB	F-USE
F-ESS	F-LOG	
F-EST	F-LOP	

Four letters to five

F-ABLE

F-ACED

F-ACER

F-AERY

F-AIRY

F-AKED

F-ARED

F-AXED

F-AYRE

F-EAST

F-ETCH

F-EVER

F-EWER

F-ILLY

F-INCH

F-ITCH

F-LACK

F-LAIR

F-LAKE

F-LAKY

F-LAME

F-LANE

F-LANK

F-LARE

F-LASH

F-LAVA

F-LEER

F-LEET

F-LICK

F-LIER

F-LING

F-LINT

F-LITE

F-LOCK

F-LOOR

F-LOSS

F-LOUR

F-LOUT

F-LOWN

F-LUFF

F-LUKE

F-LUNG

F-LUNK

F-LUSH

F-LUTE

F-OLIO

F-OYER

F-RAIL

F-RANK

F-REED

F-RILL

F-RISK

F-RITZ

F-ROCK

F-RUMP

F-USED

Five letters to six

F-ABLED

F-ACING

F-ACTOR

F-AILED

F-ALLOW

F-ALTER

F-AMINE

F-ARMED

F-ARMER

F-ARROW

F-AXING

F-EARED

F-ENDED

F-ENDER

F-ESTER

F-ICKLE

F-INNER

F-LAKED

F-LAKER

F-LAMED

F-LAMER

F-LAWED

F-LAYED

F-LAYER

F-LEDGE

F-LETCH

F-LIGHT

F-LINCH

F-LINTY

F-LOWED

F-LOWER

F-LUTED

F-LUTER

F

F-LYING   F-OUGHT   F-RISKY
F-ODDER   F-RIDGE   F-USING
F-OILED   F-RIGHT   F-UTILE
F-OLDER   F-RIGID

Six letters to seven

F-ABLING	F-LAKING	F-LUBBER
F-ACTION	F-LAMING	F-LUMMOX
F-ACTUAL	F-LANKER	F-LUMPED
F-ADDLED	F-LAPPED	F-LUSHED
F-AILING	F-LAPPER	F-LUSTER
F-AIRIER	F-LASHED	F-LUTING
F-AIRILY	F-LASHER	F-LUTIST
F-AIRING	F-LASKET	F-OILING
F-AIRWAY	F-LATTER	F-OXLIKE
F-ANGLED	F-LAYING	F-OXTAIL
F-ARMING	F-LEDGED	F-RAGGED
F-ATTEST	F-LEERED	F-RAILER
F-AWNING	F-LEGGED	F-RANKED
F-EARFUL	F-LENSED	F-RANKER
F-EARING	F-LICKED	F-RANKLY
F-EASTER	F-LICKER	F-RAPPED
F-EATING	F-LIMPED	F-RAZZLE
F-ENDING	F-LINGER	F-RIDGED
F-ETCHED	F-LIPPED	F-RINGED
F-ETCHER	F-LIPPER	F-RIPPER
F-ICKLER	F-LITTER	F-RISKED
F-INCHED	F-LOCKED	F-RISKER
F-INNING	F-LOGGED	F-ROCKED
F-LACKED	F-LOGGER	F-RUSHED
F-LACKER	F-LOPPED	F-UNFAIR
F-LAGGED	F-LOPPER	
F-LAGGER	F-LOWING	

F

97

Seven letters to eight

F-AIRIEST	F-LAWLESS	F-RAPPING
F-ALLOWED	F-LETCHED	F-RIDGING
F-ALTERED	F-LICKING	F-RIGHTEN
F-ALTERER	F-LIGHTED	F-RIGIDER
F-EARLESS	F-LINTING	F-RIGIDLY
F-EASTING	F-LIPPING	F-RINGING
F-ETCHING	F-LOCKING	F-RISKIER
F-ICKLEST	F-LOGGING	F-RISKILY
F-IRELESS	F-LOPPING	F-RISKING
F-LACKING	F-LOUTING	F-ROCKING
F-LAGGING	F-LOWERED	F-UNCTION
F-LAKIEST	F-LUSHEST	F-USELESS
F-LANKING	F-RAGGING	F-UTILITY
F-LAPPING	F-RANKEST	
F-LASHING	F-RANKING	

Some end-hooks

Two letters to three

AL-F	ER-F	OO-F
AR-F	GI-F	OR-F
DE-F	IF-F	RE-F
DI-F	KA-F	SI-F
DO-F	KI-F	TE-F
EF-F	NE-F	WO-F
EL-F	OF-F	

Three letters to four

BAR-F	CUR-F	GOO-F
BEE-F	DIF-F	GUL-F
CHE-F	DOF-F	HOO-F
CON-F	FIE-F	HOW-F

HUM-F	REE-F	SOW-F
LEA-F	RIF-F	SUR-F
LIE-F	ROO-F	WAI-F
LOO-F	SEL-F	WOO-F
PRO-F	SER-F	

Four letters to five

BRIE-F	MOTI-F	SKEE-F
GANE-F	PILA-F	SNAR-F
GONE-F	PROO-F	SPIF-F
HOUF-F	SCAR-F	TRAY-F
HOWF-F	SCUR-F	
KALI-F	SHEA-F	

Five letters to six

BELIE-F	GONIF-F	RELIE-F
DECAF-F	PILAF-F	

Six letters to seven

SHERIF-F

BLOCKERS

It is useful to know which words are blockers and can't therefore be extended before or after. You may want to play a blocker that your opponent can't extend, or you may want to avoid playing a blocker because you want to keep the board open.

Two-letter blocker beginning with F

FY

The three-letter blockers beginning with F

FAE	FAX	FLY
FAP	FEZ	FRY

Some four-letter blockers beginning with F

FAAN	FLIX	FROM
FASH	FLUX	FUMY
FAUX	FOGY	FURY
FEET	FONE	FUSC
FIXT	FOXY	
FLED	FRAE	

Some five-letter blockers beginning with F (except words ending in '-ED', '-J', '-S', '-X', '-Y' or '-Z')

FATAL	FETCH	FLUNG
FAUGH	FETID	FOLIC
FAURD	FEWER	FRENA
FECIT	FINCH	FURTH
FETAL	FLOWN	

Some six-letter blockers beginning with F (except words ending in '-ED', '-J', '-S', '-X', '-Y' or '-Z')

FACEUP	FAZING	FILIAL
FACILE	FECUND	FILMIC
FAIRER	FEEING	FINISH
FAKING	FERINE	FINITO
FALLEN	FERRIC	FITFUL
FAMING	FERVID	FLAXEN
FAMISH	FETISH	FLEMIT
FARING	FEUDAL	FLETCH
FATTER	FEWEST	FLIEST
FAXING	FEYEST	FLINCH

FLOOIE	FOOBAR	FRUGAL
FLORID	FOREGO	FUMING
FLUIER	FORGOT	FUNGIC
FLUISH	FOULER	FUNNER
FLYEST	FOXIER	FUSILE
FOETAL	FREEST	FUSING
FOETID	FRIGID	
FONDER	FROZEN	

BONUS WORDS

Bonus words on your rack can be hard to spot, especially for the less experienced player. One way to help find them is by using prefixes and suffixes.

Many larger words include a common prefix or suffix – remembering these and using them where you can is a good way to discover any longer words on your rack, including any potential bonus words. The key prefixes to remember beginning with F are FOOT- and FOR- and the key suffixes are -FISH, -FORM and -FUL.

Some words beginning with FOOT-

Seven-letter words

FOOT-AGE	FOOT-BOY	FOOT-ROT
FOOT-BAG	FOOT-MAN	FOOT-WAY
FOOT-BAR	FOOT-MEN	
FOOT-BED	FOOT-PAD	

Eight-letter words

| FOOT-BALL | FOOT-FALL | FOOT-HOLD |
| FOOT-BATH | FOOT-HILL | FOOT-LESS |

FOOT-LIKE	FOOT-PATH	FOOT-STEP
FOOT-LING	FOOT-PUMP	FOOT-WALL
FOOT-LONG	FOOT-RACE	FOOT-WEAR
FOOT-MARK	FOOT-REST	FOOT-WORK
FOOT-NOTE	FOOT-SORE	FOOT-WORN

Some words beginning with FOR-

F

Seven-letter words

FOR-BADE	FOR-GAVE	FOR-SAID
FOR-BEAR	FOR-GETS	FOR-SAKE
FOR-BIDS	FOR-GIVE	FOR-SOOK
FOR-BODE	FOR-GOER	FOR-WARD
FOR-CEPS	FOR-GOES	FOR-WARN
FOR-DONE	FOR-GONE	FOR-WENT
FOR-EVER	FOR-LORE	FOR-WORN
FOR-FEND	FOR-LORN	

Eight-letter words

FOR-BODED	FOR-SOOTH	FOR-SWEAR
FOR-GIVEN	FOR-SPEAK	FOR-SWORN
FOR-GIVER	FOR-SPEND	
FOR-GOING	FOR-SPOKE	

Some words ending with -FISH

Seven-letter words

BAT-FISH	FIN-FISH	ICE-FISH
BOX-FISH	FOX-FISH	MAY-FISH
CAT-FISH	GAR-FISH	MUD-FISH
COD-FISH	GEM-FISH	OAR-FISH
COW-FISH	HAG-FISH	OUT-FISH
DOG-FISH	HOG-FISH	PAN-FISH

PIG-FISH   RAT-FISH   SUN-FISH
PIN-FISH   RED-FISH
PUP-FISH   SAW-FISH

Eight-letter words

BAIT-FISH   GAME-FISH   SAIL-FISH
BAND-FISH   GOLD-FISH   SALT-FISH
BLOW-FISH   GRAY-FISH   SAND-FISH
BLUE-FISH   KELP-FISH   SCAR-FISH
BONE-FISH   KING-FISH   SOAP-FISH
CAVE-FISH   LION-FISH   STAR-FISH
CRAW-FISH   LUNG-FISH   SUCK-FISH
CRAY-FISH   MONK-FISH   SURF-FISH
DEAL-FISH   MOON-FISH   TOAD-FISH
FLAT-FISH   OVER-FISH   WOLF-FISH
FOOL-FISH   PIPE-FISH
FROG-FISH   ROCK-FISH

Some words ending with -FORM

Seven-letter words

ACI-FORM   DEI-FORM   OVI-FORM
ALI-FORM   DIF-FORM   PER-FORM
AUS-FORM   DIS-FORM   PRE-FORM
AVI-FORM   ISO-FORM   TRI-FORM
CON-FORM   MIS-FORM   UNI-FORM

Eight-letter words

AERI-FORM   FUSI-FORM   PALI-FORM
CONI-FORM   LAND-FORM   PARA-FORM
CUBI-FORM   LYRI-FORM   PLAN-FORM
FLAT-FORM   MANI-FORM   PLAT-FORM
FREE-FORM   OMNI-FORM   POST-FORM

PYRI-FORM	TUBI-FORM	WAVE-FORM
ROTI-FORM	URSI-FORM	
SLIP-FORM	VARI-FORM	

Some words ending with -FUL
Seven-letter words

F

ARMS-FUL	FRET-FUL	PITI-FUL
BALE-FUL	GAIN-FUL	PLAY-FUL
BANE-FUL	GLEE-FUL	RACK-FUL
BASH-FUL	GUTS-FUL	RAGE-FUL
BOAT-FUL	HAND-FUL	REST-FUL
BOWL-FUL	HARM-FUL	RISK-FUL
BRIM-FUL	HATE-FUL	SACK-FUL
CARE-FUL	HEED-FUL	SINK-FUL
DARE-FUL	HELP-FUL	SKIL-FUL
DEED-FUL	HOPE-FUL	SKIN-FUL
DIRE-FUL	HURT-FUL	SOUL-FUL
DOLE-FUL	LUNG-FUL	TACT-FUL
DUTI-FUL	LUST-FUL	TANK-FUL
FACT-FUL	MIND-FUL	TEAR-FUL
FATE-FUL	NEED-FUL	TUNE-FUL
FEAR-FUL	PAIL-FUL	VASE-FUL
FIST-FUL	PAIN-FUL	WAKE-FUL
FORK-FUL	PALM-FUL	WILL-FUL

Eight-letter words

BELLY-FUL	DIRGE-FUL	FORCE-FUL
BLAME-FUL	DOUBT-FUL	FRUIT-FUL
BLISS-FUL	DREAD-FUL	GHAST-FUL
BOAST-FUL	EVENT-FUL	GLASS-FUL
CHEER-FUL	FAITH-FUL	GOURD-FUL
COLOR-FUL	FANCI-FUL	GRACE-FUL

GRATE-FUL	POWER-FUL	TRUST-FUL
GUILE-FUL	RIGHT-FUL	TRUTH-FUL
HASTE-FUL	SCORN-FUL	UNLAW-FUL
MERCI-FUL	SHAME-FUL	VENGE-FUL
MIRTH-FUL	SKILL-FUL	WASTE-FUL
MOURN-FUL	SPITE-FUL	WATCH-FUL
MOUTH-FUL	SPOON-FUL	WRATH-FUL
PEACE-FUL	TASTE-FUL	WRONG-FUL
PLATE-FUL	THANK-FUL	YOUTH-FUL

F

Handy Hint: Shuffle the rackful

A useful way to visualise your options is to shuffle the tiles on your rack. If you rearrange tiles, place them in alphabetical order or try to form prefixes, suffixes or verb inflections, so that you stand a better chance of spotting good words, or even bonus words to play.

UNUSUAL WORDS FROM OVERSEAS ENGLISH

If you have an awkward combination of letters on your rack then words from overseas English may come in handy. Here are some beginning with F.

Australian words

FASTIE	deceitful act
FESTY	dirty or smelly
FIGJAM	very conceited person
FIZGIG	frivolous or flirtatious girl
FOULIE	bad mood
FRIB	short heavy-conditioned piece of wool
FURPHY	rumour or fictitious story

South African words

FOEFIE	of a type of rope slide

Essential info
Value: 2 points
Number in set: 3

G begins only three two-letter words in Scrabble:
GI (a suit worn by martial arts practitioners, 3 points),
GO and GU (a kind of violin from Shetland, 3 points).
G also combines well with Y to form quite a few short
words including GAY, GEY (a Scots word for very,
7 points), GOY (a Yiddish word for a person who is
not Jewish, 7 points), GUY and also GYM and GYP
(9 points each).

Two-letter words beginning with G

GI   GO   GU

Some three-letter words beginning with G

GAB	GER	GOO
GAD	GHI	GOR
GAE	GIB	GOV
GAK	GID	GOX
GAL	GIE	GOY
GAM	GIF	GUB
GAN	GIO	GUE
GAR	GIP	GUL
GAT	GIT	GUP
GAW	GJU	GUR
GED	GNU	GUV
GEE	GOA	GYM
GEL	GOE	GYP
GEN	GON	

HOOKS

Hooking requires a subtle change in a player's thought process, in that they must look at words already on the board without becoming distracted by their pronunciation.

Some front-hooks
Two letters to three

G-AB	G-AL	G-AS
G-AD	G-AM	G-AT
G-AE	G-AN	G-AW
G-AG	G-AR	G-AY

G-ED	G-IN	G-OR
G-EE	G-IO	G-OS
G-EL	G-IS	G-OX
G-EM	G-IT	G-OY
G-EN	G-NU	G-UM
G-ER	G-OB	G-UN
G-ET	G-OD	G-UP
G-HI	G-OE	G-UR
G-ID	G-ON	G-US
G-IF	G-OO	G-UT

Three letters to four

G-AFF	G-ILL	G-OUT
G-AGA	G-LAD	G-OWN
G-AGE	G-LAM	G-RAD
G-AIN	G-LEE	G-RAM
G-AIT	G-LIB	G-RAN
G-ALA	G-LID	G-RAY
G-ALE	G-LOB	G-REW
G-ALL	G-LOW	G-RID
G-APE	G-LUG	G-RIM
G-ARB	G-LUM	G-RIN
G-ASH	G-NAT	G-RIP
G-ASP	G-NAW	G-RIT
G-ATE	G-OAT	G-RIZ
G-AVE	G-OES	G-ROT
G-EAR	G-OLD	G-ROW
G-EEK	G-ONE	G-RUB
G-ELD	G-OOF	G-RUE
G-ELT	G-OON	G-URN
G-ENE	G-ORE	

Four letters to five

| G-ABLE | G-AGER | G-APED |
| G-AGED | G-ALLY | G-APER |

G-AUNT
G-AVEL
G-EMMY
G-HAST
G-HOST
G-ILLS
G-ILLY
G-INCH
G-IRON
G-ITCH
G-LACE
G-LADE
G-LADY
G-LAND
G-LARE
G-LASS
G-LAZE
G-LAZY

G-LEAM
G-LEAN
G-LINT
G-LOAM
G-LOBE
G-LODE
G-LOOM
G-LOOP
G-LORY
G-LOSS
G-LOST
G-LOUT
G-LOVE
G-LUTE
G-NOME
G-OLDY
G-ONER
G-OOFY

G-OOSE
G-OOSY
G-OUCH
G-RACE
G-RADE
G-RAFT
G-RAIL
G-RAIN
G-RAND
G-RANT
G-RASP
G-RATE
G-RAVE
G-RAZE
G-REED
G-REEK
G-REEN

Five letters to six

G-ABLED
G-ABOON
G-ADDED
G-ADDER
G-AGGER
G-AGING
G-ALLEY
G-ALLOW
G-AMBIT
G-AMBLE
G-AMINE
G-AMMON
G-APING
G-ARGLE
G-ASHED

G-ASPER
G-ASTER
G-AUGER
G-EARED
G-ELATE
G-ELDER
G-ENDER
G-ENTRY
G-INNER
G-LANCE
G-LAZED
G-LOBED
G-LOOPY
G-LOSSY
G-LOVED

G-LOWER
G-NOMIC
G-OLDEN
G-OLDER
G-RACED
G-RAINY
G-RANGE
G-RATED
G-RATER
G-RAVED
G-RAVEL
G-RAVEN
G-RAVER
G-RAYED
G-RAZED

G-REAVE
G-REEDY
G-RIMED
G-RIPED
G-ROPED
G-ROUND

G-ROUSE
G-ROVED
G-ROWER
G-RUBBY
G-RUING
G-RUMPY

G-UNMAN
G-URNED
G-USHER
G-UTTER

Six letters to seven

G-ABLING
G-ADDING
G-ALLIED
G-AMBLED
G-AMBLER
G-ANGLED
G-ASHING
G-AUNTLY
G-EARING
G-ELATED
G-ELDING
G-ESTATE
G-HOSTED
G-HOSTLY
G-IGGING
G-IZZARD
G-LACIER
G-LADDER
G-LANCED
G-LANCER
G-LAZIER
G-LAZILY
G-LAZING
G-LEAMED
G-LEANED
G-LEANER
G-LEEING

G-LIBBED
G-LIBBER
G-LIMMER
G-LINTED
G-LISTEN
G-LISTER
G-LITTER
G-LOOMED
G-LOOPED
G-LOVING
G-LOWING
G-OLDEST
G-OLDISH
G-OWNING
G-RACING
G-RAFTED
G-RAFTER
G-RAINED
G-RANGER
G-RANTED
G-RANTER
G-RAPIER
G-RAPING
G-RASPED
G-RASPER
G-RATIFY
G-RATING

G-RAVING
G-RAYING
G-RAZING
G-REAVED
G-REEKED
G-RIDDED
G-RIDDER
G-RIDDLE
G-RIFTED
G-RILLED
G-RIMMER
G-RINDED
G-RIPING
G-RIPPED
G-RIPPER
G-ROCKED
G-ROOMED
G-ROOMER
G-ROPING
G-ROUSED
G-ROUSER
G-ROUTED
G-ROUTER
G-ROWING
G-RUBBED
G-RUBBER
G-RUFFED

G-RUFFLY   G-RUMPED   G-UNSHOT
G-RUMBLE   G-RUNTED
G-RUMMER   G-UNLESS

Seven letters to eight

G-ALLOWED   G-LOAMING   G-REEDILY
G-AMBLING   G-LOOMING   G-RIDDLED
G-ANGLING   G-LOOPIER   G-RIEVING
G-ARGLING   G-LOOPING   G-RIFTING
G-EARLESS   G-LOWERED   G-RILLING
G-ELASTIC   G-LUGGING   G-RIPPING
G-ELATING   G-NATTIER   G-ROCKING
G-ESTATED   G-OATLIKE   G-ROOMING
G-HASTING   G-OFFERED   G-ROUNDED
G-HOSTING   G-OLDENED   G-ROUNDER
G-LANCING   G-ONENESS   G-ROUSING
G-LAZIEST   G-RAFTING   G-ROUTING
G-LEAMING   G-RAINIER   G-ROWABLE
G-LEANERS   G-RAINING   G-RUMBLED
G-LEANING   G-RANTING   G-UNMAKER
G-LIBBING   G-RANULAR   G-UNSTOCK
G-LINTIER   G-RASPING   G-UTTERED
G-LINTING   G-RAVELLY
G-LITTERY   G-REEDIER

> ### Handy Hint: Gee! Are those really words?
>
> Some unusual and high-scoring words beginning
> with G are GJU (a variant spelling of GU, 11 points),
> GOX (form of gaseous oxygen, 11 points), GUANXI
> (Chinese social concept based on the exchange of
> favours, 14 points) and GYOZA (Japanese fried
> dumplings, 18 points).

Some end-hooks
Two letters to three

BA-G	IN-G	OR-G
BE-G	JA-G	PE-G
BI-G	JO-G	PI-G
BO-G	LA-G	RE-G
DA-G	LI-G	SI-G
DE-G	LO-G	SO-G
DI-G	MA-G	TA-G
DO-G	ME-G	TE-G
EN-G	MI-G	TI-G
ER-G	MO-G	TO-G
FA-G	MU-G	WO-G
FE-G	NA-G	YA-G
GI-G	NE-G	YU-G
HA-G	NO-G	ZA-G
HO-G	NU-G	

Three letters to four

AGO-G	FRO-G	QUA-G
BAN-G	GAN-G	RAN-G
BIN-G	GON-G	RIN-G
BIO-G	HAN-G	RUN-G
BON-G	HUN-G	SAN-G
BRA-G	KIN-G	SIN-G
BUN-G	LIN-G	SON-G
BUR-G	MAR-G	SUN-G
DAN-G	MUN-G	TAN-G
DIN-G	NAN-G	TIN-G
DON-G	PAN-G	TON-G
DUN-G	PIN-G	WIN-G
FAN-G	PLU-G	ZIN-G
FRA-G	PRO-G	

G

Four letters to five

AGIN-G	GULA-G	THAN-G
BEIN-G	MOON-G	THIN-G
BLIN-G	RUIN-G	THON-G
BRIN-G	SPAN-G	TYIN-G
CHIN-G	STUN-G	
CLAN-G	SWAN-G	

Five letters to six

ACTIN-G	LAWIN-G	RAVIN-G
BASIN-G	LAYIN-G	RICIN-G
BELON-G	LIKIN-G	ROBIN-G
CONIN-G	LININ-G	ROSIN-G
COVIN-G	MATIN-G	SAVIN-G
ELFIN-G	MIRIN-G	SEWIN-G
GAMIN-G	PAVIN-G	TAKIN-G
LAKIN-G	PURIN-G	TAMIN-G

Six letters to seven

BOBBIN-G	HOGGIN-G	OUTWIN-G
BUGGIN-G	JERKIN-G	OVERDO-G
BUSKIN-G	MERLIN-G	PARKIN-G
COPPIN-G	MUFFIN-G	PIPPIN-G
CUFFIN-G	MUNTIN-G	PUFFIN-G
CYCLIN-G	MURLIN-G	RAISIN-G
DENTIN-G	NOGGIN-G	RENNIN-G
DUBBIN-G	OUTRAN-G	ROBBIN-G
GRADIN-G	OUTRUN-G	TANNIN-G
GRATIN-G	OUTSIN-G	TIFFIN-G

Seven letters to eight

ASPIRIN-G	CREATIN-G	GELATIN-G
CHITLIN-G	CRISPIN-G	LITTLIN-G

MAHJONG-G	RAVELIN-G	SPELDIN-G
MORPHIN-G	RELAXIN-G	SPONGIN-G
PUMPKIN-G	RESILIN-G	UNDERDO-G
RATTLIN-G	SCULPIN-G	

G

BLOCKERS

It is useful to know which words are blockers and can't therefore be extended before or after. You may want to play a blocker that your opponent can't extend, or you may want to avoid playing a blocker because you want to keep the board open.

The three-letter blockers beginning with G

GEY	GOX

Some four-letter blockers beginning with G

GAGA	GAZY	GLEG
GAMY	GEEZ	GORY
GASH	GERT	

Some five-letter blockers beginning with G (except words ending in '-ED', '-J', '-S', '-X', '-Y' or '-Z')

GARNI	GNASH	GROWN
GEESE	GNAWN	GRUND
GELID	GOBBO	GULCH
GENAL	GONNA	GURSH
GEYER	GOTTA	GWINE
GHEST	GOYIM	GYRAL
GLIAL	GREEK	

Some six-letter blockers beginning with G (except words ending in '-ED', '-J', '-S', '-X', '-Y' or '-Z')

GAIJIN	GEMINI	GOOIER
GAMEST	GENIAL	GORIER
GAMIER	GHUBAR	GOTTEN
GARDAI	GIBING	GOWDER
GARISH	GIDDUP	GRAVEN
GASHER	GLOBAL	GRAYER
GASLIT	GLUIER	GREEBO
GATVOL	GLUING	GREYER
GAYEST	GNAMMA	GRINCH
GEDDIT	GNOMIC	GYRANT
GEEING	GOLDER	

G

BONUS WORDS

Bonus words on your rack can be hard to spot, especially for the less experienced player. One way to help finding them is by using prefixes and suffixes.

Many larger words include a common prefix or suffix – remembering these and using them where you can is a good way to discover any longer words on your rack, including any potential bonus words. The key suffixes to remember ending with G are -GEN and -GRAM.

Some words ending with -GEN
Seven-letter words

ANTI-GEN	HALO-GEN	MUTA-GEN
CRYO-GEN	INDI-GEN	ONCO-GEN
ENDO-GEN	LOXY-GEN	PYRO-GEN

Eight-letter words

ALLER-GEN	ESTRO-GEN	NITRO-GEN
ANDRO-GEN	HISTO-GEN	OBESO-GEN
COLLA-GEN	HYDRO-GEN	PATHO-GEN
CYANO-GEN	MISCE-GEN	PHOTO-GEN

Some words ending with -GRAM
Seven-letter words

ANA-GRAM	MYO-GRAM	TRI-GRAM
DIA-GRAM	PAN-GRAM	URO-GRAM
EPI-GRAM	PRO-GRAM	
ISO-GRAM	TAN-GRAM	

Eight-letter words

AERO-GRAM	HEXA-GRAM	MONO-GRAM
DATA-GRAM	HOLO-GRAM	NANO-GRAM
DECA-GRAM	IDEO-GRAM	SONO-GRAM
DECI-GRAM	IDIO-GRAM	TELE-GRAM
ETHO-GRAM	KILO-GRAM	
GENO-GRAM	LEXI-GRAM	

UNUSUAL WORDS FROM OVERSEAS ENGLISH

If you have an awkward combination of letters on your rack then words from overseas English may come in handy. Here are some beginning with G.

Australian words

GALAH	grey-and-pink cockatoo
GARBO	dustman
GEEBUNG	tree with edible but tasteless fruit

GIDGEE	small acacia tree that sometimes emits an unpleasant smell
GILGAI	natural water hole
GING	child's catapult
GNOW	ground-dwelling bird
GOANNA	monitor lizard
GOOG	egg
GUNYAH	bush hut or shelter
GYMPIE	tall tree with stinging hairs on its leaves

Hindi words

GAUR	large wild cow
GARIAL	fish-eating crocodilian with long slender snout
GHARRI	horse-drawn vehicle for hire
GHAT	stairs or passage leading down to a river
GHEE	clarified butter
GHERAO	industrial action in which workers imprison their employers
GINGILI	oil obtained from sesame seeds
GORAL	small goat antelope
GUAR	plant that produces gum
GUNNY	coarse fabric used for sacks

New Zealand word

GRAUNCH	crush or destroy

South African word

GEELBEK	yellow-jawed fish

Essential info
Value: 4 points
Number in set: 2

H begins a two-letter word with every vowel except for U (although it can form UH, a sound that people make when they are unsure about something, 5 points), making it very useful for forming short multi-word plays. As H is worth 4 points, these words HA, HE, HI and HO (all 5 points) can return healthy scores in conjunction with premium squares with little effort.

Two-letter words beginning with H

HA	HI	HO
HE	HM	

Some three-letter words beginning with H

HAE	HEY	HON
HAH	HIC	HOO
HAJ	HIE	HOX
HAN	HIN	HOY
HAO	HIS	HUB
HAP	HMM	HUH
HAW	HOA	HUN
HEH	HOC	HUP
HEP	HOD	HYE
HET	HOH	HYP
HEW	HOI	
HEX	HOM	

HOOKS

Hooking requires a subtle change in a player's thought process, in that they must look at words already on the board without becoming distracted by their pronunciation.

Some front-hooks
Two letters to three

H-AD	H-AS	H-EN
H-AE	H-AT	H-ER
H-AG	H-AW	H-ES
H-AH	H-AY	H-ET
H-AM	H-EH	H-EX
H-AN	H-EM	H-ID

H-IN	H-OI	H-OY
H-IS	H-OM	H-UG
H-IT	H-ON	H-UH
H-MM	H-OO	H-UM
H-OB	H-OP	H-UN
H-OD	H-OS	H-UP
H-OE	H-OW	H-UT
H-OH	H-OX	H-YE

Three letters to four

H-AFT	H-ARM	H-IRE
H-AHA	H-ART	H-ISH
H-AIL	H-ASP	H-OAR
H-AIN	H-ATE	H-OBO
H-AIR	H-AVE	H-OLD
H-AKA	H-EAR	H-OLE
H-AKE	H-EAT	H-ONE
H-ALE	H-EEL	H-OOF
H-ALF	H-EFT	H-OOP
H-ALL	H-ELL	H-OOT
H-ALT	H-ELM	H-OPE
H-AND	H-ERE	H-OSE
H-ARD	H-ICK	H-OUR
H-ARE	H-IDE	H-OWL
H-ARK	H-ILL	H-UMP

Four letters to five

H-AIRY	H-AWED	H-EDGY
H-ARDS	H-EARD	H-EXED
H-ARED	H-EAST	H-EXES
H-ASHY	H-EATH	H-EYED
H-AULD	H-EAVE	H-INKY
H-AUNT	H-ECHT	H-IRED
H-AVER	H-EDGE	H-ITCH

H-OARY   H-ONER   H-OVER
H-OAST   H-OVEN

Five letters to six

H-ACKER   H-ASHED   H-INTER
H-AILED   H-AUGHT   H-IRING
H-AIRED   H-AWING   H-ITCHY
H-ALLOW   H-EARTH   H-OLDEN
H-ALTER   H-EATER   H-OLDER
H-ANGER   H-EAVED   H-OTTER
H-ANGRY   H-EDGED   H-OWLED
H-ARBOR   H-EDGER   H-OWLER
H-ARMED   H-EIGHT   H-USHER
H-ARMER   H-EXING
H-ARROW   H-ILLER

Six letters to seven

H-AILING   H-ASHIER   H-EIGHTH
H-AIRIER   H-ASHING   H-ERRING
H-AIRILY   H-AUNTER   H-INKIER
H-AIRING   H-AUTEUR   H-ITCHED
H-AMBLED   H-EARING   H-OVERED
H-ARBOUR   H-EATING   H-OWLING
H-ARKING   H-EAVING   H-UPPING
H-ARMFUL   H-EDGIER
H-ARMING   H-EDGING

Seven letters to eight

H-AIRIEST   H-ANGRIER   H-ITCHIER
H-AIRLESS   H-ARBORED   H-ITCHILY
H-AIRLIKE   H-ARMLESS   H-ITCHING
H-AIRLINE   H-ARROWED   H-OVERFLY
H-AIRLOCK   H-EATABLE   H-OVERING
H-ALLOWED   H-EDGIEST   H-USHERED
H-ALTERED   H-INKIEST

Some end-hooks
Two letters to three

AA-H	HA-H	PE-H
AS-H	HE-H	PO-H
BA-H	HO-H	RE-H
BO-H	IS-H	SH-H
DA-H	LA-H	SO-H
DO-H	ME-H	UG-H
ED-H	NA-H	YA-H
ET-H	NO-H	YE-H
FA-H	OO-H	
FE-H	PA-H	

Three letters to four

ARC-H	HAS-H	PAS-H
BAC-H	HAT-H	PAT-H
BAS-H	HET-H	PEC-H
BAT-H	HIS-H	PIT-H
BOO-H	HOG-H	POO-H
BOT-H	KIT-H	POS-H
BUS-H	LAS-H	PUS-H
CAZ-H	LAT-H	RAS-H
COS-H	MAC-H	SHA-H
DAS-H	MAS-H	SIT-H
DIS-H	MAT-H	SUK-H
DOS-H	MES-H	TAS-H
DOT-H	MET-H	TEC-H
EAT-H	MOS-H	UMP-H
FAS-H	MOT-H	WAS-H
GAS-H	MUS-H	WIS-H
GOS-H	NIS-H	WIT-H
GOT-H	NOS-H	YEA-H
GUS-H	OAT-H	

Four letters to five

BOOT-H	HUMP-H	SOUT-H
BRAS-H	LEAS-H	SWAT-H
BRUS-H	MARC-H	SYNC-H
BUMP-H	MARS-H	TENT-H
BURG-H	MERC-H	THIG-H
CLOT-H	MYNA-H	TOOT-H
CRUS-H	NEAT-H	TORA-H
FLUS-H	PLUS-H	TORC-H
FORT-H	SCAT-H	WOOS-H
FRIT-H	SLOT-H	WORT-H
GIRT-H	SMIT-H	
HEAT-H	SOOT-H	

Five letters to six

COMET-H	HOOKA-H	POLIS-H
DELIS-H	HURRA-H	PUNKA-H
EIGHT-H	HUZZA-H	SHEIK-H
FATWA-H	LOOFA-H	SHIVA-H
FELLA-H	MULLA-H	SUNNA-H
FINIS-H	PARIS-H	WALLA-H
HEART-H	PERIS-H	

Six letters to seven

AARRGH-H	OUTWIT-H	SABBAT-H
HAGGIS-H	QABALA-H	

Seven letters to eight

BEGORRA-H	MADRASA-H	PEISHWA-H
HOSANNA-H	MESHUGA-H	SAVANNA-H
HYDRANT-H	NARGILE-H	SCAMPIS-H
KHALIFA-H	OCTOPUS-H	VERANDA-H

BLOCKERS

It is useful to know which words are blockers and can't therefore be extended before or after. You may want to play a blocker that your opponent can't extend, or you may want to avoid playing a blocker because you want to keep the board open.

The three-letter blockers beginning with H

HEX   HOX

Some four-letter blockers beginning with H

HAZY	HOHA	HWAN
HELD	HOLY	HYTE
HIYA	HUED	
HOAX	HUNG	

Some five-letter blockers beginning with H (except words ending in '-ED', '-J', '-S', '-X', '-Y' or '-Z')

HAITH	HEWGH	HUGER
HARSH	HOING	HUMID
HAULT	HOOCH	HUNCH
HEAME	HOVEN	HUTCH

Some six-letter blockers beginning with H (except words ending in '-ED', '-J', '-S', '-X', '-Y' or '-Z')

HABILE	HELIAC	HORRID
HALERU	HIKING	HOSING
HANGUL	HOLDEN	HOWZAT
HARDER	HOLIER	HUGEST
HATING	HOOROO	HYENIC
HAUNCH	HOOTCH	HYMNIC
HAWKIT	HOOVEN	
HAZIER	HOPING	

BONUS WORDS

Bonus words on your rack can be hard to spot, especially for the less experienced player. One way to help find them is by using prefixes and suffixes.

Many larger words include a common prefix or suffix – remembering these and using them where you can is a good way to discover any longer words on your rack, including any potential bonus words. The key suffixes to remember ending with H are -HOLE, -HOOD and -HORN.

Some words ending with -HOLE
Seven-letter words

AIR-HOLE	FOX-HOLE	PIN-HOLE
ARM-HOLE	KEY-HOLE	POT-HOLE
BOG-HOLE	LUG-HOLE	SPY-HOLE
EAR-HOLE	MAN-HOLE	
EYE-HOLE	PIE-HOLE	

Eight-letter words

BLOW-HOLE	HELL-HOLE	SINK-HOLE
BOLT-HOLE	KNOT-HOLE	WELL-HOLE
BORE-HOLE	LOOP-HOLE	WOOD-HOLE
BUNG-HOLE	PEEP-HOLE	WORM-HOLE
CAKE-HOLE	PLUG-HOLE	
FEED-HOLE	PORT-HOLE	

Some words ending with -HOOD
Seven-letter words

BOY-HOOD	LAD-HOOD	SON-HOOD
GOD-HOOD	MAN-HOOD	

Eight-letter words

AUNT-HOOD	KING-HOOD	PUMP-HOOD
BABY-HOOD	LADY-HOOD	SAGE-HOOD
CALF-HOOD	MAID-HOOD	SELF-HOOD
COLT-HOOD	MISS-HOOD	SERF-HOOD
DOLL-HOOD	MONK-HOOD	WIFE-HOOD
GIRL-HOOD	PAGE-HOOD	WIVE-HOOD
IDLE-HOOD	POPE-HOOD	

Some words ending with -HORN

Seven-letter words

ALP-HORN	ELK-HORN	LEG-HORN
BIG-HORN	FOG-HORN	SAX-HORN
DIS-HORN	INK-HORN	TIN-HORN

Eight-letter words

BULL-HORN	LONG-HORN	SHOE-HORN
DEER-HORN	RAMS-HORN	STAG-HORN

> **Handy Hint: Powerful H words**
>
> Some short, useful words starting with H and using power tiles are HAJ (Muslim pilgrimage to Mecca, 13 points, also its variant form HADJ), HAJI (one who goes on a haj, 14 points), HAZE (16 points), HAZY (19 points), HEX (a curse or spell, 13 points) and HOX (a Shakespearean word meaning to cut a horse's hamstring, also 13).

H

UNUSUAL WORDS FROM OVERSEAS ENGLISH

If you have an awkward combination of letters on your rack then words from overseas English may come in handy. Here are some beginning with H.

Australian words

HAKEA	type of shrub or tree
HOVEA	plant with purple flowers
HUTCHIE	groundsheet draped over an upright stick as a shelter

Hindi words

HARTAL	act of closing shop or stopping work as a political protest
HOWDAH	seat for riding on an elephant's back

New Zealand words

Many Maori words start with the letter H, and if you have an H alongside a selection of vowels you may be able to play some of the following:

HAKA	war dance
HANGI	open-air cooking pit
HAPU	subtribe
HAPUKA	large fish
HEITIKI	neck ornament
HIKOI	protest march
HOKONUI	illicit whisky
HONGI	nose-touching greeting
HUHU	hairy beetle
HUI	conference or meeting
HUIA	extinct New Zealand bird

I

Essential info
Value: 1 point
Number in set: 9

I can be a tricky letter to use in multiples so you need to try and use an I as soon as you can to avoid getting two of them. There are plenty of two-letter words beginning with I to help you make good-scoring parallel plays as shown below. The higher-scoring three letter words beginning with I are worth making note of, such as ICY (8 points), IVY (9 points) and IMP (7 points). The I can also be vital for reaping points with a Q or X with QI or XI. The I is also one of the letters of the RETAIN set so may be worth keeping if you have others of those letters to work towards a bonus word, but not at the expense of scoring meanwhile.

Two-letter words beginning with I

ID	IN	IS
IF	IO	IT

Some three-letter words beginning with I

ICH	ING	ISM
ICK	ION	ISO
IDE	IRE	ITA
IFF	ISH	

I

HOOKS

Hooking requires a subtle change in a player's thought process, in that they must look at words already on the board without becoming distracted by their pronunciation.

Some front-hooks
Two letters to three

I-CH	I-OS	I-SO
I-DE	I-RE	I-TA
I-ON	I-SH	

Three letters to four

I-BIS	I-KON	I-RES
I-CON	I-LEA	I-RID
I-DEE	I-LEX	I-SIT
I-DOL	I-MAM	I-SOS
I-GAD	I-MID	I-TAS
I-KAT	I-RED	I-URE

Four letters to five

I-DANT	I-MAGE	I-RATE
I-DEAL	I-MINE	I-RING
I-DEES	I-MINO	I-RONE
I-DENT	I-NANE	I-SLED
I-GAPO	I-ODIC	I-VIED
I-LEAL	I-RADE	

Five letters to six

I-CONIC	I-ODISM	I-SATIN
I-GUANA	I-ONIUM	I-SLING
I-LEXES	I-RATER	I-TEMED
I-NYALA	I-RISES	

Six letters to seven

I-MAGISM	I-RISING	I-SOLATE

Seven letters to eight

I-CONICAL	I-SLANDER
I-SABELLA	I-SOLATED

Handy Hint: Looking, thinking, bonusing

If you have the letters to form the suffix -ING, you could be well on the way to scoring a bonus word for 50 points. Look at the other letters on your rack and try to form a word ending in -ING (there are thousands!). But don't hang on to -ING at all costs, as by doing so you are restricting yourself to playing with just four letters, with the consequent likelihood of low scores.

Some end-hooks

Two letters to three

AH-I	HO-I	PO-I
AM-I	JA-I	RE-I
AN-I	KA-I	TA-I
BO-I	KO-I	UN-I
CH-I	MO-I	
DE-I	OB-I	

Three letters to four

I

ANT-I	HAJ-I	PER-I
ART-I	IMP-I	PIP-I
BAN-I	KAK-I	PUR-I
BEN-I	LOB-I	QUA-I
BID-I	LOT-I	RAG-I
BUD-I	MAG-I	RAM-I
CAD-I	MAL-I	RAN-I
CAM-I	MAN-I	REF-I
CAP-I	MAX-I	ROT-I
CHA-I	MID-I	RUD-I
CON-I	MIR-I	SAD-I
DAL-I	MOD-I	SAR-I
DEF-I	MOM-I	SAT-I
DEL-I	MOT-I	SIR-I
DEN-I	MUN-I	SUM-I
DIV-I	NID-I	SUN-I
FEN-I	NOD-I	TAB-I
FIN-I	NON-I	TAX-I
GAD-I	PAD-I	TIP-I
GAR-I	PAL-I	TOP-I
GOB-I	PEN-I	TOR-I

Four letters to five

ARCH-I	DILL-I	LUNG-I
BASS-I	DISC-I	MACH-I
BARF-I	FAST-I	MYTH-I
BAST-I	FERM-I	PARK-I
BEST-I	FILM-I	PART-I
BIND-I	FUND-I	POOR-I
BUFF-I	FUNG-I	PRIM-I
CAMP-I	GLOB-I	PULL-I
CARD-I	HADJ-I	PUTT-I
CARP-I	HAJJ-I	ROST-I
CELL-I	HANG-I	SENS-I
COAT-I	HONG-I	SENT-I
COMB-I	HOUR-I	SWAM-I
CORN-I	JINN-I	TANG-I
CROC-I	LASS-I	TARS-I
CULT-I	LENT-I	TEMP-I
CURL-I	LIMB-I	VILL-I
DEMO-I	LOGO-I	VOLT-I

Five letters to six

ANNUL-I	FRACT-I	SCAMP-I
AVANT-I	GARDA-I	SENSE-I
CAROL-I	GLUTE-I	SHALL-I
CHICH-I	HAIKA-I	SILEN-I
CHILL-I	JEHAD-I	SMALT-I
COLON-I	JIHAD-I	SOLID-I
CUBIT-I	KAIKA-I	STELA-I
DENAR-I	MANAT-I	TAPET-I
DJINN-I	POLYP-I	YOGIN-I
EQUAL-I	RHOMB-I	

Six letters to seven

ACANTH-I	DENARI-I	REVERS-I
AFGHAN-I	HALLAL-I	RHYTHM-I
BANDAR-I	JAMPAN-I	SECOND-I
CHIASM-I	MARTIN-I	SHIKAR-I
DACTYL-I	PAESAN-I	SIGNOR-I
DEMENT-I	QAWWAL-I	TYMPAN-I

Seven letters to eight

BRAHMAN-I	DRACHMA-I	PENSION-I
CALAMAR-I	FASCISM-I	PERFECT-I
CAPITAN-I	FASCIST-I	QUADRAT-I
CONCEPT-I	HETAIRA-I	SIGNIOR-I
CONCERT-I	MARCHES-I	TANDOOR-I
CONDUCT-I	PARCHES-I	

I

BLOCKERS

It is useful to know which words are blockers and can't therefore be extended before or after. You may want to play a blocker that your opponent can't extend, or you may want to avoid playing a blocker because you want to keep the board open.

Some four-letter blockers beginning with I

IBIS	IDLY	INRO
IDEM	INLY	

Some five-letter blockers beginning with I (except words ending in '-ED', '-J', '-S', '-X', '-Y' or '-Z')

ICTIC	ILEAL	IMIDO
ILEAC	ILIAC	IMINO

IMSHI	INFRA	IODIC
INAPT	INNIT	ISNAE
INBYE	INTIL	IXNAY
INEPT	INTRA	
INERM	INUST	

Some six-letter blockers beginning with I
(except words ending in '-ED', '-J', '-S', '-X', '-Y' or '-Z')

ICONIC	INFELT	INTIRE
IDLEST	INFERE	INWITH
IMMANE	INFIMA	INWORN
INANER	INLAID	IRATER
INBENT	INMESH	IRIDAL
INBORN	INMOST	IRIDIC
INCUBI	INRUSH	IRITIC
INCULT	INTACT	IRREAL
INDIGN	INTIME	ITSELF

I

BONUS WORDS

Bonus words on your rack can be hard to spot, especially for the less experienced player. One way to help find them is by using prefixes and suffixes.

Many larger words include a common prefix or suffix – remembering these and using them where you can is a good way to discover any longer words on your rack, including any potential bonus words. The key prefixes to remember beginning with I are IM-, IN- and ISO- and the key suffixes are -IBLE, -IFY, -INGS, -ISE, -ISH, -ISM, -IST, -ITY and -IUM.

Some words beginning with IM-

Seven-letter words

IM-BURSE	IM-PARTS	IM-PORTS
IM-MENSE	IM-PASSE	IM-POSED
IM-MORAL	IM-PEACH	IM-POUND
IM-PACTS	IM-PEDES	IM-PRESS
IM-PAIRS	IM-PENDS	IM-PRINT
IM-PALED	IM-PERIL	IM-PROVE
IM-PALER	IM-PLANT	IM-PULSE
IM-PANEL	IM-PLIED	IM-PURER

Eight-letter words

IM-BARKED	IM-PARTED	IM-PROPER
IM-BODIED	IM-PENDED	IM-PROVED
IM-MATURE	IM-PLYING	IM-PROVER
IM-MOBILE	IM-POLITE	IM-PUDENT
IM-MODEST	IM-PORTED	IM-PURELY
IM-MORTAL	IM-POSING	IM-PUREST
IM-PAIRED	IM-POSTER	IM-PURITY
IM-PALING	IM-POTENT	
IM-PARITY	IM-PRISON	

Some words beginning with IN-

Seven-letter words

IN-BOUND	IN-DENTS	IN-FIGHT
IN-BOXES	IN-DICTS	IN-FIRMS
IN-BUILT	IN-DOORS	IN-FLAME
IN-CASED	IN-DORSE	IN-FORCE
IN-CENSE	IN-DUCTS	IN-FORMS
IN-CITED	IN-EXACT	IN-FRACT
IN-COMER	IN-FAMED	IN-FUSED
IN-DEEDY	IN-FESTS	IN-GESTS

IN-GRAIN	IN-SECTS	IN-TAKES
IN-GRAMS	IN-SIDER	IN-TENDS
IN-GRATE	IN-SIGHT	IN-TENSE
IN-GROWN	IN-SISTS	IN-TERNS
IN-HABIT	IN-SNARE	IN-TONER
IN-HALED	IN-SOFAR	IN-VADED
IN-HUMAN	IN-SOLES	IN-VALID
IN-LAYER	IN-SPIRE	IN-VENTS
IN-MATES	IN-STALL	IN-VERSE
IN-NARDS	IN-STATE	IN-VESTS
IN-QUEST	IN-STEAD	IN-VOLVE
IN-QUIRE	IN-STEPS	IN-WARDS
IN-ROADS	IN-STILL	
IN-SANER	IN-SURED	

Eight-letter words

IN-ACTION	IN-EQUITY	IN-SANELY
IN-ACTIVE	IN-EXPERT	IN-SANITY
IN-BREEDS	IN-FAMOUS	IN-SCRIBE
IN-CENSED	IN-FESTER	IN-SECURE
IN-CITING	IN-FILLED	IN-SHRINE
IN-CLOSED	IN-FINITE	IN-SISTER
IN-COMING	IN-FIRMER	IN-SOURCE
IN-CREASE	IN-FLIGHT	IN-STANCE
IN-CURRED	IN-FORMAL	IN-STATED
IN-DEBTED	IN-FORMED	IN-TERNAL
IN-DECENT	IN-FRINGE	IN-THRALL
IN-DENTED	IN-FUSION	IN-TREPID
IN-DIGEST	IN-GROUND	IN-VENTED
IN-DIRECT	IN-GROWTH	IN-VIABLE
IN-DOLENT	IN-HUMANE	
IN-EDIBLE	IN-PUTTED	

Some words beginning with ISO-
Seven-letter words

ISO-BARS	ISO-LATE	ISO-TOPE
ISO-DOSE	ISO-MERE	ISO-TRON
ISO-FORM	ISO-PODS	ISO-TYPE
ISO-GRAM	ISO-TONE	

Eight-letter words

ISO-BARIC	ISO-GRAPH	ISO-TONIC
ISO-BUTYL	ISO-LATED	ISO-TOPIC
ISO-GAMIC	ISO-MORPH	ISO-TYPIC
ISO-GENIC	ISO-NOMIC	
ISO-GRAFT	ISO-THERM	

Some words ending with -IBLE
Seven-letter words

ADD-IBLE	FUS-IBLE	RIS-IBLE
AUD-IBLE	LEG-IBLE	VIS-IBLE
DEL-IBLE	MIX-IBLE	
DOC-IBLE	PAT-IBLE	

Eight-letter words

CRED-IBLE	GULL-IBLE	SENS-IBLE
CRUC-IBLE	HORR-IBLE	TANG-IBLE
ELIG-IBLE	INED-IBLE	TENS-IBLE
FALL-IBLE	MAND-IBLE	TERR-IBLE
FEAS-IBLE	POSS-IBLE	VINC-IBLE
FLEX-IBLE	RINS-IBLE	
FORC-IBLE	RUNC-IBLE	

I

Some words ending with -IFY
Seven-letter words

ACID-IFY	GRAT-IFY	REUN-IFY
AMPL-IFY	HORR-IFY	SACR-IFY
BEAT-IFY	JUST-IFY	SALS-IFY
CERT-IFY	LIQU-IFY	SCAR-IFY
CLAR-IFY	MAGN-IFY	SIGN-IFY
CRUC-IFY	MORT-IFY	SPEC-IFY
DIGN-IFY	NULL-IFY	TERR-IFY
FALS-IFY	PETR-IFY	TEST-IFY
FORT-IFY	QUAL-IFY	YUPP-IFY
GLOR-IFY	RECT-IFY	ZOMB-IFY

Eight-letter words

BEAUT-IFY	PRETT-IFY	SANCT-IFY
CLASS-IFY	QUANT-IFY	SIMPL-IFY
DETOX-IFY	REMOD-IFY	SOLID-IFY
EMULS-IFY	RENOT-IFY	STRAT-IFY
GENTR-IFY	REPUR-IFY	STULT-IFY
HUMID-IFY	RESIN-IFY	
IDENT-IFY	RIGID-IFY	

Some words ending with -INGS
Seven-letter words

ACH-INGS	COK-INGS	FAD-INGS
ADD-INGS	COM-INGS	FIX-INGS
ARM-INGS	DAT-INGS	GAP-INGS
BID-INGS	DIN-INGS	GAT-INGS
BUS-INGS	DRY-INGS	HID-INGS
BUY-INGS	EAR-INGS	INN-INGS
CAN-INGS	EAS-INGS	JOK-INGS
COD-INGS	END-INGS	LAD-INGS

MER-INGS	RAG-INGS	TIM-INGS
MIX-INGS	RAT-INGS	TOY-INGS
OUT-INGS	SAY-INGS	TRY-INGS
PAC-INGS	SIT-INGS	TUB-INGS
PAR-INGS	SPY-INGS	WAD-INGS
PAY-INGS	TAP-INGS	WAN-INGS

Eight-letter words

BAIT-INGS	FAST-INGS	LONG-INGS
BANG-INGS	FEED-INGS	MALT-INGS
BATH-INGS	FELL-INGS	MAUL-INGS
BEAR-INGS	FIND-INGS	MEAN-INGS
BEAT-INGS	FISH-INGS	MEET-INGS
BOMB-INGS	FOOT-INGS	MOOR-INGS
BOND-INGS	GASP-INGS	MORN-INGS
BOWL-INGS	GELD-INGS	NAGG-INGS
BUCK-INGS	GOLF-INGS	NEST-INGS
CAMP-INGS	GRAD-INGS	ONGO-INGS
CAST-INGS	HEAD-INGS	OUTS-INGS
COAT-INGS	HEAR-INGS	PAIR-INGS
COIN-INGS	HINT-INGS	PARK-INGS
COMB-INGS	HOOK-INGS	PAST-INGS
COPY-INGS	HUNT-INGS	PEAK-INGS
COST-INGS	JOLT-INGS	PELT-INGS
DAWN-INGS	JUMP-INGS	PRIM-INGS
DEAL-INGS	KIDD-INGS	RAIL-INGS
DRAW-INGS	KILL-INGS	READ-INGS
DUNK-INGS	LAND-INGS	REAP-INGS
EARN-INGS	LASH-INGS	REEL-INGS
EDIT-INGS	LEAN-INGS	RING-INGS
ETCH-INGS	LIMP-INGS	ROCK-INGS
EVEN-INGS	LIST-INGS	ROLL-INGS
FAIL-INGS	LOAN-INGS	ROOF-INGS

ROUT-INGS	SNIP-INGS	WARN-INGS
SACK-INGS	STAG-INGS	WASH-INGS
SEAL-INGS	STAR-INGS	WEEP-INGS
SEAT-INGS	TEXT-INGS	WHIN-INGS
SHOW-INGS	TRAD-INGS	WHIT-INGS
SIGH-INGS	TWIN-INGS	WIND-INGS
SIGN-INGS	UNDO-INGS	WORK-INGS
SING-INGS	UNIT-INGS	WRIT-INGS
SLID-INGS	VETT-INGS	YAPP-INGS

Some words ending with -ISE (these can also be spelt -IZE)

Seven-letter words

AGON-ISE	IDOL-ISE	OXID-ISE
ATOM-ISE	IRON-ISE	POET-ISE
BAPT-ISE	ITEM-ISE	REAL-ISE
DUAL-ISE	LION-ISE	UNIT-ISE
ICON-ISE	ODOR-ISE	

Eight-letter words

ACTIV-ISE	FINAL-ISE	PARAD-ISE
BANAL-ISE	HUMAN-ISE	PENAL-ISE
CALOR-ISE	IDEAL-ISE	POLAR-ISE
CANON-ISE	IMMUN-ISE	SANIT-ISE
CIVIL-ISE	LEGAL-ISE	SATIR-ISE
COLON-ISE	LOCAL-ISE	TREAT-ISE
COLOR-ISE	MAXIM-ISE	UNION-ISE
DEMON-ISE	MINIM-ISE	VAPOR-ISE
DEPUT-ISE	MORAL-ISE	VITAL-ISE
EQUAL-ISE	MOTOR-ISE	VOCAL-ISE
ETHER-ISE	ORGAN-ISE	VOWEL-ISE

Some words ending with -ISH
Seven-letter words

BOOK-ISH   HAWK-ISH   REDD-ISH
BULL-ISH   HOTT-ISH   SELF-ISH
COLD-ISH   LEFT-ISH   SLAV-ISH
DARK-ISH   LONG-ISH   SLOW-ISH
DORK-ISH   MILD-ISH   SOFT-ISH
FOOL-ISH   MORE-ISH   SOON-ISH
FOPP-ISH   NEAR-ISH   TALL-ISH
GIRL-ISH   PECK-ISH   WAIF-ISH
GOOD-ISH   PEEV-ISH

Eight-letter words

BLACK-ISH   DRUNK-ISH   SANDY-ISH
BLOKE-ISH   FEVER-ISH   SHARP-ISH
BLOND-ISH   FIEND-ISH   SHEEP-ISH
BLUNT-ISH   HEAVY-ISH   SMALL-ISH
CHILD-ISH   LIGHT-ISH   SWEET-ISH
CLEAN-ISH   NANNY-ISH   THICK-ISH
CLOWN-ISH   PLAIN-ISH   YOUNG-ISH
DEVIL-ISH   ROUGH-ISH

Some words ending with -ISM
Seven-letter words

AGON-ISM   EGOT-ISM   REAL-ISM
BRUT-ISM   FASC-ISM   SIZE-ISM
CULT-ISM   GEEK-ISM   TEXT-ISM
DADA-ISM   IDOL-ISM   TOUR-ISM
DUAL-ISM   LADD-ISM

Eight-letter words

ACTIV-ISM	FEMIN-ISM	NATIV-ISM
ALARM-ISM	FUTUR-ISM	NIHIL-ISM
ALIEN-ISM	GIPSY-ISM	OPTIM-ISM
ANEUR-ISM	HEDON-ISM	ORGAN-ISM
BOTUL-ISM	HUMAN-ISM	PACIF-ISM
CLASS-ISM	IDEAL-ISM	POPUL-ISM
CRONY-ISM	JINGO-ISM	ROYAL-ISM
CYNIC-ISM	LOCAL-ISM	STOIC-ISM
DYNAM-ISM	LOYAL-ISM	TOKEN-ISM
EMBOL-ISM	LYRIC-ISM	UNION-ISM
ESCAP-ISM	MINIM-ISM	VEGAN-ISM
FATAL-ISM	MORAL-ISM	

I

Some words ending with -IST
Seven-letter words

ATOM-IST	DIET-IST	LEFT-IST
BASS-IST	DUAL-IST	PALM-IST
CELL-IST	DUEL-IST	RANK-IST
CHEM-IST	FLOR-IST	REAL-IST
COOL-IST	FOIL-IST	TOUR-IST
DIAR-IST	HARP-IST	

Eight-letter words

ALARM-IST	ESSAY-IST	JINGO-IST
ARSON-IST	FAMIL-IST	KENDO-IST
BANJO-IST	FINAL-IST	LOBBY-IST
CANOE-IST	HOBBY-IST	LOYAL-IST
CHART-IST	HUMAN-IST	LYRIC-IST
CLASS-IST	HUMOR-IST	MEDAL-IST
COLOR-IST	IDEAL-IST	MINIM-IST
COMED-IST	JIHAD-IST	MORAL-IST

MOTOR-IST	POPUL-IST	ROYAL-IST
OPTIM-IST	PUGIL-IST	SHOOT-IST
ORGAN-IST	RALLY-IST	STOCK-IST
PACIF-IST	REGAL-IST	TOTAL-IST
PANEL-IST	RIGHT-IST	TOTEM-IST

Some words ending with -ITY

Seven-letter words

ACID-ITY	DUAL-ITY	QUAL-ITY
AMEN-ITY	JOLL-ITY	REAL-ITY
ARID-ITY	NULL-ITY	TENS-ITY
CHAR-ITY	OBES-ITY	TRIN-ITY
DENS-ITY	PRIV-ITY	UTIL-ITY
DIGN-ITY	PROB-ITY	VACU-ITY

Eight-letter words

ACRID-ITY	GRATU-ITY	POLAR-ITY
ACTIV-ITY	HUMAN-ITY	PRIOR-ITY
AFFIN-ITY	HUMID-ITY	RABID-ITY
BANAL-ITY	HUMIL-ITY	RAPID-ITY
CALAM-ITY	IDENT-ITY	REGAL-ITY
CHAST-ITY	IMMUN-ITY	RIGID-ITY
CONIC-ITY	INSAN-ITY	RURAL-ITY
CUBIC-ITY	LEGAL-ITY	SANCT-ITY
ENORM-ITY	LIVID-ITY	SECUR-ITY
EQUAL-ITY	LOCAL-ITY	SENIL-ITY
FACIL-ITY	LUCID-ITY	SEREN-ITY
FATAL-ITY	MAJOR-ITY	SEVER-ITY
FIDEL-ITY	MINOR-ITY	SOLID-ITY
FINAL-ITY	MOBIL-ITY	TIMID-ITY
FLUID-ITY	MORAL-ITY	TONAL-ITY
FUTIL-ITY	NATIV-ITY	TONIC-ITY

| TOTAL-ITY | VALID-ITY | VITAL-ITY |
| TOXIC-ITY | VIRAL-ITY | |

Some words ending with -IUM

Seven-letter words

CALC-IUM	IRID-IUM	RHOD-IUM
CRAN-IUM	LITH-IUM	STAD-IUM
FERM-IUM	PALL-IUM	TERT-IUM
GALL-IUM	PLAG-IUM	TRIT-IUM
HASS-IUM	PREM-IUM	URAN-IUM
HOLM-IUM	PROT-IUM	YTTR-IUM

Eight-letter words

ACTIN-IUM	EULOG-IUM	REFUG-IUM
AEROB-IUM	FRANC-IUM	ROSAR-IUM
ALLUV-IUM	GERAN-IUM	RUBID-IUM
AMMON-IUM	IMPER-IUM	SELEN-IUM
AQUAR-IUM	INGEN-IUM	SOLAR-IUM
BRACH-IUM	LIMON-IUM	SOLAT-IUM
CHROM-IUM	MOTOR-IUM	THALL-IUM
CORON-IUM	NOBEL-IUM	TITAN-IUM
DELIR-IUM	OSSAR-IUM	TRILL-IUM
DILUV-IUM	PHORM-IUM	VIVAR-IUM
EMPOR-IUM	POLON-IUM	

UNUSUAL WORDS FROM OVERSEAS ENGLISH

If you have an awkward combination of letters on your rack then words from overseas English may come in handy. Here are some beginning with I.

New Zealand word

IWI   a Maori tribe

Canadian word

ICEWINE   dessert wine made from frozen grapes
INUKSUK   a stone used by the Inuits to mark a location

Urdu word

INQILAB   revolution

I

Essential info
Value: 8 points
Number in set: 1

POWER TILE

J alone is worth 8 points, making it an extremely valuable tile. However, it can be difficult to play: for example, there are only two two-letter words beginning with J (JA, a South African word for yes, and JO, a Scots word for sweetheart, both 9 points). When used in conjunction with the other power tiles X and Z, however, there is scope for huge scoring, especially if words are played judiciously on double- or triple-letter squares. Good short words to use J alongside X and Z include JINX (18 points) and JAZY (23 points), but such words are unlikely to occur given there is only one of each power tile in the set. Note that you will need a blank tile to take advantage of words with two Js (e.g. JUJU, 10 points, HAJJ, 13 points).

Two-letter words beginning with J

JA   JO

Some three-letter words beginning with J

JAB	JEE	JOL
JAG	JEU	JOR
JAI	JIB	JOW
JAK	JIN	JUD
JAP	JIZ	JUN
JAY	JOE	JUS

The three-letter words using J

| AJI | HAJ | TAJ |
| GJU | RAJ | |

Some four-letter words using J

Some four-letter words using J that you may not know are
DOJO (room or hall for the practice of martial arts, 12 points),
JEHU (a fast driver, 14 points), JIAO (Chinese currency unit,
11 points) and JIRD (another word for gerbil, 12 points)

AJAR	JADE	JASP
AJEE	JAFA	JASS
BAJU	JAGA	JASY
BENJ	JAGG	JATO
DJIN	JAIL	JAUK
DOJO	JAKE	JAUP
FUJI	JAMB	JAVA
GAJO	JANE	JAXY
GOJI	JANN	JAZY
HADJ	JAPE	JAZZ
HAJI	JARK	JEAN
JAAP	JARL	JEAT
JACK	JARP	JEDI

JEED	JIRD	JUDO
JEEL	JIVE	JUDY
JEEP	JIVY	JUGA
JEER	JOBE	JUJU
JEEZ	JOCK	JUKE
JEFE	JOCO	JUKU
JEFF	JOEY	JUMP
JEHU	JOHN	JUNK
JELL	JOIN	JUPE
JEON	JOKE	JURA
JERK	JOKY	JURE
JESS	JOLE	JURY
JEST	JOLL	JUST
JETE	JOLT	JUTE
JEUX	JOMO	JUVE
JIAO	JONG	JYNX
JIBB	JOOK	KOJI
JIBE	JOSH	MOJO
JIFF	JOSS	PUJA
JILL	JOTA	RAJA
JILT	JOUK	SIJO
JIMP	JOUR	SJOE
JINK	JOWL	SOJA
JINN	JUBA	SOJU
JINS	JUBE	
JINX	JUCO	

J

HOOKS

Hooking requires a subtle change in a player's thought process, in that they must look at words already on the board without becoming distracted by their pronunciation.

Some front-hooks

Two letters to three

J-AB	J-EE	J-OY
J-AG	J-ET	J-UG
J-AI	J-IN	J-UN
J-AM	J-OB	J-US
J-AR	J-OE	J-UT
J-AW	J-OR	
J-AY	J-OW	

Three letters to four

J-AGA	J-EAT	J-IVY
J-AIL	J-EEL	J-OBE
J-AKE	J-EFF	J-OKE
J-ANE	J-ELL	J-OLE
J-ANN	J-ERK	J-OUK
J-APE	J-ESS	J-OUR
J-ARK	J-EST	J-OWL
J-ASP	J-IFF	J-UDO
J-ASS	J-ILL	J-UKE
J-AUK	J-IMP	J-UMP
J-AVA	J-INK	J-URE
J-EAN	J-INN	J-UTE

Four letters to five

J-AGER	J-EMMY	J-OWED
J-ALAP	J-ESSE	J-OWLY
J-AMBO	J-IFFY	J-UMBO
J-APED	J-ILLS	J-UMPY
J-APER	J-IMMY	J-UNCO
J-AUNT	J-INGO	J-UNTO
J-AVEL	J-NANA	J-UPON
J-AWED	J-OINT	
J-EELY	J-OUST	

Five letters to six

J-ABBED	J-ASSES	J-OTTER
J-ACKER	J-AUNTY	J-OUNCE
J-AGGER	J-AWING	J-OWING
J-AILED	J-EANED	J-OWLED
J-AMBER	J-EFFED	J-OWLER
J-ANGLE	J-ESSES	J-UDDER
J-ANKER	J-ESTER	J-UGGED
J-APERY	J-IGGED	J-UMBLE
J-APING	J-IMPLY	J-UMPED
J-ARGON	J-INGLE	J-UNKED
J-ARRAH	J-INKED	J-UNKET
J-ASPER	J-INKER	

J

Six letters to seven

J-AGGIES	J-IMMIES	J-OUSTER
J-AILING	J-INGOES	J-OWLIER
J-ANGLED	J-INKING	J-OWLING
J-ANGLER	J-OCULAR	J-UGGING
J-AUNTIE	J-OINTED	J-UMPING
J-AWLESS	J-OLLIES	J-UNCATE
J-EFFING	J-OSTLER	J-UNCOES
J-IGGING	J-OUSTED	J-UNKING

Seven letters to eight

J-ANGLING	J-OUSTING	J-UNCTION
J-APERIES	J-OWLIEST	
J-OINTING	J-UDDERED	

Some end-hooks
Two letters to three

HA-J	TA-J

151

Three letters to four

BEN-J   HAD-J   HAJ-J

BLOCKERS

It is useful to know which words are blockers and can't therefore be extended before or after. You may want to play a blocker that your opponent can't extend, or you may want to avoid playing a blocker because you want to keep the board open.

J

Some four-letter blockers beginning with J

JASS	JEUX	JOSH
JASY	JINX	JOSS
JAZY	JIVY	JURY
JEED	JOKY	JYNX

Some five-letter blockers beginning with J (except words ending in '-ED', '-J', '-S', '-X', '-Y' or '-Z')

JAMON	JINGO	JURAL
JEEZE	JIRRE	
JEUNE	JOKOL	

Some six-letter blockers beginning with J (except words ending in '-ED', '-J', '-S', '-X', '-Y' or '-Z')

JACENT	JIMPER	JOCUND
JADING	JINGKO	JOKIER
JADISH	JINNEE	JOKING
JANTEE	JIVIER	JOLING
JEEING	JIVING	JOVIAL
JEJUNE	JOBING	JOWING
JIBING	JOCOSE	JOYFUL

JOYING   JUGATE
JUBATE   JUKING

Handy Hint: Not just J- words

When holding a power tile try looking beyond the easy
two and three-letter words that might jump out at
you. Also look for words that might score more
embedding the power tile rather than starting with it
– a few containing a J are RAJA (11 points), MAJOR (14),
CAJOLE (15), OUIJA (12), BANJO (14).

J

Bonus words
Seven-letter words

JABBERS	JAILORS	JARRING
JABBING	JAMJARS	JASMINE
JACKALS	JAMLIKE	JASPERS
JACKASS	JAMMERS	JASPERY
JACKDAW	JAMMIER	JAUNTED
JACKERS	JAMMIES	JAUNTEE
JACKETS	JAMMING	JAUNTIE
JACKING	JAMPOTS	JAUPING
JACKPOT	JANDALS	JAVELIN
JACKSIE	JANGLED	JAWBONE
JADEDLY	JANGLER	JAWINGS
JAGGERS	JANGLES	JAWLESS
JAGGERY	JANITOR	JAWLINE
JAGGIER	JARFULS	JAYBIRD
JAGGIES	JARGONS	JAYWALK
JAGGING	JARGONY	JAZZIER
JAGUARS	JARHEAD	JAZZILY
JAILERS	JARPING	JAZZING
JAILING	JARRAHS	JAZZMAN

153

JAZZMEN	JETPACK	JOBBERS
JEALOUS	JETSAMS	JOBBING
JEEPERS	JETSOMS	JOBLESS
JEEPING	JETTIED	JOCKEYS
JEERERS	JETTIER	JOCULAR
JEERING	JETTIES	JODHPUR
JEHADIS	JETTING	JOGGERS
JELLIED	JEWELED	JOGGING
JELLIFY	JEWELER	JOHNNIE
JELLING	JEWELRY	JOHNSON
JEMIMAS	JEZEBEL	JOINERS
JEMMIED	JIBBERS	JOINERY
JEMMIER	JIBBING	JOINING
JEMMIES	JIFFIES	JOINTED
JENNIES	JIGGERS	JOINTER
JEOPARD	JIGGIER	JOINTLY
JERBILS	JIGGING	JOISTED
JERBOAS	JIGGLED	JOJOBAS
JEREEDS	JIGSAWS	JOKIEST
JERKERS	JIHADIS	JOKINGS
JERKIER	JILTERS	JOLLERS
JERKIES	JILTING	JOLLEYS
JERKILY	JIMJAMS	JOLLIED
JERKING	JIMMIED	JOLLIER
JERKINS	JIMMIES	JOLLIES
JERRIES	JIMMINY	JOLLIFY
JERSEYS	JINGLED	JOLLILY
JESSIES	JINGLER	JOLLITY
JESTEES	JINGLET	JOLTILY
JESTERS	JINGOES	JOLTING
JESTFUL	JINXING	JONESED
JESTING	JITTERS	JONESES
JESUITS	JITTERY	JOSHERS
JETLAGS	JIVIEST	JOSHING
JETLIKE	JOANNAS	JOSTLED

JOSTLER	JUDOIST	JUMPILY
JOTTERS	JUGFULS	JUMPING
JOTTIER	JUGGLED	JUNGLED
JOTTING	JUGGLER	JUNGLES
JOURNAL	JUGHEAD	JUNIORS
JOURNEY	JUGSFUL	JUNIPER
JOURNOS	JUGULAR	JUNKETS
JOUSTED	JUICERS	JUNKIER
JOUSTER	JUICIER	JUNKMAN
JOWLIER	JUICILY	JUNKMEN
JOWLING	JUICING	JURISTS
JOYLESS	JUJITSU	JURYING
JOYPADS	JUJUIST	JURYMAN
JOYRIDE	JUKEBOX	JURYMEN
JUBILEE	JULIETS	JUSTICE
JUDASES	JUMBLED	JUSTIFY
JUDDERS	JUMBLER	JUTTIER
JUDDERY	JUMBUCK	JUTTING
JUDGERS	JUMPERS	
JUDGING	JUMPIER	

J

Eight-letter words

JABBERED	JAILLESS	JAUNTIER
JABBERER	JALAPENO	JAUNTILY
JACKAROO	JAMBOREE	JAUNTING
JACKBOOT	JAMMABLE	JAVELINA
JACKEROO	JAMMIEST	JAWBONED
JACKETED	JANGLIER	JAWBONER
JADELIKE	JANGLING	JAZZIEST
JAGGEDER	JANITRIX	JAZZLIKE
JAGGEDLY	JAPANISE	JEALOUSY
JAGGIEST	JAPANIZE	JEANETTE
JAILABLE	JAPINGLY	JEHADEEN
JAILBAIT	JARGONED	JEHADISM
JAILBIRD	JAUNDICE	JEHADIST

155

JELLYING	JOINTURE	JUGGLERY
JEMMIEST	JOISTING	JUGGLING
JEMMYING	JOKESOME	JUGULATE
JEOPARDY	JOKESTER	JUICIEST
JERKIEST	JOKINESS	JULIENNE
JEROBOAM	JOKINGLY	JUMBLIER
JERRICAN	JOLLEYER	JUMBLING
JERRYCAN	JOLLIEST	JUMPABLE
JERSEYED	JOLLYING	JUMPIEST
JESTBOOK	JOLTHEAD	JUMPSIES
JESUITIC	JOLTIEST	JUMPSUIT
JESUITRY	JOLTINGS	JUNCTION
JETPACKS	JONESING	JUNCTURE
JIGGLIER	JONGLEUR	JUNGLIER
JIGGLING	JOSHINGS	JUNGLIST
JIGSAWED	JOSTLING	JUNKETED
JIHADEEN	JOTTIEST	JUNKETER
JIHADISM	JOUNCIER	JUNKIEST
JIHADIST	JOUNCING	JUNKYARD
JILLAROO	JOUSTING	JURASSIC
JIMCRACK	JOVIALLY	JURATORY
JIMMYING	JOVIALTY	JURISTIC
JINGLIER	JOWLIEST	JURYLESS
JINGLING	JOYFULLY	JURYMAST
JINGOISM	JOYOUSLY	JUSTICER
JINGOIST	JOYRIDER	JUSTLING
JITTERED	JOYSTICK	JUSTNESS
JOBSHARE	JUBILANT	JUTELIKE
JOCKETTE	JUBILATE	JUTTIEST
JOCKEYED	JUDDERED	JUTTYING
JOGGLING	JUDGINGS	JUVENILE
JOINABLE	JUDGMENT	
JOINTING	JUDICIAL	

J

UNUSUAL WORDS FROM OVERSEAS ENGLISH

If you have an awkward combination of letters on your rack then words from overseas English may come in handy. Here are some beginning with J.

Australian words

JARRAH   type of eucalyptus tree
JEFF   downsize or close down an organization
JUMBUCK   sheep

Canadian word

JOUAL   nonstandard Canadian French dialect

Hindi words

JAGGERY   coarse brown sugar
JAI   victory

Essential info
Value: 5 points
Number in set: 1

K is a valuable tile at 5 points and is particularly useful if you also have a C on your rack because of the abundance of words ending in -CK. There is a selection of useful two-letter words beginning with K: KA, KI, KO (6 points each) and KY (9 points). Three-letter words beginning with K include common words such as KEG and KID (8 points), KIP (9 points) and KEY (10 points). Others tend to be more unusual words but nevertheless very useful: KEB (9 points), KEX (14 points), KIF (10 points).

Two-letter words beginning with K

KA	KO
KI	KY

Some three-letter words beginning with K

KAB	KED	KOA
KAE	KEF	KOB
KAF	KEN	KOI
KAI	KEP	KON
KAM	KET	KOP
KAT	KEX	KOR
KAW	KHI	KOW
KAY	KIF	KYE
KEA	KIN	KYU
KEB	KIR	

K

HOOKS

Hooking requires a subtle change in a player's thought process, in that they must look at words already on the board without becoming distracted by their pronunciation.

Some front-hooks
Two letters to three

K-AB	K-EF	K-OI
K-AE	K-ET	K-ON
K-AI	K-EX	K-OP
K-AM	K-HI	K-OR
K-AS	K-ID	K-OS
K-AT	K-IF	K-OW
K-AW	K-IN	K-YE
K-AY	K-IS	K-YU
K-EA	K-IT	
K-ED	K-OB	

Three letters to four

K-AGO	K-EEN	K-NAP
K-AID	K-ELL	K-NEE
K-AIL	K-ELT	K-NEW
K-AIM	K-ERF	K-NIT
K-AIN	K-ERN	K-NOT
K-AKA	K-EST	K-NOW
K-ALE	K-ETA	K-NUB
K-AMA	K-HAN	K-NUR
K-AMI	K-HAT	K-NUT
K-ANA	K-HET	K-OBO
K-ANE	K-ICK	K-OFF
K-ANT	K-IFF	K-ORA
K-ARK	K-ILL	K-ORE
K-ART	K-INK	K-RAY
K-AVA	K-IRK	K-SAR
K-AWA	K-ISH	K-UDO
K-BAR	K-IWI	K-UTA
K-EEK	K-LAP	K-UTU
K-EEL	K-NAG	K-YAK

K

Four letters to five

K-ALIF	K-HETH	K-NOCK
K-ANGA	K-ICKY	K-NOLL
K-ARSY	K-INKY	K-NOUT
K-ARTS	K-LANG	K-NOWN
K-AVAS	K-LAPS	K-NURL
K-AWED	K-LICK	K-NURR
K-EDGE	K-LONG	K-OKRA
K-EDGY	K-LOOF	K-OMBU
K-EECH	K-LUGE	K-RAFT
K-EMPT	K-LUTZ	K-RAIT
K-ERNE	K-NAVE	K-RANG
K-ETCH	K-NEED	K-RILL
K-EVIL	K-NIFE	K-RONE
K-EYED	K-NISH	K-ROON

K-ULAN   K-YACK
K-VELL   K-YANG

Five letters to six

K-AINGA	K-EGGED	K-INGLE
K-ALONG	K-EGGER	K-INKED
K-ANTAR	K-EIGHT	K-INKLE
K-ANTED	K-EMBED	K-IRKED
K-ARKED	K-ENTIA	K-ISHES
K-ARRIS	K-ERNED	K-LATCH
K-ARSEY	K-ETTLE	K-LUGED
K-AWING	K-EYING	K-NAGGY
K-EBBED	K-ICKER	K-NIGHT
K-EDGED	K-ILLER	K-RATER
K-EDGER	K-INDIE	K-VETCH

Six letters to seven

K-ANTING	K-INKIER	K-NISHES
K-ARKING	K-INKING	K-NOBBLE
K-EBBING	K-INSHIP	K-NOCKED
K-EDGERS	K-IRKING	K-NUBBLE
K-EDGIER	K-LAPPED	K-NUBBLY
K-EDGING	K-LINKER	K-NURLED
K-EECHES	K-LISTER	K-ONNING
K-EGGING	K-LUGING	K-RATERS
K-ENOSIS	K-LUTZES	K-RIMMER
K-ERNING	K-NAPPED	K-RISING
K-ICKIER	K-NAPPER	K-VETCHY
K-IDLING	K-NICKER	

Seven letters to eight

K-ALEWIFE	K-INKIEST	K-NAPPING
K-EDGIEST	K-INSHIPS	K-NIGHTED
K-ETAMINE	K-LAPPING	K-NIGHTLY
K-ETCHING	K-LATCHES	K-NOBBIER
K-ICKIEST	K-NAGGIER	K-NOBBLED

K

K-NOCKING   K-NUBBLED   K-OSMOSES
K-NUBBIER   K-NURLING   K-RUMPING

Some end-hooks
Two letters to three

AR-K   IN-K   SI-K
AS-K   JA-K   TA-K
AW-K   KA-K   TI-K
BO-K   MA-K   WO-K
DA-K   NE-K   YA-K
EE-K   OI-K   YO-K
EL-K   OU-K   YU-K
ER-K   PA-K

Three letters to four

BAC-K   DOC-K   JAR-K
BAL-K   DOR-K   JUN-K
BAN-K   DUN-K   KIN-K
BAR-K   FAN-K   KIR-K
BAS-K   FIL-K   LAC-K
BON-K   FIN-K   LAR-K
BOO-K   FIR-K   LAW-K
BUN-K   FOR-K   LEA-K
BUR-K   FUN-K   LEE-K
BUS-K   GEE-K   LIN-K
CAR-K   GIN-K   LIS-K
CAW-K   GON-K   LOO-K
CHI-K   GUN-K   LUR-K
CON-K   HAN-K   MAC-K
COO-K   HIC-K   MAR-K
COR-K   HOC-K   MAS-K
COW-K   HON-K   MAW-K
DAN-K   HOO-K   MEE-K
DIN-K   HOW-K   MIL-K
DIS-K   HUN-K   MIR-K

MOC-K	PIN-K	SOC-K
MON-K	PUN-K	SUN-K
MOO-K	RAN-K	TAN-K
MUS-K	REE-K	TAS-K
NOO-K	RIN-K	TEA-K
NOR-K	ROC-K	TEE-K
PAC-K	ROO-K	TIC-K
PAR-K	RUC-K	TOC-K
PEA-K	SAC-K	TON-K
PEC-K	SAN-K	TOO-K
PEE-K	SEE-K	WEE-K
PER-K	SIC-K	WIN-K
PIC-K	SIN-K	

K

Four letters to five

ABAC-K	CLON-K	SKIN-K
ALEC-K	CRAN-K	SLEE-K
BLIN-K	CREE-K	SMIR-K
BLOC-K	CROC-K	SPAN-K
BRAN-K	FLAN-K	SPAR-K
BRIN-K	FLIC-K	SPEC-K
BRIS-K	FLOC-K	SPIN-K
BROO-K	FRIS-K	STAR-K
BRUS-K	GREE-K	STIR-K
CHAL-K	PLAN-K	STUN-K
CHIC-K	SCUL-K	SWAN-K
CHIN-K	SHAN-K	THAN-K
CHOC-K	SHIR-K	THIN-K
CLAN-K	SHOO-K	TWIN-K

Five letters to six

ANTIC-K	IMBAR-K	MUSIC-K
ASPIC-K	JAMBO-K	PACHA-K
BEGUN-K	KALPA-K	PANIC-K
DEBAR-K	MEDIC-K	REBEC-K
EMBAR-K	MELIC-K	RESEE-K

SQUAW-K	UNBAR-K
UMIAC-K	ZEBEC-K

Six letters to seven

AMTRAC-K	FINNAC-K	OUTBAR-K
BOOBOO-K	GWEDUC-K	OUTRAN-K
CALPAC-K	LIMBEC-K	TIETAC-K
DISBAR-K	OOMIAC-K	TOMBAC-K

Seven letters to eight

ALMANAC-K	OVERRAN-K	SHOEPAC-K
BALDRIC-K	POLITIC-K	TAMARIS-K
BAUDRIC-K	PRACTIC-K	
FORERAN-K	SHELLAC-K	

K

BLOCKERS

It is useful to know which words are blockers and can't therefore be extended before or after. You may want to play a blocker that your opponent can't extend, or you may want to avoid playing a blocker because you want to keep the board open.

The three-letter blocker beginning with K

KEX

Some four-letter blockers beginning with K

KAAL	KILD	KRIS
KEPT	KISH	KUNA
KEWL	KNEW	KUNE

Some five-letter blockers beginning with K (except words ending in '-ED', '-J', '-S', '-X', '-Y' or '-Z')

KACHA	KEECH	KEMPT

KENCH	KNELT	KORAI
KIDGE	KNISH	KOTCH
KINDA	KOHEN	KRONA

Some six-letter blockers beginning with K (except words ending in '-ED', '-J', '-S', '-X', '-Y' or '-Z')

KAPUTT	KIBOSH	KRONEN
KARMIC	KIPPEN	KRONER
KAWING	KIRSCH	KROONI
KEIGHT	KLATCH	KULAKI
KEPPIT	KNITCH	KUTCHA
KEWLER	KOUROI	KYBOSH

BONUS WORDS

Bonus words on your rack can be hard to spot, especially for the less experienced player. One way to help find them is by using prefixes and suffixes.

Many larger words include a common prefix or suffix – remembering these and using them where you can is a good way to discover any longer words on your rack, including any potential bonus words. The key suffix to remember beginning with K is -KIN.

Some words ending with -KIN
Seven-letter words

BUMP-KIN	LUMP-KIN	NUMP-KIN
LADY-KIN	MANA-KIN	PUMP-KIN
LAMB-KIN	MANI-KIN	WOLF-KIN
LORD-KIN	MINI-KIN	

Eight-letter words

BOOTI-KIN	CIDER-KIN	DEVIL-KIN

LARRI-KIN   MOUSE-KIN
MANNI-KIN   MUNCH-KIN

UNUSUAL WORDS FROM OVERSEAS ENGLISH

If you have an awkward combination of letters on your rack then words from overseas English may come in handy. Here are some beginning with K.

Australian words

KARRI	type of eucalyptus tree
KYBO	temporary lavatory
KYLIE	boomerang that is flat on one side and convex on the other

Canadian words

KAMOTIQ	a sled with wooden runners

Hindi words

KADAI	a cooking pan like a wok
KHADDAR	cotton cloth
KHEDA	enclosure for captured elephants
KOEL	parasitic cuckoo
KRAIT	brightly coloured venomous snake
KULFI	Indian dessert
KURTA	long loose garment

New Zealand words

KAHAWAI	large fish
KARANGA	call or chant of welcome
KATIPO	small venomous spider
KAUPAPA	strategy, policy or cause
KAURI	coniferous tree
KAWA	protocol or etiquette

K

KOHA	gift or donation
KORU	curved pattern
KOWHAI	small tree
KUIA	female elder
KURI	mongrel dog
KUTU	body louse

South African words

KEREL	chap or fellow
KRAAL	stockaded village
KWAITO	type of pop music

Urdu words

KAMEEZ	long tunic
KHARIF	crop harvested at beginning of winter
KHAYAL	kind of Indian classical vocal music
KINCOB	fine silk fabric embroidered with gold or silver threads
KOFTA	Indian dish of seasoned minced meat shaped into balls
KOFTGAR	person skilled in inlaying steel with gold
KOFTGARI	art of inlaying steel with gold
KORMA	Indian dish of meat or vegetables braised with yoghurt or cream

Handy Hint: K is OK outside the UK

The letter K features prominently in many variants of World English. Along with its frequency of use in the Maori-derived words of New Zealand English, the use of Ks is common in Australian English (QUOKKA, 18 points), Hindi (PUKKA, 10 points), Inuit words (MUKTUK, 11 points) and Urdu (KHAKI, 11 points). As there is only one K in the Scrabble set, you will need to have a handy blank tile to play these fascinating words, but don't foolishly waste your blank.

Essential info
Value: 1 point
Number in set: 4

The **L** is a very flexible letter for playing words because it combines with many other consonants such as BL-, CL-, FL-, PL-. If you have two of them there are also many words ending in -LL to help you out. Be aware of the following two-letter words for making parallel plays involving an L: LA (in music, the sixth note of a major scale, 2 points), LI (a Chinese unit of length, 2 points) and LO (a command that means look, 2 points). There's a great selection of three-letter words for combining the L with another higher-scoring consonant such as: LAW, LAY, LOW and LYE, all worth 6 points. There is also a handy selection of words which use X: LAX, LEX, LOX and LUX, all worth 10 points.

Two-letter words beginning with L

LA	LI	LO

Some three-letter words beginning with L

LAB	LEX	LOX
LAC	LEZ	LOY
LAH	LIB	LUG
LAM	LIG	LUM
LAR	LIN	LUN
LAT	LOD	LUR
LAV	LOP	LUX
LEA	LOR	LUZ
LEE	LOS	LYE
LES	LOU	LYM

L

HOOKS

Hooking requires a subtle change in a player's thought process, in that they must look at words already on the board without becoming distracted by their pronunciation.

Some front-hooks
Two letters to three

L-AB	L-AX	L-IN
L-AD	L-AY	L-IS
L-AG	L-EA	L-IT
L-AH	L-ED	L-OB
L-AM	L-EE	L-OD
L-AR	L-ES	L-OO
L-AS	L-ET	L-OP
L-AT	L-EX	L-OR
L-AW	L-ID	L-OS

L-OU	L-OY	L-UN
L-OW	L-UG	L-UR
L-OX	L-UM	L-YE

Three letters to four

L-ACE	L-EFT	L-OON
L-AID	L-END	L-OOP
L-AIN	L-ENS	L-OOT
L-AIR	L-ESS	L-OPE
L-AKE	L-EST	L-ORD
L-ALL	L-ICE	L-ORE
L-AMP	L-ICH	L-OSE
L-ANA	L-ICK	L-OUD
L-AND	L-IMP	L-OUP
L-ANE	L-INK	L-OUR
L-ARD	L-ION	L-OUT
L-ARK	L-OAF	L-OWE
L-ASH	L-OBE	L-OWN
L-ASS	L-OBO	L-OWT
L-ATE	L-OCH	L-UDO
L-AVA	L-ODE	L-UKE
L-AWN	L-OFT	L-UMP
L-EAN	L-ONE	L-URE
L-EAR	L-OOF	L-UTE
L-EEK	L-OOM	

Four letters to five

L-ACED	L-AWED	L-EDGE
L-ACER	L-AWNY	L-EDGY
L-ADDY	L-AYIN	L-EECH
L-AGER	L-EACH	L-EERY
L-AIRY	L-EARN	L-EGAL
L-AKED	L-EASE	L-EGGY
L-ANCE	L-EAST	L-EISH
L-APSE	L-EAVE	L-ETCH

171

L-EVER	L-OATH	L-OWED
L-INCH	L-ONER	L-OWER
L-INGO	L-OOSE	L-OWLY
L-INKY	L-OPED	L-OWSE
L-ISLE	L-OTTO	L-UMPY
L-LAMA	L-OVER	L-USER

Five letters to six

L-ACING	L-EASER	L-IZARD
L-ACKER	L-EAVED	L-OCKER
L-ADDER	L-EDGED	L-OCULI
L-AGGER	L-EDGER	L-OFTER
L-AIRED	L-EGGED	L-OLLER
L-AMBER	L-EGGER	L-ONELY
L-AMENT	L-ENDER	L-OOPED
L-AMPED	L-ETHAL	L-OPING
L-ANGER	L-ICKER	L-ORATE
L-ANKER	L-IGGED	L-OTHER
L-ARKED	L-IMBED	L-OTTER
L-ARVAL	L-IMPED	L-OUPED
L-ASHED	L-IMPLY	L-OUTED
L-ASTER	L-INKED	L-OWING
L-AWFUL	L-INKER	L-OWNED
L-AWING	L-INTEL	L-UGGED
L-EANED	L-INTER	L-UMBER
L-EARED	L-IRKED	L-UMPED
L-EASED	L-ITHER	L-USHER

Six letters to seven

L-AIDING	L-AUDING	L-EARNED
L-AIRIER	L-AWLESS	L-EARNER
L-AIRING	L-AWNIER	L-EASING
L-AMPING	L-AWNING	L-EAVING
L-ARKING	L-EANING	L-ECHING
L-ASHING	L-EARING	L-EDGIER

L-EECHED	L-IGNIFY	L-OUTING
L-EERIER	L-IMPING	L-OVERED
L-EERILY	L-INKING	L-OVERLY
L-EFTEST	L-INNING	L-OWLIER
L-EGALLY	L-IONISE	L-OWNING
L-EGGIER	L-IONIZE	L-OXYGEN
L-EGGING	L-IRKING	L-UGGING
L-ENDING	L-OCULAR	L-ULLING
L-ETCHED	L-OOPING	L-UMPING
L-IGGING	L-OUPING	

Seven letters to eight

L-ABILITY	L-EDGIEST	L-IONISER
L-ACERATE	L-EECHING	L-IONIZED
L-AIRIEST	L-EERIEST	L-IONIZER
L-AMBLING	L-EGALITY	L-ITERATE
L-ANGERED	L-EGGIEST	L-OCULATE
L-ANGUISH	L-ETCHING	L-OMENTUM
L-AUREATE	L-EVITATE	L-ONENESS
L-AWFULLY	L-IGNEOUS	L-OURIEST
L-AWNIEST	L-INCHPIN	L-OWLIEST
L-EARNING	L-IONISED	L-UMBERED

Some end-hooks
Two letters to three

AA-L	EE-L	OW-L
AI-L	EL-L	PA-L
AL-L	GU-L	PE-L
AW-L	JO-L	PO-L
BA-L	MA-L	SO-L
BE-L	ME-L	TE-L
DA-L	MI-L	TI-L
DE-L	MO-L	ZO-L
DO-L	OI-L	

Three letters to four

AXE-L	GOA-L	PUL-L
BAL-L	GRR-L	PUR-L
BOW-L	HOW-L	SEA-L
CEL-L	JAI-L	SOU-L
COO-L	JOW-L	TAI-L
COW-L	MAL-L	TEA-L
CUR-L	MEL-L	TEL-L
DAH-L	MEW-L	TIL-L
DOL-L	MIL-L	TOO-L
DOW-L	MOL-L	VIA-L
DUE-L	NIL-L	WAI-L
EAR-L	ORA-L	WOO-L
FEE-L	OVA-L	YOW-L
FOU-L	PAL-L	ZEA-L
FUR-L	PEA-L	
GAL-L	POL-L	

Four letters to five

ALKY-L	GAVE-L	MOTE-L
ALLY-L	GNAR-L	MURA-L
ANNA-L	GROW-L	NAVE-L
AURA-L	GRUE-L	OCTA-L
BABE-L	HAZE-L	PANE-L
BRAW-L	HOTE-L	PEAR-L
CABA-L	HOVE-L	PERI-L
CAME-L	IDEA-L	PROW-L
CRAW-L	IDYL-L	PUPA-L
CREE-L	KAVA-L	QUAI-L
CRUE-L	KNEE-L	RAVE-L
DRAW-L	LEVE-L	RIVA-L
DURA-L	LOCA-L	ROTA-L
EASE-L	META-L	RUBE-L
FAVE-L	MODE-L	SCOW-L
FETA-L	MORA-L	SHAW-L

L

SNAR-L	VENA-L	WHIR-L
SPIE-L	VINY-L	YODE-L
UREA-L	VITA-L	YOKE-L
VASA-L	WHEE-L	ZONA-L

Five letters to six

ANIMA-L	FLOTE-L	REDIA-L
AORTA-L	GRAVE-L	REGNA-L
APPAL-L	GROVE-L	SCRAW-L
ATRIA-L	LARVA-L	SEPTA-L
BARBE-L	MAMMA-L	SHOVE-L
BARRE-L	MANGE-L	SIGNA-L
CARTE-L	MEDIA-L	SPINA-L
CAUSA-L	MENTA-L	SWIVE-L
COSTA-L	MONGO-L	TASSE-L
DERMA-L	MORSE-L	TEASE-L
DORSA-L	MUSSE-L	TIBIA-L
DRIVE-L	NORMA-L	TRAVE-L
ENROL-L	PASTE-L	VANDA-L
EXTOL-L	PETRE-L	VESTA-L
FACIA-L	PORTA-L	VISTA-L
FAUNA-L	PRIMA-L	
FLORA-L	RECAL-L	

Six letters to seven

ANGINA-L	CRESTA-L	LATERA-L
BARBEL-L	CUBICA-L	LEXICA-L
CAMERA-L	DISTIL-L	LINGUA-L
CAPITA-L	EPOCHA-L	MAXIMA-L
CENTRA-L	FASCIA-L	MIASMA-L
CHANCE-L	FEMORA-L	MINIMA-L
CHROMY-L	FULFIL-L	NATURA-L
COLONE-L	GENERA-L	NOMINA-L
CORNEA-L	INSTAL-L	OPTIMA-L
CORONA-L	INSTIL-L	ORBITA-L

L

| RETINA-L | STADIA-L | TRIVIA-L |
| SALIVA-L | STIGMA-L | |

Seven letters to eight

ALLUVIA-L	CRIMINA-L	MINUTIA-L
AMPHORA-L	ENTHRAL-L	PERINEA-L
ANTENNA-L	HYDROXY-L	PERSONA-L
BRACHIA-L	IMPERIA-L	RESIDUA-L
BRIMFUL-L	INERTIA-L	SKILFUL-L
CAROUSE-L	MALARIA-L	SPECTRA-L
CEREBRA-L	MANDRIL-L	STAMINA-L
CORPORA-L	MARSHAL-L	VISCERA-L

L

BLOCKERS

It is useful to know which words are blockers and can't therefore be extended before or after. You may want to play a blocker that your opponent can't extend, or you may want to avoid playing a blocker because you want to keep the board open.

Some three-letter blockers beginning with L

| LEZ | LUZ |

Some four-letter blockers beginning with L

LACY	LEVY	LORN
LEKE	LEWD	LYNX
LEVO	LIRE	

Some five-letter blockers beginning with L (except words ending in '-ED', '-J', '-S', '-X', '-Y' or '-Z')

LAEVO	LEANT	LEEZE
LAITH	LEAPT	LEISH
LAXER	LEASH	LIART

LIVID	LURCH	LYART
LOYAL	LURID	LYNCH
LUCID	LYARD	

Some six-letter blockers beginning with L
(except words ending in '-ED', '-J', '-S', '-X', '-Y' or '-Z')

LACTIC	LEFTER	LOIPEN
LAKISH	LEWDER	LOOSER
LAMEST	LIMBIC	LORATE
LARGER	LIMPID	LOUDER
LARVAE	LINEAL	LOUPIT
LARVAL	LINEAR	LOWSER
LAWFUL	LIROTH	LUBING
LAXEST	LITTEN	
LEARNT	LIVEST	

L

BONUS WORDS

Bonus words on your rack can be hard to spot, especially for the less experienced player. One way to help find them is by using prefixes and suffixes.

Many larger words include a common prefix or suffix – remembering these and using them where you can is a good way to discover any longer words on your rack, including any potential bonus words. The key suffixes to remember beginning with L are -LAND, -LESS, -LET, -LIKE, -LOGY and -LY.

Some words ending with -LAND
Seven-letter words

| BAD-LAND | DRY-LAND | GAR-LAND |
| BOG-LAND | FEN-LAND | HIE-LAND |

HOL-LAND	MID-LAND	SUN-LAND
LAW-LAND	NOR-LAND	TOY-LAND
LOW-LAND	OUT-LAND	WET-LAND

Eight-letter words

BACK-LAND	FLAT-LAND	PARK-LAND
BARE-LAND	FOOD-LAND	PEAT-LAND
BOOK-LAND	GANG-LAND	PINE-LAND
BUSH-LAND	HEAD-LAND	PORT-LAND
CLUB-LAND	HIGH-LAND	SHET-LAND
CROP-LAND	HOME-LAND	SNOW-LAND
DOCK-LAND	LAKE-LAND	TIDE-LAND
DUNE-LAND	MAIN-LAND	WILD-LAND
EURO-LAND	MOOR-LAND	WOOD-LAND
FARM-LAND	OVER-LAND	YARD-LAND

L

Some words ending with -LESS

Seven-letter words

AGE-LESS	GUN-LESS	MAP-LESS
AIM-LESS	GUT-LESS	PIN-LESS
AIR-LESS	HAP-LESS	RIB-LESS
ARM-LESS	HAT-LESS	SEX-LESS
ART-LESS	HUB-LESS	SKY-LESS
BAG-LESS	IRE-LESS	SUN-LESS
EAR-LESS	JOB-LESS	TAG-LESS
END-LESS	JOY-LESS	USE-LESS
EYE-LESS	LAW-LESS	WIT-LESS
GOD-LESS	LEG-LESS	ZIP-LESS

Eight-letter words

BACK-LESS	CHIN-LESS	DECK-LESS
BONE-LESS	CLUE-LESS	DRUG-LESS
CARE-LESS	CORD-LESS	FACE-LESS
CASH-LESS	DEBT-LESS	FEAR-LESS

FLAW-LESS
FORM-LESS
GAIN-LESS
GOAL-LESS
HAIR-LESS
HARM-LESS
HEAD-LESS
HELP-LESS
HOST-LESS
LAMP-LESS

LIFE-LESS
LIST-LESS
LOVE-LESS
MIND-LESS
NAME-LESS
PAIN-LESS
PEER-LESS
REST-LESS
RUTH-LESS
SEAM-LESS

SEED-LESS
SELF-LESS
STEP-LESS
TACT-LESS
TAIL-LESS
TIME-LESS
WHIP-LESS
WIRE-LESS

Some words ending with -LET

Seven-letter words

BOOK-LET
CORM-LET
COUP-LET
DOUB-LET
EPAU-LET
LAKE-LET
LEAF-LET

NECK-LET
NOTE-LET
RING-LET
RIVU-LET
ROOT-LET
SERV-LET
SING-LET

STAR-LET
TOAD-LET
TART-LET
TRIO-LET
TWIG-LET

Eight-letter words

BRACE-LET
COVER-LET
FRUIT-LET
GAUNT-LET

GLOBU-LET
PAMPH-LET
PISTO-LET
PLATE-LET

SPROG-LET
VALVE-LET

Some words ending with -LIKE

Seven-letter words

APE-LIKE
AXE-LIKE
BAT-LIKE
CAN-LIKE

CAT-LIKE
DIS-LIKE
DOG-LIKE
FAN-LIKE

GOD-LIKE
HOG-LIKE
MAN-LIKE
MIS-LIKE

PAN-LIKE   TOY-LIKE   WIG-LIKE
POD-LIKE   WAR-LIKE
SKY-LIKE   WAX-LIKE

Eight-letter words

AUNT-LIKE   HAWK-LIKE   ROCK-LIKE
BABY-LIKE   HERD-LIKE   SILK-LIKE
BEAR-LIKE   KING-LIKE   SWAN-LIKE
BIRD-LIKE   LADY-LIKE   TEAR-LIKE
CLAW-LIKE   LIFE-LIKE   TWIG-LIKE
DOME-LIKE   LORD-LIKE   VICE-LIKE
FISH-LIKE   MAZE-LIKE   WHIP-LIKE
GAME-LIKE   OVEN-LIKE   WOLF-LIKE
GERM-LIKE   REED-LIKE

L Some words ending with -LY

Seven-letter words

ACUTE-LY   FALSE-LY   NIGHT-LY
AGILE-LY   FLUID-LY   ORDER-LY
AWFUL-LY   FRESH-LY   PLAIN-LY
BEAST-LY   GHOST-LY   PRICK-LY
BLACK-LY   GREAT-LY   QUICK-LY
BLANK-LY   GROSS-LY   QUIET-LY
BLUNT-LY   HARSH-LY   RAPID-LY
BRAVE-LY   IDEAL-LY   RIGHT-LY
BROAD-LY   INEPT-LY   ROUGH-LY
CHEAP-LY   JOINT-LY   SHAPE-LY
CHIEF-LY   LARGE-LY   SIDED-LY
CLEAR-LY   LEGAL-LY   SIGHT-LY
CRACK-LY   LITHE-LY   SMART-LY
DAZED-LY   LOCAL-LY   SOUND-LY
DEATH-LY   MISER-LY   STATE-LY
EAGER-LY   MONTH-LY   STERN-LY
ELDER-LY   MUTED-LY   TACIT-LY
FAINT-LY   NASAL-LY   TENSE-LY

TOTAL-LY	USUAL-LY	WEIRD-LY
TOUGH-LY	UTTER-LY	WORLD-LY
TRICK-LY	VAGUE-LY	
TWINK-LY	VIRAL-LY	

Eight-letter words

ABRUPT-LY	GINGER-LY	PROPER-LY
ABSURD-LY	HEATED-LY	QUAINT-LY
ACTIVE-LY	HEAVEN-LY	RECENT-LY
AUGUST-LY	INSANE-LY	REMOTE-LY
BENIGN-LY	JOYFUL-LY	SCARCE-LY
BOYISH-LY	KNIGHT-LY	SECOND-LY
BRUTAL-LY	LAWFUL-LY	SECURE-LY
CANDID-LY	MANFUL-LY	SOLEMN-LY
CARING-LY	MANNER-LY	TRIBAL-LY
CASUAL-LY	MANUAL-LY	TURGID-LY
DEMURE-LY	MENTAL-LY	UNEVEN-LY
DIRECT-LY	MINDED-LY	UNFAIR-LY
ENTIRE-LY	MINUTE-LY	VERBAL-LY
EXPERT-LY	NATIVE-LY	WESTER-LY
FACIAL-LY	ONWARD-LY	WINTER-LY
FORMAL-LY	PATENT-LY	WOODEN-LY
FRIEND-LY	PRIMAL-LY	

L

UNUSUAL WORDS FROM OVERSEAS ENGLISH

If you have an awkward combination of letters on your rack then words from overseas English may come in handy. Here are some beginning with L.

Australian words

| LOPPY | man employed to do maintenance work on a ranch |
| LOWAN | ground-dwelling bird |

Canadian words

LOGAN	backwater
LOONIE	Canadian dollar coin with loon bird on one face

Hindi words

LAKH	100,000
LANGUR	arboreal monkey
LASSI	yoghurt drink
LATHI	long heavy stick used as a weapon
LUNGI	long piece of cloth worn as loincloth or turban

South African word

LEGUAAN	large monitor lizard

Urdu word

LASCAR	sailor from the East Indies

L

Handy Hint: Do your homework

A game of Scrabble can go either way and a less prepared player will always be at a disadvantage. A few simple steps can improve your chances before even starting the game, for example:

• Learn two and three-letter words, especially those with a tile worth 4 or more points (FHJKQVWXYZ), for scoring well in tight situations and milking the premium squares

• Don't forget using all your letters at once gets you a 50-point bonus

Essential info
Value: 3 points
Number in set: 2

M is a good letter for forming short words as it begins
a two-letter word with every vowel, as well as with Y
and with another M. M combines well with power tiles
X and Z: MAX, MIX and MUX (an old American word
meaning to make a mess of something) are all worth
12 points and MIZ (informal short form of misery) and
MOZ (a curse of jinx) are both worth 14. It is also worth
remembering the three-letter words ending in W: MAW,
MEW and MOW (8 points each).

Two-letter words beginning with M

MA	MM	MY
ME	MO	
MI	MU	

Some three-letter words beginning with M

MAA	MEU	MOE
MAC	MEW	MOG
MAE	MHO	MOI
MAG	MIB	MOL
MAK	MIC	MOM
MAL	MID	MON
MAM	MIG	MOR
MAW	MIL	MOT
MAX	MIM	MOU
MED	MIR	MOY
MEE	MIZ	MOZ
MEG	MNA	MUN
MEH	MOA	MUT
MEL	MOC	MUX
MEM	MOD	MYC

M

HOOKS

Hooking requires a subtle change in a player's thought process, in that they must look at words already on the board without becoming distracted by their pronunciation.

Some front-hooks
Two letters to three

M-AA	M-AE	M-AL
M-AD	M-AG	M-AM

M-AN	M-ES	M-OP
M-AR	M-ET	M-OR
M-AS	M-HO	M-OS
M-AT	M-ID	M-OU
M-AW	M-IS	M-OW
M-AX	M-NA	M-OY
M-AY	M-OB	M-UG
M-ED	M-OD	M-UM
M-EE	M-OE	M-UN
M-EH	M-OI	M-US
M-EL	M-OM	M-UT
M-EM	M-ON	
M-EN	M-OO	

Three letters to four

M-ACE	M-ASK	M-IRE
M-ACH	M-ASS	M-IRK
M-AGE	M-ATE	M-ISO
M-AHA	M-EAN	M-OAT
M-AID	M-EAT	M-ODE
M-AIL	M-EEK	M-OKE
M-AIM	M-ELD	M-OLD
M-AIN	M-ELL	M-OLE
M-AIR	M-ELT	M-ONO
M-AKE	M-EME	M-OON
M-ALE	M-EMO	M-OOR
M-ALL	M-END	M-OOT
M-ALT	M-ERE	M-OPE
M-AMA	M-ESS	M-ORE
M-ANE	M-ETA	M-ORT
M-ANY	M-ETH	M-OWN
M-ARE	M-ICE	M-ULE
M-ARK	M-IFF	M-UMP
M-ART	M-ILK	M-UMU
M-ARY	M-ILL	M-USE
M-ASH	M-INK	M-UTE

Four letters to five

M-ACED	M-ETIC	M-ORAL
M-ACER	M-IFFY	M-OSES
M-ACHE	M-IRED	M-OTTO
M-AGMA	M-IRID	M-OUCH
M-AMBO	M-ITCH	M-OULD
M-ANGA	M-OBEY	M-OURN
M-ANNA	M-ODAL	M-OUST
M-ANTA	M-OLDY	M-OVER
M-ARCH	M-OLLA	M-OWED
M-ASHY	M-ONER	M-OWER
M-AWED	M-ONIE	M-USED
M-AXED	M-OOSE	M-USER
M-AXES	M-OPED	
M-AXIS	M-OPUS	

Five letters to six

M-ACERS	M-ANTIC	M-ELDER
M-ACING	M-ANTIS	M-EMBER
M-ADDED	M-ANTRA	M-ENDED
M-ADDER	M-ARKED	M-ENDER
M-ADMAN	M-ARROW	M-ERING
M-ADMEN	M-ASCOT	M-ESSES
M-AGISM	M-ASHED	M-ESTER
M-AIDED	M-ASHES	M-ETHOS
M-AILED	M-ASKED	M-ETHYL
M-AIMED	M-ASKER	M-ETTLE
M-AIMER	M-ASTER	M-ICKLE
M-AKING	M-AWING	M-ILLER
M-ALIGN	M-AXING	M-INGLE
M-ALLOW	M-EAGER	M-INION
M-AMMON	M-EAGRE	M-INTER
M-ANGEL	M-EANED	M-IRING
M-ANGER	M-EASED	M-ISLED
M-ANGLE	M-EASLE	M-ITHER

M-OCKER
M-ODDER
M-OILED
M-OILER
M-OLDER
M-OLLIE
M-OPING
M-ORGAN
M-ORGUE

M-ORRIS
M-OTHER
M-OUGHT
M-OUPED
M-OUTER
M-OWING
M-OZZIE
M-UDDER
M-UGGED

M-UMBLE
M-UMPED
M-UNIFY
M-UNITE
M-USHER
M-USING
M-UTTER

Six letters to seven

M-ADDING
M-AGNATE
M-AIDING
M-AILING
M-AIMING
M-ANGLED
M-ANGLER
M-ARCHED
M-ARCHER
M-ARCHES
M-ARGENT
M-ARKING
M-ARROWY
M-ASHIER
M-ASHING

M-ASKING
M-EANING
M-EARING
M-EASING
M-ELDING
M-ENDING
M-ETHANE
M-ETHOXY
M-ETTLED
M-ICKLER
M-IFFIER
M-ITCHED
M-OILING
M-OMENTA
M-ONEYER

M-OPUSES
M-ORALLY
M-ORPHIC
M-OUCHED
M-OUCHES
M-OULDER
M-OUPING
M-OUSTED
M-OUTHER
M-OZZIES
M-UGGING
M-ULLING
M-UMPING
M-UNITED
M-USEFUL

Seven letters to eight

M-ACERATE
M-ADWOMAN
M-ADWOMEN
M-AGISTER
M-AIDLESS
M-ALIGNED
M-ALIGNER

M-ANGLING
M-ARCHING
M-ARRIAGE
M-ARROWED
M-ASHIEST
M-EAGERER
M-EAGERLY

M-ENOLOGY
M-ERISTIC
M-ETHANOL
M-ETHOXYL
M-ETHYLIC
M-ICKLEST
M-IFFIEST

M

M-ISOGAMY   M-ORALISM   M-UNITING
M-ITCHING   M-ORALIST   M-UNITION
M-OATLIKE   M-ORALITY   M-UTTERED
M-OMENTUM   M-ORATORY   M-UTTERER
M-OORIEST   M-UNIFIED

Some end-hooks

Two letters to three

AI-M	HO-M	OO-M
AR-M	IS-M	PA-M
BA-M	JA-M	PO-M
DA-M	KA-M	RE-M
DI-M	LA-M	SI-M
DO-M	MA-M	SO-M
EL-M	ME-M	TA-M
ER-M	MI-M	TO-M
FE-M	MO-M	UM-M
GU-M	MU-M	WE-M
HA-M	NA-M	YA-M
HE-M	NO-M	YO-M
HI-M	NY-M	YU-M
HM-M	OH-M	

Three letters to four

BAL-M	FAR-M	HER-M
BAR-M	FER-M	IDE-M
BOO-M	FIL-M	LEA-M
BOR-M	FIR-M	LOO-M
CHA-M	FOR-M	MAL-M
COO-M	FRO-M	MAR-M
COR-M	GAU-M	MUM-M
DEE-M	GOR-M	NEE-M
DOO-M	HAE-M	NOR-M
DOR-M	HAW-M	PAL-M

M

PER-M	SHA-M	TOO-M
PLU-M	SKI-M	WAR-M
PRE-M	SOW-M	WAS-M
PRO-M	SPA-M	WEE-M
ROO-M	TEA-M	WHA-M
SEA-M	TEE-M	WHO-M
SEE-M	THE-M	ZOO-M

Four letters to five

ABRI-M	GOLE-M	REAR-M
ABYS-M	HAKA-M	RETE-M
ALAR-M	HARE-M	SATE-M
BREE-M	HAUL-M	SEIS-M
BROO-M	MALA-M	SHAW-M
CHAR-M	MAXI-M	SPAS-M
CHAS-M	MINI-M	STUM-M
DENI-M	MODE-M	THAR-M
FLAM-M	PASH-M	THRU-M
FLEA-M	PURI-M	TOTE-M
FORA-M	REAL-M	

M

Five letters to six

BALSA-M	LINGA-M	PURIS-M
BAZOO-M	MALIS-M	SADIS-M
BESEE-M	MERIS-M	SCRAW-M
CENTU-M	MESTO-M	SHTUM-M
CHIAS-M	MONTE-M	SPIRE-M
CONDO-M	MURRA-M	TELES-M
COPAL-M	MUTIS-M	YOGIS-M
DODGE-M	PARTI-M	

Six letters to seven

ANIMIS-M	GOPURA-M	MISTER-M
BUCKRA-M	MANTRA-M	PREWAR-M
FASCIS-M	MISSEE-M	SENSIS-M

Seven letters to eight

CLASSIS-M	JEHADIS-M	TITANIS-M
CYMBALO-M	JIHADIS-M	
FINALIS-M	TELECOM-M	

> ## BLOCKERS
>
> It is useful to know which words are blockers and can't therefore be extended before or after. You may want to play a blocker that your opponent can't extend, or you may want to avoid playing a blocker because you want to keep the board open.

The three-letter blockers beginning with M

MEH   MUX

Some four-letter blockers beginning with M

MADE	MENO	MONY
MAHA	MINX	MOOI
MANY	MIXY	MOPY
MARY	MOAI	MOSH
MATY	MOBY	MOWN
MAZY	MOMI	MWAH

Some five-letter blockers beginning with M
(except words ending in '-ED', '-J', '-S', '-X', '-Y' or '-Z')

MACHI	MERCH	MUCHO
MANET	MICRA	MULCH
MARCH	MIKRA	MULSH
MARIA	MITCH	MUSHA
MAYAN	MIXTE	MUTER
MEANT	MOLTO	
MENSH	MOOSE	

Some six-letter blockers beginning with M
(except words ending in '-ED', '-J', '-S', '-X', '-Y' or '-Z')

MACING	MEEKER	MODISH
MAGYAR	MEIKLE	MODULI
MAINER	MEREST	MOIRAI
MALIBU	METING	MOOING
MALOTI	MEWING	MOPIER
MANFUL	MILDER	MOPING
MANTIC	MILKEN	MORBID
MATIER	MIMING	MORISH
MAWGER	MINIER	MORYAH
MAXING	MIRING	MURKER
MAYEST	MISDID	MUTEST
MAYHAP	MISLIT	MUTING
MAZIER	MITRAL	MYSELF
MEAGER	MIXIER	MYTHIC

M

> **Handy Hint: M is for mnemonic**
>
> You may find it useful to use memory aids when
> trying to remember long lists of Scrabble words.
> Some more experienced players prefer to remember
> words in their entirety, but for beginners a mnemonic
> or two can be a great help. Eg, the initial letters of the
> words in the mnemonic: Please Don't Holler So, Be
> Nice For Once gives the front hooks for the two-letter
> word OH. You'll have fun making up your own
> mnemonics to suit your needs.

BONUS WORDS

Bonus words on your rack can be hard to spot, especially for the less experienced player. One way to help find them is by using prefixes and suffixes.

Many larger words include a common prefix or suffix – remembering these and using them where you can is a good way to discover any longer words on your rack, including any potential bonus words. The key prefixes to remember beginning with M are MAN- and MIS- and the key suffixes are -MAN and -MEN.

Some words beginning with MAN-

Seven-letter words

MAN-BAGS	MAN-HUNT	MAN-LIKE
MAN-BAND	MAN-JACK	MAN-MADE
MAN-GOLD	MAN-KIND	MAN-TRAP
MAN-HOLE	MAN-KINI	MAN-WARD
MAN-HOOD	MAN-LIER	

Eight-letter words

MAN-FULLY	MAN-POWER	MAN-SHIFT
MAN-GROVE	MAN-SCAPE	MAN-SWORN

Some words beginning with MIS-

Seven-letter words

MIS-ALLY	MIS-DIAL	MIS-HAPS
MIS-CALL	MIS-DOER	MIS-HEAR
MIS-CAST	MIS-FILE	MIS-LAID
MIS-CODE	MIS-FIRE	MIS-LEAD
MIS-CUED	MIS-FITS	MIS-MARK
MIS-DEED	MIS-GIVE	MIS-NAME

MIS-READ	MIS-SOLD	MIS-TIME
MIS-RULE	MIS-STEP	MIS-TOOK
MIS-SELL	MIS-TAKE	MIS-USED

Eight-letter words

MIS-ALIGN	MIS-GUIDE	MIS-SPELL
MIS-APPLY	MIS-HEARD	MIS-SPEND
MIS-BEGOT	MIS-JUDGE	MIS-SPOKE
MIS-CARRY	MIS-MATCH	MIS-TAKEN
MIS-CHIEF	MIS-PLACE	MIS-TIMED
MIS-CHOSE	MIS-PRICE	MIS-TREAT
MIS-COLOR	MIS-PRINT	MIS-TRIAL
MIS-COUNT	MIS-QUOTE	MIS-TRUST
MIS-FILED	MIS-RULED	MIS-TRUTH
MIS-FIRED	MIS-SHAPE	MIS-USAGE
MIS-GIVEN	MIS-SPEAK	MIS-USING

M

Some words ending with -MAN (all have -MEN plurals)
Seven-letter words

AUTO-MAN	FOOT-MAN	PLOW-MAN
BIRD-MAN	FORE-MAN	POST-MAN
BOAT-MAN	FREE-MAN	RAIL-MAN
BOND-MAN	FROG-MAN	REPO-MAN
BOOK-MAN	HANG-MAN	SAND-MAN
BUSH-MAN	HARD-MAN	SHIP-MAN
CAVE-MAN	HEAD-MAN	SHOW-MAN
COAL-MAN	JAZZ-MAN	SNOW-MAN
CREW-MAN	JURY-MAN	SWAG-MAN
DEAD-MAN	LENS-MAN	WING-MAN
DOOR-MAN	LINE-MAN	WORK-MAN
DUST-MAN	MAIL-MAN	
FIRE-MAN	MILK-MAN	

Eight-letter words

BARGE-MAN	FRESH-MAN	SHORE-MAN
BOGEY-MAN	FRONT-MAN	SOUND-MAN
BRINK-MAN	HANDY-MAN	SPACE-MAN
CHAIR-MAN	HENCH-MAN	STUNT-MAN
CLASS-MAN	HORSE-MAN	SUPER-MAN
COACH-MAN	KNIFE-MAN	SWORD-MAN
DOORS-MAN	NOBLE-MAN	TRASH-MAN
EARTH-MAN	POINT-MAN	WATCH-MAN
EVERY-MAN	RANCH-MAN	WHEEL-MAN
FERRY-MAN	RIFLE-MAN	
FREED-MAN	ROADS-MAN	

Some words ending in S and -MAN (all have -MEN plurals)

Seven-letter words

ARTS-MAN	MAGS-MAN	ODDS-MAN
BATS-MAN	MESS-MAN	PASS-MAN
DAYS-MAN	MOBS-MAN	RODS-MAN
KINS-MAN	NEWS-MAN	TAPS-MAN
LENS-MAN	OARS-MAN	TOPS-MAN

Eight-letter words

BAILS-MAN	DOOMS-MAN	HUNTS-MAN
BANDS-MAN	DOORS-MAN	ISLES-MAN
BANKS-MAN	GAMES-MAN	LANDS-MAN
BLUES-MAN	GANGS-MAN	LINES-MAN
BOATS-MAN	GILDS-MAN	LINKS-MAN
BONDS-MAN	GLASS-MAN	LOCKS-MAN
CHESS-MAN	GOWNS-MAN	MARKS-MAN
CLANS-MAN	HEADS-MAN	PRESS-MAN
CLASS-MAN	HELMS-MAN	PUNTS-MAN
CORPS-MAN	HERDS-MAN	RAFTS-MAN

RAMPS-MAN	SIDES-MAN	TIDES-MAN
ROADS-MAN	SWAGS-MAN	TOWNS-MAN
SALES-MAN	TALIS-MAN	WOODS-MAN

UNUSUAL WORDS FROM OVERSEAS ENGLISH

If you have an awkward combination of letters on your rack then words from overseas English may come in handy. Here are some beginning with M.

Australian words

MALLEE	low shrubby eucalyptus tree
MARRI	type of eucalyptus
MIDDY	middle-sized glass of beer
MOLOCH	spiny lizard
MOPOKE	small spotted owl
MUGGA	eucalyptus tree with pink flowers
MULGA	acacia shrub
MULLOCK	waste material from a mine
MUSO	musician
MYALL	acacia with hard scented wood
MYXO	myxomatosis

M

Canadian words

MECHOUI	a meal of spit-roasted meat
MUCKAMUCK	food
MUKTUK	beluga skin used as food

Hindi words

MACHAN	platform used in tiger hunting
MAHOUT	elephant driver
MAHSEER	large freshwater fish
MANDI	big market

MANDIR	Hindu or Jain temple
MAUND	unit of weight
MELA	cultural or religious festival
MOHUR	old gold coin
MONAL	Asian pheasant
MORCHA	hostile demonstration
MRIDANG	drum used in Indian music
MYNAH	tropical starling

New Zealand words

MANUKA	myrtaceous tree
MATAI	evergreen tree
MIHI	ceremonial greeting
MOKI	edible sea fish
MOKO	Maori tattoo or tattoo pattern
MOOLOO	person from Waikato
MOPOKE	small spotted owl
MUNGA	army canteen

South African words

MEERKAT	sociable mongoose
MENEER	Mr or Sir
MEVROU	Mrs or Madam
MOOI	pleasing
MUTI	herbal medicine

Urdu words

MAIDAN	open space used for meetings and sports
MASALA	mixed spices ground into a paste
MOOLVI	Muslim doctor of the law

M

Essential info
Value: 1 point
Number in set: 6

There are six **N** tiles in the Scrabble set, making it one of the most common consonants alongside R and T. N is very useful for short words to facilitate parallel plays as it begins a two-letter word with every vowel except I. While three-letter words beginning with N are common, there are fewer high-scoring ones than you might think. These include NAB (5 points) and NAY, NEW and NOW (all 6 points). N is one of the letters of the RETAIN set and is therefore a good letter to keep if trying to get a bonus word.

Two-letter words beginning with N

NA	NO	NY
NE	NU	

Some three-letter words beginning with N

NAE	NEK	NOR
NAH	NEP	NOT
NAM	NID	NOX
NAT	NIS	NOY
NAV	NIT	NUB
NAW	NIX	NUG
NAY	NOB	NUR
NEB	NOG	NYE
NED	NOH	NYM
NEE	NOM	NYS
NEF	NON	
NEG	NOO	

HOOKS

Hooking requires a subtle change in a player's thought process, in that they must look at words already on the board without becoming distracted by their pronunciation.

Some front-hooks
Two letters to three

N-AB	N-AN	N-ED
N-AE	N-AS	N-EE
N-AG	N-AT	N-EF
N-AH	N-AW	N-ET
N-AM	N-AY	N-ID

N-IS
N-IT
N-OB
N-OD
N-OH
N-OM
N-ON

N-OO
N-OR
N-OS
N-OW
N-OX
N-OY
N-UG

N-UN
N-UR
N-US
N-UT
N-YE

Three letters to four

N-AFF
N-AGA
N-AIL
N-ANA
N-ANE
N-APE
N-ARC
N-ARE
N-ARK
N-ARY
N-AVE
N-EAR
N-EAT

N-EON
N-ERK
N-ESS
N-EST
N-EUK
N-EWT
N-ICE
N-ICK
N-ILL
N-ISH
N-ITS
N-ODE
N-ONE

N-OON
N-OPE
N-OSE
N-OUS
N-OUT
N-OVA
N-OWL
N-OWN
N-OWT
N-UKE
N-YAH

Four letters to five

N-ACHE
N-AILS
N-AKED
N-APED
N-ARCO
N-AUNT
N-AVAL
N-AVEL
N-EATH
N-EDDY

N-EMPT
N-EVER
N-EWER
N-ICER
N-ICKY
N-IFFY
N-ODAL
N-OILY
N-OINT
N-OMEN

N-ONCE
N-ONES
N-OOSE
N-OPAL
N-OULD
N-OUPS
N-OVEL
N-OVUM
N-OWED

Five letters to six

N-ABBED
N-AGGER
N-AILED
N-APERY
N-APING
N-APRON
N-ARKED
N-ARROW
N-AUGHT
N-EARED
N-EARLY
N-EATEN

N-EATER
N-EBBED
N-ESSES
N-ESTER
N-ETHER
N-ETTLE
N-EWEST
N-ICHED
N-ICKER
N-ICKLE
N-IMBED
N-ITHER

N-ODDER
N-OGGIN
N-OSIER
N-OTARY
N-OTHER
N-OUGHT
N-OVATE
N-UMBER
N-UMPTY
N-UNCLE
N-UTTER

Six letters to seven

N-AILING
N-APHTHA
N-ARKING
N-ASCENT
N-ATRIUM
N-EARING
N-EBBING
N-EDDISH
N-EITHER

N-EMESES
N-EMESIS
N-EOLITH
N-ETTLED
N-ICHING
N-IFFIER
N-OINTED
N-ONUSES
N-OOLOGY

N-OVATED
N-OYESES
N-ULLING
N-UNDINE
N-UNHOOD
N-UNLIKE
N-UNSHIP

Seven letters to eight

N-AINSELL
N-APERIES
N-ARRASES
N-ARROWED
N-ATRIUMS

N-EARLIER
N-ETTLING
N-IFFIEST
N-OINTING
N-OTARIES

N-OVATING
N-OVATION
N-ULLINGS
N-UMBERED
N-YAFFING

Some end-hooks
Two letters to three

AI-N	GU-N	OW-N
AN-N	HA-N	PA-N
AW-N	HE-N	PE-N
BA-N	HI-N	PI-N
BE-N	HO-N	QI-N
BI-N	IN-N	RE-N
BO-N	IO-N	SI-N
DA-N	KI-N	SO-N
DE-N	KO-N	TA-N
DI-N	LI-N	TE-N
DO-N	MA-N	TI-N
EA-N	ME-N	TO-N
EE-N	MO-N	UR-N
ER-N	MU-N	WE-N
FA-N	NA-N	WO-N
FE-N	NO-N	YE-N
GI-N	NU-N	YO-N
GO-N	OO-N	

Three letters to four

BAR-N	EAR-N	LOO-N
BEE-N	EVE-N	MOA-N
BOO-N	FAW-N	MOO-N
BOR-N	FER-N	MOR-N
BRA-N	GOO-N	MOW-N
BUR-N	GUR-N	NOO-N
CHI-N	HEW-N	OPE-N
COR-N	HOO-N	PAW-N
DAW-N	JIN-N	RAI-N
DEE-N	LAW-N	SAW-N
DOO-N	LEA-N	SEE-N
DOW-N	LIE-N	SEW-N

SHE-N	TEE-N	TOW-N
SKI-N	THE-N	UPO-N
SOW-N	TOO-N	YAR-N
SPA-N	TOR-N	YAW-N

> **Handy Hint: No more arguments**
>
> Use a dictionary when playing Scrabble to check the validity of words when a play is challenged (and to avoid any arguments!). We recommend Collins Official Scrabble Dictionary, where you will find the meanings for all the words listed in this book.

Four letters to five

BASE-N	GROW-N	SARI-N
BLOW-N	HALO-N	SATI-N
BRAW-N	HERO-N	SHAW-N
BROW-N	HOSE-N	SHOW-N
CHAI-N	HUMA-N	SIRE-N
CLOW-N	KNOW-N	SPAW-N
COVE-N	LADE-N	SPUR-N
CROW-N	LEAR-N	STOW-N
DEMO-N	LIKE-N	TAKE-N
DJIN-N	LINE-N	TOKE-N
DOVE-N	LOGO-N	TWEE-N
DOZE-N	MAYA-N	VEGA-N
DRAW-N	PARE-N	WAKE-N
FLOW-N	RAVE-N	WIDE-N
FROW-N	RIPE-N	WOKE-N
GIVE-N	RISE-N	WOVE-N
GNAW-N	RIVE-N	YEAR-N
GREE-N	ROMA-N	

N

Five letters to six

ALTER-N	GLUTE-N	RESEW-N
ARISE-N	GRAVE-N	RESOW-N
ASTER-N	HASTE-N	ROTTE-N
AWAKE-N	HEAVE-N	SCREE-N
AWOKE-N	HOOVE-N	SHAKE-N
BABOO-N	INTER-N	SHAMA-N
BARRE-N	LARGE-N	SHAPE-N
BITTE-N	LEAVE-N	SHAVE-N
BRAZE-N	LOOSE-N	SPOKE-N
BROKE-N	MACRO-N	STOLE-N
CARBO-N	MEDIA-N	STONE-N
CARVE-N	MICRO-N	STRAW-N
CAVER-N	MODER-N	STREW-N
CHOSE-N	NORMA-N	STROW-N
CLOVE-N	PANDA-N	SYLVA-N
COMMO-N	PHOTO-N	THRAW-N
CRAVE-N	PROVE-N	THROW-N
DRIVE-N	RATIO-N	WHITE-N
FROZE-N	RESEE-N	WICCA-N

N

Six letters to seven

ACKNOW-N	MEDUSA-N	REGIME-N
ALKALI-N	NUCLEI-N	REGIVE-N
BRONZE-N	OUTSEE-N	REGROW-N
CAPITA-N	PAPAYA-N	RERISE-N
CHASTE-N	PASTER-N	RESHOW-N
COARSE-N	PATTER-N	RETAKE-N
EASTER-N	POSTER-N	REWAKE-N
EMBRYO-N	PREWAR-N	REWOVE-N
ENVIRO-N	PROTEA-N	RIPSAW-N
GELATI-N	PROTEI-N	SIERRA-N
HOARSE-N	REDRAW-N	SMIDGE-N
JIGSAW-N	REFLOW-N	STONER-N

STRIVE-N	UNDRAW-N	URANIA-N
STROKE-N	UNWOVE-N	UTOPIA-N
TERTIA-N	UPGROW-N	WESTER-N
THRIVE-N	UPRISE-N	WRITHE-N
TRUDGE-N	UPTAKE-N	ZITHER-N

Seven letters to eight

AQUARIA-N	FORGIVE-N	OVERSEE-N
ARCADIA-N	FORSAKE-N	PANACEA-N
AURELIA-N	HACKSAW-N	PARAZOA-N
BEREAVE-N	LEATHER-N	PARTAKE-N
BESPOKE-N	MAGNETO-N	PRESHOW-N
BESTREW-N	MALARIA-N	QUARTER-N
BOHEMIA-N	MISDRAW-N	REAWAKE-N
CODRIVE-N	MISGIVE-N	REFROZE-N
COLLAGE-N	MISGROW-N	REGALIA-N
DEFROZE-N	MISKNOW-N	RESHAVE-N
DILUVIA-N	MISTAKE-N	ROSARIA-N
DISLIKE-N	NORTHER-N	RUBELLA-N
ELECTRO-N	OUTDRAW-N	SLATTER-N
ENGRAVE-N	OUTFLOW-N	SOUTHER-N
ENLARGE-N	OUTGIVE-N	UNBROKE-N
FLYBLOW-N	OUTGROW-N	UNFROZE-N
FORESEE-N	OUTTAKE-N	UNSPOKE-N

N

BLOCKERS

It is useful to know which words are blockers and can't therefore be extended before or after. You may want to play a blocker that your opponent can't extend, or you may want to avoid playing a blocker because you want to keep the board open.

The three-letter blockers beginning with N

NAH	NOX	NYM
NOH	NTH	NYS

Some four-letter blockers beginning with N

NANG	NIXY	NOTT
NAVY	NOPE	NOUS
NESS	NOSH	NYAH
NIDI	NOSY	

Some five-letter blockers beginning with N
(except words ending in '-ED', '-J', '-S', '-X', '-Y' or '-Z')

NATAL	NEWER	NUDZH
NAVAL	NICER	NUMEN
NEMPT	NOHOW	
NEVER	NOTUM	

Some six-letter blockers beginning with N
(except words ending in '-ED', '-J', '-S', '-X', '-Y' or '-Z')

NAFFER	NEWEST	NONPAR
NAIFER	NEWISH	NORDIC
NAIVER	NICEST	NOSIER
NAPING	NICISH	NOSTRO
NARINE	NIENTE	NOTING
NEARER	NIGHER	NOTOUR
NEATER	NITRIC	NOUNAL
NEBISH	NIXING	NOWISE
NEFAST	NOBBUT	NUKING
NERVAL	NOBLER	NUTANT
NETHER	NOGAKU	
NEURAL	NONFAT	

BONUS WORDS

Bonus words on your rack can be hard to spot, especially for the less experienced player. One way to help find them is by using prefixes and suffixes.

Many larger words include a common prefix or suffix – remembering these and using them where you can is a good way to discover any longer words on your rack, including any potential bonus words. The key suffix to remember beginning with N is -NESS.

Some words ending with -NESS

Seven-letter words

APT-NESS	HIP-NESS	ONE-NESS
BAD-NESS	HOT-NESS	RAW-NESS
BIG-NESS	ICI-NESS	RED-NESS
COY-NESS	ILL-NESS	SAD-NESS
DIM-NESS	LOW-NESS	SHY-NESS
DRY-NESS	MAD-NESS	WET-NESS
FAT-NESS	NEW-NESS	WIT-NESS
FIT-NESS	ODD-NESS	WRY-NESS
FUL-NESS	OLD-NESS	

Eight-letter words

AGED-NESS	CURT-NESS	FOND-NESS
ARCH-NESS	DAMP-NESS	GLAD-NESS
BALD-NESS	DARK-NESS	GOOD-NESS
BARE-NESS	DEAF-NESS	GOOI-NESS
BOLD-NESS	DEFT-NESS	GREY-NESS
BUSI-NESS	DUDE-NESS	HARD-NESS
CALM-NESS	EVIL-NESS	HIGH-NESS
COLD-NESS	FAIR-NESS	HUGE-NESS
COSI-NESS	FIRM-NESS	IDLE-NESS

KIND-NESS	OPEN-NESS	TALL-NESS
LADY-NESS	PALE-NESS	TAME-NESS
LATE-NESS	POSH-NESS	TAUT-NESS
LIKE-NESS	PURE-NESS	VAST-NESS
MEAN-NESS	RARE-NESS	WARM-NESS
MILD-NESS	RIPE-NESS	WEAK-NESS
MUCH-NESS	SAME-NESS	WELL-NESS
NEAT-NESS	SICK-NESS	WILD-NESS
NUMB-NESS	SLOW-NESS	
OAKI-NESS	SURE-NESS	

UNUSUAL WORDS FROM OVERSEAS ENGLISH

If you have an awkward combination of letters on your rack then words from overseas English may come in handy. Here are some beginning with N.

N

Australian words

NARDOO	cloverlike fern
NEDDY	horse
NOAH	shark
NONG	stupid or incompetent person
NUMBAT	small marsupial with long snout

Canadian word

NANOOK	polar bear

Hindi words

NAUCH	intricate Indian dance
NAWAB	Muslim prince in India
NEEM	large tree
NILGAI	large Indian antelope
NULLAH	stream or drain
NUMDAH	coarse felt

New Zealand words

NGAIO	small tree
NGATI	tribe or clan
NIKAU	palm tree

South African words

NAARTJIE	tangerine
NKOSI	master or chief

N

Essential info
Value: 1 point
Number in set: 8

O is a common letter in Scrabble, with eight tiles in the set. It forms a two-letter word with every other vowel except for A, and is useful when it comes to forming short words in order to score in two directions at once using premium squares, or in tight corners, or for parallel plays, for example OB, OM and OP (4 points each) and OF, OH, OW (5 points each). O also combines well with X to form short words such as OXO (10 points) and OXY (13 points) as well as numerous words ending in -OX.

Two-letter words beginning with O

OB	OM	OU
OD	ON	OW
OE	OO	OX
OF	OP	OY
OH	OR	
OI	OS	

Some three-letter words beginning with O

OBA	ONY	ORF
OBE	OOF	ORG
OBI	OOH	ORT
OBO	OOM	OSE
OCH	OON	OUD
ODA	OOP	OUK
OFF	OOR	OUP
OFT	OOT	OUS
OHM	OPA	OWT
OHO	OPE	OXO
OIK	ORA	OXY
OKA	ORB	OYE
OMA	ORC	
ONO	ORD	

O

HOOKS

Hooking requires a subtle change in a player's thought process, in that they must look at words already on the board without becoming distracted by their pronunciation.

Some front-hooks
Two letters to three

O-AR	O-IS	O-OS
O-AT	O-KA	O-PA
O-BA	O-MA	O-PE
O-BE	O-NE	O-RE
O-BI	O-NO	O-UP
O-BO	O-NY	O-UR
O-CH	O-OF	O-US
O-DA	O-OH	O-UT
O-DE	O-OM	O-WE
O-ES	O-ON	O-YE
O-HM	O-OP	
O-HO	O-OR	

Three letters to four

O-ARY	O-GEE	O-PEN
O-BEY	O-INK	O-PUS
O-BIT	O-KAY	O-RAD
O-CHE	O-LEA	O-RES
O-DAH	O-LES	O-SAR
O-DAL	O-LID	O-TIC
O-DOR	O-MEN	O-URN
O-DSO	O-OSE	O-VUM
O-FAY	O-PAL	O-WED
O-GAM	O-PED	O-YES

Four letters to five

O-AKED	O-CHER	O-GLED
O-ARED	O-DOUR	O-HING
O-AVES	O-FLAG	O-LIVE
O-BANG	O-GEED	O-LOGY
O-BOLE	O-GIVE	O-MEGA

O-OBIT
O-OHED
O-OPED
O-OSES
O-PINE
O-PING
O-PIUM
O-RACH
O-RACY
O-RANG
O-RANT
O-RATE
O-READ
O-RIEL
O-SCAR
O-UNCE
O-UNDY
O-VARY
O-VERT
O-VINE
O-VOID
O-WING
O-ZONE

Five letters to six

O-BITER
O-BLAST
O-BLATE
O-BOLUS
O-CELLI
O-EDEMA
O-GAMIC
O-GIVES
O-INKED
O-LINGO
O-LIVER
O-MENED
O-MENTA
O-OHING
O-OLOGY
O-OPING
O-OSIER
O-PALED
O-PENED
O-PINED
O-PUSES
O-RACHE
O-RALLY
O-RANGE
O-RANGY
O-RATED
O-STEAL
O-STENT
O-TITIS
O-UNCES
O-WRIER
O-YESES

Six letters to seven

O-CARINA
O-CELLAR
O-CREATE
O-DONATE
O-DORISE
O-DORIZE
O-ESTRAL
O-ESTRUM
O-INKING
O-KIMONO
O-LOGIES
O-MENING
O-MENTAL
O-MENTUM
O-MICRON
O-MIKRON
O-PACIFY
O-PENING
O-PINING
O-PINION
O-POSSUM
O-RANGER
O-RATING
O-RATION
O-ROTUND
O-STRICH
O-UGLIED
O-UGLIES
O-UTMOST
O-VARIES
O-VERBID
O-VERSET
O-WRIEST
O-YESSES
O-ZONATE

O

Seven letters to eight

O-DORISED	O-ESTRONE	O-RANGIER
O-DORIZED	O-ESTROUS	O-STOMATE
O-ECOLOGY	O-MISSION	O-UROLOGY
O-EDEMATA	O-MISSIVE	O-VARIOLE
O-ENOLOGY	O-OLOGIES	O-VARIOUS
O-ESTRIOL	O-OLOGIST	O-ZONATED

Some end-hooks
Two letters to three

AB-O	HA-O	PO-O
AD-O	HO-O	RE-O
AG-O	IS-O	SH-O
BI-O	LO-O	TA-O
BO-O	MO-O	TO-O
DO-O	NO-O	UP-O
EM-O	OB-O	WO-O
EX-O	OH-O	ZO-O
GI-O	ON-O	
GO-O	OX-O	

O

Three letters to four

ALS-O	CIT-O	FIG-O
ALT-O	DAD-O	FIL-O
ANN-O	DEF-O	FIN-O
BIT-O	DIN-O	HER-O
BOB-O	DIV-O	HOB-O
BOH-O	DOC-O	HYP-O
BOY-O	DOD-O	JUD-O
BUB-O	ECH-O	KAY-O
BUD-O	ERG-O	KIN-O
CAM-O	FAR-O	LID-O
CAP-O	FID-O	LIN-O

LIP-O	MON-O	SOH-O
LOB-O	MUS-O	SOL-O
LOG-O	NAN-O	SUM-O
LOT-O	PES-O	TAR-O
LUD-O	PIS-O	TOP-O
MAK-O	POL-O	TOR-O
MAN-O	RED-O	VEG-O
MAY-O	REG-O	VET-O
MEM-O	REP-O	VIN-O
MIC-O	ROT-O	WIN-O
MIL-O	SAD-O	
MIS-O	SAG-O	

Four letters to five

AMIN-O	CHIC-O	GECK-O
BANC-O	CHIN-O	GISM-O
BARD-O	CHOC-O	GUAN-O
BASH-O	COMB-O	GUST-O
BEAN-O	COMM-O	HALL-O
BENT-O	COMP-O	HELL-O
BERK-O	COND-O	HILL-O
BIFF-O	CORN-O	HOWS-O
BING-O	CRED-O	HULL-O
BOFF-O	CUFF-O	JELL-O
BOMB-O	DECK-O	JOCK-O
BONG-O	DING-O	KEEN-O
BUCK-O	DIPS-O	LASS-O
BUFF-O	DISC-O	LENT-O
BUNK-O	DITT-O	LIMB-O
BURR-O	DRAC-O	LING-O
CACA-O	DUMB-O	MACH-O
CAME-O	FANG-O	MANG-O
CARB-O	FATS-O	MENT-O
CELL-O	FUNG-O	METH-O
CHIA-O	GAMB-O	MEZZ-O

O

MILK-O	PINK-O	SANT-O
MIME-O	PINT-O	SICK-O
MOTT-O	PONG-O	SOCK-O
MUCH-O	POSH-O	STEN-O
NACH-O	POTT-O	TANG-O
NARC-O	PRIM-O	TEMP-O
NUTS-O	PROM-O	TORS-O
PANT-O	PROS-O	VERS-O
PEST-O	PULA-O	VIDE-O
PHON-O	PUNT-O	WACK-O
PHOT-O	RODE-O	WALD-O
PIAN-O	RUMP-O	WHAM-O

Five letters to six

AMMON-O	FRANC-O	REECH-O
BILLY-O	HALLO-O	RIGHT-O
BRILL-O	HOLLO-O	ROMAN-O
BRONC-O	HULLO-O	SHACK-O
CARDI-O	LIBER-O	SHEEP-O
CHARR-O	LIVED-O	SOLAN-O
CHEAP-O	MEDIC-O	SPEED-O
CHEER-O	MORPH-O	STERE-O
CHOCK-O	NYMPH-O	STINK-O
CHURR-O	PEDAL-O	THICK-O
CONCH-O	PLONK-O	TOLED-O
CRYPT-O	PREST-O	TRILL-O
DINER-O	PSEUD-O	VIGOR-O
DORAD-O	PSYCH-O	WEIRD-O
DUETT-O	QUART-O	WHACK-O
ERING-O	RABAT-O	WHATS-O
FASCI-O	RANCH-O	

Six letters to seven

BANDIT-O	BRACER-O	CANTIC-O
BATTER-O	BUDGER-O	CYMBAL-O

O

GRADIN-O	PIMENT-O	SERRAN-O
MAGNET-O	PRIMER-O	TAMARA-O
MOMENT-O	PUMMEL-O	TYMPAN-O
NITROS-O	RABBIT-O	VERISM-O
PAESAN-O	REVERS-O	WHERES-O
PAISAN-O	SCREAM-O	
PAMPER-O	SECOND-O	

Seven letters to eight

ARMIGER-O	FASCISM-O	PRELUDI-O
CAPITAN-O	FLAMING-O	RANCHER-O
CLASSIC-O	INTAGLI-O	SESTETT-O
COMMAND-O	LEGGIER-O	SOMBRER-O
CONCERT-O	MONTANT-O	STAMPED-O
CORNETT-O	PEEKABO-O	VIGOROS-O
COURANT-O	PERFECT-O	ZECCHIN-O
EXPRESS-O	POLITIC-O	

O

BLOCKERS

It is useful to know which words are blockers and can't therefore be extended before or after. You may want to play a blocker that your opponent can't extend, or you may want to avoid playing a blocker because you want to keep the board open.

Three-letter blocker beginning with O

OXO

The four-letter blockers beginning with O

OAKY	OLEA	ORYX
OCCY	ONST	OSAR
ODEA	ONYX	OYEZ

Some five-letter blockers beginning with O
(except words ending in '-ED', '-J', '-S', '-X', '-Y' or '-Z')

OATEN	ONCET	OUTGO
OHONE	ORGIC	OUTTA
OLEIC	OUTDO	

Some six-letter blockers beginning with O
(except words ending in '-ED', '-J', '-S', '-X', '-Y' or '-Z')

OAFISH	OGRISH	OSTIUM
OAKIER	OMIGOD	OTARID
OBESER	ONAGRI	OUTBYE
OBITER	ONRUSH	OUTDID
OBTECT	OPTING	OUTSAT
OCHONE	ORBIER	OUTSAW
OCTOPI	ORGANA	OUTWON
ODDEST	ORGIAC	OWLISH
ODDISH	OSTEAL	OXIDIC
OFFKEY	OSTIAL	OZONIC

O

BONUS WORDS

Bonus words on your rack can be hard to spot, especially for the less experienced player. One way to help find them is by using prefixes and suffixes.

Many larger words include a common prefix or suffix – remembering these and using them where you can is a good way to discover any longer words on your rack, including any potential bonus words. The key prefixes to remember beginning with O are OUT- and OVER- and the key suffixes are -OID, -OR, -OUS and -OUT.

Some words beginning with OUT-

Seven-letter words

OUT-ACTS
OUT-AGES
OUT-BACK
OUT-BIDS
OUT-CAST
OUT-COME
OUT-CROP
OUT-DOER
OUT-DONE
OUT-DOOR
OUT-DRAW
OUT-EARN
OUT-FALL
OUT-FISH
OUT-FITS
OUT-FLOW
OUT-FOOT
OUT-GAVE
OUT-GOER

OUT-GROW
OUT-GUNS
OUT-GUSH
OUT-KEEP
OUT-LAID
OUT-LAND
OUT-LAST
OUT-LAWS
OUT-LAYS
OUT-LETS
OUT-LIES
OUT-LIVE
OUT-LOOK
OUT-MODE
OUT-PACE
OUT-PLAY
OUT-POST
OUT-PUTS
OUT-RAGE

OUT-RANK
OUT-RIDE
OUT-RUNS
OUT-SELL
OUT-SIDE
OUT-SING
OUT-SIZE
OUT-SOLD
OUT-SPAN
OUT-STAY
OUT-TAKE
OUT-TALK
OUT-VOTE
OUT-WAIT
OUT-WARD
OUT-WITH
OUT-WITS

Eight-letter words

OUT-ACTED
OUT-ARGUE
OUT-BOARD
OUT-BOUND
OUT-BREAK
OUT-CHARM
OUT-CLASS
OUT-CRIES
OUT-DANCE
OUT-DATED
OUT-DOING

OUT-DRINK
OUT-FACED
OUT-FENCE
OUT-FIELD
OUT-FLANK
OUT-FLING
OUT-FLUNG
OUT-FOXED
OUT-GOING
OUT-GROWN
OUT-LAWED

OUT-LINED
OUT-MATCH
OUT-PACED
OUT-PRICE
OUT-PSYCH
OUT-RAGED
OUT-REACH
OUT-RIDER
OUT-SCORE
OUT-SIDER
OUT-SIZED

O

OUT-SPEAK	OUT-STARE	OUT-VOICE
OUT-SPOKE	OUT-SWEPT	OUT-WEIGH
OUT-STAND	OUT-THINK	

Some words beginning with OVER-

Seven-letter words

OVER-ACT	OVER-DUB	OVER-LAY
OVER-AGE	OVER-DUE	OVER-PAY
OVER-ALL	OVER-EAT	OVER-RAN
OVER-ATE	OVER-EGG	OVER-SAW
OVER-AWE	OVER-FED	OVER-SEE
OVER-CUT	OVER-JOY	OVER-TAX
OVER-DID	OVER-LAP	OVER-USE

Eight-letter words

OVER-ARCH	OVER-GOES	OVER-PAGE
OVER-AWED	OVER-GROW	OVER-PAID
OVER-BANK	OVER-HAND	OVER-PLAY
OVER-BEAR	OVER-HANG	OVER-RATE
OVER-BITE	OVER-HAUL	OVER-RODE
OVER-BRED	OVER-HEAR	OVER-RULE
OVER-BUSY	OVER-HEAT	OVER-SEEN
OVER-CAME	OVER-HYPE	OVER-SELL
OVER-CAST	OVER-IDLE	OVER-SHOT
OVER-CLUB	OVER-KEEN	OVER-SIZE
OVER-COAT	OVER-KILL	OVER-STAY
OVER-COME	OVER-LAID	OVER-STEP
OVER-COOK	OVER-LAND	OVER-TAKE
OVER-DOES	OVER-LEAF	OVER-TIME
OVER-DONE	OVER-LOAD	OVER-TONE
OVER-DOSE	OVER-LONG	OVER-TOOK
OVER-EASY	OVER-LOOK	OVER-TURN
OVER-FEED	OVER-LORD	OVER-WORK
OVER-FILL	OVER-PACK	OVER-WRAP

O

Some words ending with -OID

Seven-letter words

ADEN-OID	FACT-OID	SAUR-OID
ANDR-OID	FUNG-OID	SPOR-OID
COSM-OID	GLOB-OID	STER-OID
CYST-OID	HYDR-OID	TABL-OID
DELT-OID	NEUR-OID	THYR-OID
DISC-OID	PLUT-OID	TYPH-OID

Eight-letter words

ALKAL-OID	MANAT-OID	RETIN-OID
AMOEB-OID	MEDUS-OID	RHOMB-OID
BLAST-OID	MELAN-OID	SCHIZ-OID
CAMEL-OID	NEMAT-OID	SLEAZ-OID
CENTR-OID	NUCLE-OID	SPHER-OID
DENDR-OID	OCTOP-OID	TECHN-OID
GROUP-OID	PARAN-OID	TETAN-OID
HEMAT-OID	PLASM-OID	TREND-OID
HUMAN-OID	POLYP-OID	VARIC-OID
LEMUR-OID	PSYCH-OID	VIRUS-OID
LYMPH-OID	RESIN-OID	

Some words ending with -OLOGY

Seven-letter words

AP-OLOGY	GE-OLOGY	UR-OLOGY
BI-OLOGY	NE-OLOGY	ZO-OLOGY
EC-OLOGY	UF-OLOGY	

Eight-letter words

AER-OLOGY	IDE-OLOGY	PYR-OLOGY
AUT-OLOGY	ONC-OLOGY	SIN-OLOGY
HOM-OLOGY	ONT-OLOGY	THE-OLOGY

TOP-OLOGY   VEN-OLOGY
TYP-OLOGY   VIR-OLOGY

Some words ending with -OR
Seven-letter words

ADAPT-OR   ENACT-OR   REACT-OR
ADVIS-OR   EQUAT-OR   ROTAT-OR
AUDIT-OR   EXCIT-OR   SENAT-OR
AVIAT-OR   GRANT-OR   SETTL-OR
CREAT-OR   IGNIT-OR   SPONS-OR
CURAT-OR   JANIT-OR   SQUAL-OR
DEBIT-OR   MUTAT-OR   TRACT-OR
DILUT-OR   NEGAT-OR   TRAIT-OR
EJECT-OR   NOTAT-OR   TRUST-OR
ELECT-OR   OFFER-OR   VISIT-OR
EMPER-OR   QUEST-OR

Eight-letter words

ABDUCT-OR   DETECT-OR   OBSESS-OR
ACCENT-OR   DICTAT-OR   PREDAT-OR
ACCEPT-OR   DIRECT-OR   PROVID-OR
ADJUST-OR   EFFECT-OR   PURVEY-OR
AGITAT-OR   ELEVAT-OR   RADIAT-OR
ANIMAT-OR   EXECUT-OR   REDUCT-OR
ASSESS-OR   GOVERN-OR   REJECT-OR
ASSIGN-OR   IMITAT-OR   RESIST-OR
BISECT-OR   IMPOST-OR   SCULPT-OR
CAVEAT-OR   INFECT-OR   SECRET-OR
CODEBT-OR   INJECT-OR   SELECT-OR
CONVEN-OR   INVENT-OR   STRESS-OR
CONVEY-OR   INVEST-OR   SURVEY-OR
CREDIT-OR   ISOLAT-OR   TESTAT-OR
DEFECT-OR   NARRAT-OR   TREMBL-OR
DEPICT-OR   OBJECT-OR   VIOLAT-OR

O

Some words ending with -OUS

Seven-letter words

AMOR-OUS	GIBB-OUS	POMP-OUS
ARDU-OUS	GLOB-OUS	RAUC-OUS
BILI-OUS	HEIN-OUS	RIOT-OUS
BULB-OUS	HIDE-OUS	RUIN-OUS
CALL-OUS	IGNE-OUS	TEDI-OUS
CURI-OUS	JEAL-OUS	TENU-OUS
DEVI-OUS	NITR-OUS	TIME-OUS
DUBI-OUS	NOXI-OUS	VACU-OUS
ENVI-OUS	OBVI-OUS	VARI-OUS
FATU-OUS	ODOR-OUS	VICI-OUS
FERR-OUS	OMIN-OUS	VITI-OUS
FIBR-OUS	ONER-OUS	ZEAL-OUS
FURI-OUS	PITE-OUS	

O

> **Handy Hint: Tile tracking**
>
> This means being aware of what tiles have already
> been played and therefore what might remain in
> the bag or on your opponent's rack. Tile tracking can
> be useful to manage your expectations of what
> common vowels or consonants you are likely to pick
> from the bag, and whether there are any goodies
> (blanks Ss JQXZ) left. At the end of a game it could
> even enable you to know what your opponent is
> holding. This practice is more common at club and
> tournament level.

Eight-letter words

ARSON-OUS	COVET-OUS	DEXTR-OUS
BIBUL-OUS	DECOR-OUS	ENORM-OUS
CHROM-OUS	DESIR-OUS	FABUL-OUS

FACTI-OUS	MUTIN-OUS	STUDI-OUS
FEVER-OUS	NITRE-OUS	TIMOR-OUS
GENER-OUS	NUMER-OUS	TORTU-OUS
GORGE-OUS	ORDUR-OUS	ULCER-OUS
GRACI-OUS	PERIL-OUS	UNCTU-OUS
GRIEV-OUS	POPUL-OUS	VAPOR-OUS
LIBEL-OUS	PRECI-OUS	VENOM-OUS
LUMIN-OUS	PREVI-OUS	VIGOR-OUS
LUSCI-OUS	RIGOR-OUS	VIRTU-OUS
LUSTR-OUS	SENSU-OUS	WONDR-OUS
LYMPH-OUS	SQUAM-OUS	

Some words ending with -OUT

Seven-letter words

BACK-OUT	HAND-OUT	SELL-OUT
BAIL-OUT	HANG-OUT	SHUT-OUT
BLOW-OUT	HAUL-OUT	SPIN-OUT
BURN-OUT	HIDE-OUT	TAKE-OUT
CALL-OUT	KICK-OUT	TIME-OUT
CAMP-OUT	LOCK-OUT	TURN-OUT
CONK-OUT	LOOK-OUT	WALK-OUT
COOK-OUT	MISS-OUT	WASH-OUT
DROP-OUT	PASS-OUT	WITH-OUT
FADE-OUT	PULL-OUT	WORK-OUT
FALL-OUT	READ-OUT	
FOLD-OUT	ROLL-OUT	

Eight-letter words

BLACK-OUT	CLEAR-OUT	PRINT-OUT
BREAK-OUT	FLAME-OUT	PUNCH-OUT
BUILD-OUT	FORCE-OUT	ROUGH-OUT
CARRY-OUT	FREAK-OUT	SHAKE-OUT
CHECK-OUT	KNOCK-OUT	SHOOT-OUT
CLEAN-OUT	PHASE-OUT	SHOUT-OUT

O

SLEEP-OUT	STAND-OUT	WATCH-OUT
SPEAK-OUT	STICK-OUT	WHITE-OUT
STAKE-OUT	THERE-OUT	

UNUSUAL WORDS FROM OVERSEAS ENGLISH

If you have an awkward combination of letters on your rack then words from overseas English may come in handy. Here are some beginning with O.

Australian word

OCKER   uncultivated or boorish Australian

Hindi word

OONT   camel

South African words

OMA   a grandmother
OOM   title of respect
OPA   a grandfather

O

Essential info
Value: 3 points
Number in set: 2

There are two-letter words beginning with **P** for each vowel except U which, combined with OP and UP, make it very flexible for short words such as PE (the 17th letter in the Hebrew alphabet, 4 points) and PO (an informal word for chamber pot, also 4 points). P also combines well with X, forming three-letter words PAX, PIX and POX (12 points each) and also Z, for example the three-letter POZ (an old-fashioned short form of positive, 14 points), as well as ZEP and ZIP.

Two-letter words beginning with P

PA	PI
PE	PO

Some three-letter words beginning with P

PAC	PHI	POZ
PAH	PHO	PRE
PAK	PHT	PSI
PAM	PIA	PST
PAP	PIC	PUG
PAR	PIR	PUH
PAV	PIU	PUR
PAX	PIX	PUS
PEC	POA	PUY
PED	POH	PWN
PEH	POI	PYA
PEL	POL	PYE
PEP	POM	PYX
PER	POW	
PEW	POX	

HOOKS

Hooking requires a subtle change in a player's thought process, in that they must look at words already on the board without becoming distracted by their pronunciation.

Some front-hooks
Two letters to three

P-AD	P-AL	P-AN
P-AH	P-AM	P-AR

P-AS	P-HI	P-RE
P-AT	P-HO	P-SI
P-AW	P-IN	P-ST
P-AX	P-IS	P-UG
P-AY	P-IT	P-UH
P-EA	P-OD	P-UN
P-ED	P-OH	P-UP
P-EE	P-OI	P-UR
P-EH	P-OM	P-US
P-EL	P-OO	P-UT
P-EN	P-OP	P-YA
P-ER	P-OS	P-YE
P-ES	P-OW	
P-ET	P-OX	

Three letters to four

P-ACE	P-ASS	P-ICK
P-ACT	P-ATE	P-ILL
P-AGE	P-AVE	P-IMP
P-AID	P-AWN	P-INK
P-AIL	P-EAR	P-ION
P-AIN	P-EAT	P-ITA
P-AIR	P-EEK	P-LAT
P-AIS	P-EEL	P-LAY
P-ALE	P-EEN	P-LEA
P-ALL	P-ELT	P-LED
P-ALP	P-END	P-LEX
P-AND	P-EON	P-LIE
P-ANE	P-ERE	P-LOD
P-ANT	P-ERK	P-LOP
P-ARE	P-EST	P-LOT
P-ARK	P-HAT	P-LOW
P-ART	P-HEW	P-LOY
P-ASH	P-HUT	P-LUG

P-LUM	P-OSE	P-RIG
P-OKE	P-OUR	P-RIM
P-OLE	P-OUT	P-ROB
P-ONE	P-OXY	P-ROD
P-ONY	P-RAM	P-ROM
P-OOR	P-RAT	P-ROW
P-OPE	P-RAY	P-UKE
P-ORE	P-REP	P-UMP
P-ORT	P-REZ	P-URE

Four letters to five

P-ACED	P-INTO	P-RANG
P-ACER	P-ITCH	P-RANK
P-AEON	P-LACE	P-RAWN
P-AGED	P-LACK	P-REEN
P-AGER	P-LAID	P-RICE
P-ALAS	P-LAIN	P-RICY
P-ALLY	P-LANE	P-RIDE
P-APER	P-LANK	P-RIMA
P-ARCH	P-LANT	P-RIME
P-ARED	P-LAST	P-RISE
P-ARIS	P-LATE	P-ROBE
P-ARTY	P-LEAD	P-ROLE
P-AVER	P-LEAT	P-ROLL
P-AWED	P-LIED	P-RONG
P-EACH	P-LIER	P-ROOF
P-EARL	P-LINK	P-ROSE
P-EASE	P-LUCK	P-ROVE
P-EGGY	P-LUMP	P-RUDE
P-ESKY	P-LUSH	P-RUNE
P-HONE	P-OINT	P-SHAW
P-ICKY	P-OLIO	P-UNTO
P-INCH	P-OUCH	P-URGE
P-INKY	P-OWER	

P

Five letters to six

P-ACING	P-INION	P-OUTER
P-ACKER	P-INKED	P-RAISE
P-ADDED	P-INKER	P-RANCE
P-ADDER	P-INNED	P-RAYED
P-ADDLE	P-INNER	P-REACH
P-AGING	P-IRATE	P-REACT
P-AIRED	P-ITCHY	P-REBUY
P-AIRER	P-LACED	P-RECUT
P-ALATE	P-LACER	P-REFER
P-ANTED	P-LATED	P-REFIX
P-ARISH	P-LATER	P-REMIX
P-ARKED	P-LAYED	P-REPAY
P-ARLED	P-LAYER	P-RESET
P-ARSON	P-LEASE	P-RETAX
P-ASHED	P-LEDGE	P-REVUE
P-ASTER	P-LODGE	P-RICED
P-AWING	P-LOUGH	P-RICER
P-AWNED	P-LOVER	P-RIEVE
P-AWNER	P-LOWED	P-RIMED
P-EASED	P-LOWER	P-RIMER
P-EGGED	P-LUCKY	P-RISER
P-ELVES	P-LUMMY	P-RIVET
P-ENDED	P-LUMPY	P-ROBED
P-ESTER	P-LUNGE	P-ROPER
P-HONED	P-LYING	P-ROSED
P-HONER	P-ODIUM	P-ROTON
P-HONEY	P-OLDER	P-ROVED
P-HOOEY	P-OSIER	P-ROVEN
P-ICKER	P-OTTER	P-ROVER
P-ICKLE	P-OUNCE	P-ROWER
P-IGGED	P-OUPED	P-RUNED
P-IMPLY	P-OUTED	P-UMPED

P

P-UPPED   P-URGER   P-UTTER
P-URGED   P-USHER

Six letters to seven

P-ADDING	P-INKING	P-LUMPER
P-ADDLED	P-INNING	P-LUNGED
P-AIRING	P-ITCHED	P-LUNGER
P-ANTHER	P-LACING	P-LUNKER
P-ANTING	P-LAIDED	P-LUSHER
P-ANTLER	P-LANKED	P-LUSHLY
P-ARABLE	P-LANNER	P-OINTED
P-ARCHED	P-LASTER	P-OODLES
P-ARKING	P-LATINA	P-ORCINE
P-ARLING	P-LATTER	P-OUCHED
P-ARTIER	P-LAYING	P-OUTING
P-ASHING	P-LAYOFF	P-RAISED
P-AWNING	P-LEADED	P-RAISER
P-EANING	P-LEADER	P-RANCED
P-EASING	P-LEASED	P-RANGED
P-EERIER	P-LEASER	P-RANKED
P-EGGING	P-LEDGED	P-RANKLE
P-ENDING	P-LEDGER	P-RATTED
P-ENFOLD	P-LIABLE	P-RATTLE
P-HARMER	P-LODGED	P-RAYING
P-HATTER	P-LOTTED	P-REAVER
P-HONIED	P-LOTTER	P-REBILL
P-HONING	P-LOWING	P-REBOOK
P-ICKIER	P-LUCKED	P-RECAST
P-ICKILY	P-LUGGED	P-RECEDE
P-ICKLER	P-LUGGER	P-RECEPT
P-INCASE	P-LUMBER	P-RECOOK
P-INCHED	P-LUMPED	P-REDATE
P-INCHER	P-LUMPEN	P-REDIAL

P

P-REFACE	P-RESHIP	P-RIDING
P-REFECT	P-RESIDE	P-RISING
P-REHEAT	P-RESOLD	P-ROBING
P-REMADE	P-RESUME	P-RODDED
P-REMISE	P-RETELL	P-ROOFED
P-REMOVE	P-RETOLD	P-ROOFER
P-RENAME	P-REVERB	P-ROSILY
P-REPACK	P-REVIEW	P-ROVING
P-REPAID	P-REWASH	P-RUDISH
P-REPONE	P-REWORN	P-UPPING
P-RESALE	P-RICIER	P-URGING
P-RESELL	P-RICKLE	
P-RESENT	P-RICKLY	

Seven letters to eight

P-ADDLING	P-INCHING	P-LUGHOLE
P-ALIMONY	P-INKIEST	P-LUMPING
P-ALLYING	P-ITCHIER	P-LUMPISH
P-ALTERED	P-ITCHILY	P-LUNGING
P-ARCHING	P-ITCHING	P-LUSHEST
P-ARTICLE	P-LAIDING	P-LUSHIER
P-ARTISAN	P-LANKING	P-OTTERED
P-ARTWORK	P-LAYBACK	P-OUCHING
P-EARLIER	P-LAYTIME	P-RAISING
P-ENCHANT	P-LEADING	P-RANCING
P-ENLIGHT	P-LEASING	P-RANGING
P-ENOLOGY	P-LEASURE	P-RANKING
P-ENTICED	P-LIGHTED	P-RANKISH
P-HARMING	P-LIGHTER	P-RATTLED
P-HISHING	P-LOTTING	P-RATTLER
P-HONEYED	P-LUCKILY	P-REACHED
P-ICKIEST	P-LUCKING	P-REACHER
P-INBOARD	P-LUGGING	P-READAPT

P

P-READMIT	P-REJUDGE	P-RETRIAL
P-REAPPLY	P-REMIXED	P-RETYPED
P-REARMED	P-REMORSE	P-REUNION
P-REBIRTH	P-REMOULD	P-REUNITE
P-REBOUND	P-REMOVED	P-REVALUE
P-REBUILD	P-REORDER	P-REVISED
P-REBUILT	P-REPAVED	P-REVISIT
P-RECEDED	P-REPLACE	P-REWEIGH
P-RECITED	P-REPOSED	P-REWIRED
P-RECLEAN	P-REPRICE	P-RICIEST
P-RECURED	P-REPRINT	P-RIGGISH
P-RECYCLE	P-RESERVE	P-RILLING
P-REDATED	P-RESHOWN	P-RODDING
P-REDRAFT	P-RESIDED	P-ROOFING
P-REELECT	P-RESIDER	P-ROSIEST
P-REFACED	P-RESUMED	P-UNITIVE
P-REFIXED	P-RESUMER	P-UTTERED
P-REGNANT	P-RETRAIN	P-UTTERER

Some end-hooks

P

Two letters to three

AL-P	HA-P	NA-P
AM-P	HE-P	NE-P
AS-P	HI-P	OO-P
BA-P	HO-P	OU-P
BO-P	JA-P	PA-P
DA-P	KI-P	PE-P
DE-P	KO-P	PI-P
DI-P	LA-P	PO-P
DO-P	LI-P	RE-P
FA-P	LO-P	SI-P
GI-P	MA-P	SO-P
GU-P	MO-P	TA-P

TI-P   UR-P   YE-P
TO-P   WO-P   YU-P
UM-P   YA-P   ZA-P

Celebrity Scrabble Players

include Mel Gibson, Nicole Kidman, Chris Martin,
Madonna and Sting.

Three letters to four

BEE-P	HAS-P	POM-P
BRA-P	HEM-P	PRE-P
BUM-P	HOO-P	PRO-P
BUR-P	HUM-P	PUL-P
CAM-P	JEE-P	RAM-P
CAR-P	LAM-P	RAS-P
CHA-P	LEA-P	ROM-P
CHI-P	LEE-P	RUM-P
COO-P	LIS-P	SEE-P
COW-P	LOO-P	SKI-P
DAM-P	LOU-P	SUM-P
DEE-P	LOW-P	TAR-P
FRA-P	LUM-P	WAR-P
GAS-P	MUM-P	WAS-P
GOO-P	PAR-P	WIS-P
GUL-P	PEE-P	
GUM-P	PER-P	

Four letters to five

BICE-P	CLAM-P	CRIS-P
BLEE-P	CRAM-P	GRAM-P
CHAM-P	CREE-P	GRUM-P
CHUM-P	CRIM-P	PLUM-P

POLY-P	SKIM-P	SWAM-P
PRIM-P	SLEE-P	SWEE-P
SCAM-P	SLUM-P	TRAM-P
SCAR-P	SLUR-P	TWEE-P
SCUL-P	STUM-P	WHOM-P

Five letters to six

ESCAR-P	SCRUM-P	TRICE-P
SCRAW-P	SHLEP-P	
SCRIM-P	THREE-P	

Six letters to seven

| BEDLAM-P | MANTRA-P | SCHLEP-P |

Seven letters to eight

| AUTOCAR-P | MINICAM-P |

BLOCKERS

It is useful to know which words are blockers and can't therefore be extended before or after. You may want to play a blocker that your opponent can't extend, or you may want to avoid playing a blocker because you want to keep the board open.

The three-letter blockers beginning with P

| PAX | PLY | PYX |
| PHT | PST | |

Some four-letter blockers beginning with P

| PFFT | PHAT | PHIZ |
| PFUI | PHEW | PHOH |

PITY	POSY	PUGH
PLEX	PREZ	PUIR
POCO	PRUH	PUNY
POKY	PSST	
PONY	PTUI	

Some five-letter blockers beginning with P
(except words ending in '-ED', '-J', '-S', '-X', '-Y' or '-Z')

PACTA	PIEZO	PULIK
PADRI	PILAR	PULMO
PAISE	PILCH	PUPAE
PALER	PINCH	PUPAL
PAOLO	POOCH	PURER
PAPAL	PORCH	PUTID
PARVE	PROST	PUTTO
PEART	PROUD	PYRAL
PENAL	PUBIC	PYRIC
PERCH	PUFFA	

Some six-letter blockers begining with P
(except words ending in '-ED', '-J', '-S', '-X', '-Y' or '-Z')

PACTUM	PAWING	PLIANT
PAIRER	PEDATE	POKIER
PALEAL	PEPFUL	POLISH
PALEST	PERDIE	POLYPI
PALISH	PERISH	POMATO
PALLID	PERTER	POPRIN
PANINO	PHONAL	POSHER
PARISH	PHYLUM	POSIER
PARTIM	PINETA	POTASH
PASSEE	PIPIER	POTATO
PASSIM	PLACID	POTING
PAUSAL	PLANAR	POXIER

POXING	PROWAR	PUREST
PRELAW	PROWER	PURING
PRIMAL	PRUTAH	PUTRID
PROGUN	PULPAL	PUTTEN
PRONER	PUNIER	
PRONTO	PUNISH	

BONUS WORDS

Bonus words on your rack can be hard to spot, especially for the less experienced player. One way to help find them is by using prefixes and suffixes.

Many larger words include a common prefix or suffix – remembering these and using them where you can is a good way to discover any longer words on your rack, including any potential bonus words. The key prefixes to remember beginning with P are PER-, PRE- and PRO-.

Some words beginning with PER-

Seven-letter words

PER-CENT	PER-JURY	PER-USER
PER-CUSS	PER-PLEX	PER-VADE
PER-FORM	PER-SIST	PER-VERT
PER-FUME	PER-TAIN	
PER-HAPS	PER-TAKE	
PER-JURE	PER-USED	

Eight-letter words

PER-MUTED   PER-SUING   PER-VADED
PER-OXIDE   PER-TAKEN   PER-VERSE
PER-SPIRE   PER-USING

Some words beginning with PRE-

Seven-letter words

PRE-BOIL   PRE-FACE   PRE-SIDE
PRE-BOOK   PRE-HABS   PRE-TEEN
PRE-CAST   PRE-LOAD   PRE-TEND
PRE-CEDE   PRE-LUDE   PRE-TERM
PRE-CODE   PRE-MADE   PRE-TEXT
PRE-COOK   PRE-PACK   PRE-VAIL
PRE-DATE   PRE-PAID   PRE-VIEW
PRE-DAWN   PRE-PARE   PRE-WARN
PRE-DIAL   PRE-PLAN   PRE-WASH
PRE-DICT   PRE-SALE   PRE-WORN
PRE-EMPT   PRE-SHOW

Eight-letter words

PRE-ADAPT   PRE-FIXED   PRE-SERVE
PRE-AMBLE   PRE-JUDGE   PRE-SHAPE
PRE-BIRTH   PRE-MOLAR   PRE-SIDED
PRE-BUILT   PRE-MOULD   PRE-SLEEP
PRE-CEDED   PRE-MOULT   PRE-SOLVE
PRE-CITED   PRE-ORDER   PRE-STORE
PRE-CURED   PRE-OWNED   PRE-TASTE
PRE-CYCLE   PRE-PARED   PRE-TENSE
PRE-DATED   PRE-PLANT   PRE-TRIAL
PRE-ELECT   PRE-POSED   PRE-TYPED
PRE-EXIST   PRE-PRESS   PRE-VALUE
PRE-FACED   PRE-PRINT   PRE-VISED

Some words beginning with PRO-

Seven-letter words

PRO-BALL
PRO-BATE
PRO-CESS
PRO-CURE
PRO-DRUG

PRO-FESS
PRO-FILE
PRO-FUSE
PRO-GRAM
PRO-LONG

PRO-MOTE
PRO-NOUN
PRO-PONE
PRO-POSE
PRO-VERB

Eight-letter words

PRO-BATED
PRO-CLAIM
PRO-CURED
PRO-FILED
PRO-FILER
PRO-FOUND
PRO-LAPSE

PRO-MOTED
PRO-MOTOR
PRO-PENAL
PRO-PHASE
PRO-POSED
PRO-POUND
PRO-RATED

PRO-STYLE
PRO-TRACT
PRO-TRADE
PRO-UNION
PRO-VISOR

P

UNUSUAL WORDS FROM OVERSEAS ENGLISH

If you have an awkward combination of letters on your rack then words from overseas English may come in handy. Here are some beginning with P.

Australian words

PINDAN	desert region of Western Australia
PLONKO	alcoholic, especially one who drinks wine
PODDY	handfed calf or lamb
POSSIE	position
PRELOVED	second-hand

Canadian words

PARFLECHE	dried rawhide
PARKADE	building used as a car park
PARKETTE	small public park
PLEW	beaver skin used as a standard unit
POGEY	financial relief for the unemployed
POKELOGAN	backwater
POUTINE	chipped potatoes topped with curd cheese and tomato sauce
PUNG	horse-drawn sleigh

Hindi words

PACHISI	game resembling backgammon
PAISA	one hundredth of a rupee
PAKORA	dish of deep-fried chicken or vegetables
PANEER	soft white cheese
PARATHA	flat unleavened bread
PEEPUL	tree similar to the banyan
PUNKAH	fan made of palm leaves

P

PURDAH	custom of keeping women secluded
PURI	unleavened flaky bread
PUTTEE	strip of cloth wound around the leg

New Zealand words

PAKAHI	acid soil or land
PAKOKO	small freshwater fish
PAUA	edible abalone
PIKAU	rucksack
PIPI	shellfish
PIUPIU	leaf skirt
PONGA	tall tree fern
PORAE	edible sea fish
PORANGI	crazy
PORINA	moth larva
POTAE	hat
POWHIRI	welcoming ceremony
PUGGY	sticky
PUHA	sow thistle
PUKEKO	wading bird
PURIRI	forest tree

P

South African words

| PADKOS | snacks for a long journey |
| PLAAS | farm |

Q
10

Essential info
Value: 10 points
Number in set: 1

POWER TILE

Along with Z, **Q** is the highest-scoring letter in the
Scrabble set. However, unlike Z, Q can prove difficult
to use if it is not accompanied by the letter U. The best
method of getting around this is to commit to memory
all the short words beginning with Q which do not
require a U. This is easier than it sounds, as there is
only one two-letter word beginning with Q: QI (vital
energy believed to circulate around the body, 11 points),
and one three-letter word: QAT (evergreen shrub of
Africa and Asia whose leaves have narcotic properties).
Other three-letter Q words are the plural of QI (QIS),
QUA and SUQ.

Two-letter word beginning with Q

QI

Three-letter words beginning with Q

QAT   QIN   QUA

Three-letter word using Q

SUQ

Four-letter words

Some four-letter words using Q with which you may not be familiar include QUAG (short form of quagmire, 14 points), QUEY (a young cow, 16 points) and WAQF (endowment in Muslim law, 19 points).

AQUA	QUAG	QUIN
CINQ	QUAI	QUIP
FIQH	QUAT	QUIT
QADI	QUAY	QUIZ
QAID	QUEP	QUOD
QOPH	QUEY	QUOP
QUAD	QUID	WAQF

Q

> **Handy Hint: Q without U**
>
> Q is dependent on U for many of its words, but there is no need to panic if you have a Q and no U. If you find yourself in this situation, some useful examples to remember are: QI (11 points), QADI or QAID (14), QAT (12), QORMA (16), FAQIR (17), TALAQ (14) and TRANQ (14).

HOOKS

Hooking requires a subtle change in a player's thought process, in that they must look at words already on the board without becoming distracted by their pronunciation.

Some front-hooks
Two letters to three

Q-AT   Q-IN   Q-IS

Three letters to four

Q-AID   Q-UEY

Four letters to five

Q-AIDS   Q-UEYS

The only end-hooks

TALA-Q   TZADDI-Q

Q

BLOCKERS

It is useful to know which words are blockers and can't therefore be extended before or after. You may want to play a blocker that your opponent can't extend, or you may want to avoid playing a blocker because you want to keep the board open.

Three-letter blocker beginning with Q

QIS

Four-letter blocker beginning with Q

QUEP

The five-letter blockers beginning with Q

QUAKY	QUAYD	QURSH
QUALE	QUERY	
QUASI	QUOAD	

Some six-letter blockers beginning with Q (except words ending in '-ED', '-J', '-S', '-X', '-Y' or '-Z')

QUAINT	QUENCH	QUOTHA
QUALIA	QUETCH	QURUSH
QUATCH	QUINIC	
QUEINT	QUOOKE	

Bonus words

Seven-letter words

QABALAH	QUADRIC	QUAKING
QAMUTIK	QUAERED	QUALIFY
QAWWALI	QUAERES	QUALITY
QAWWALS	QUAFFED	QUAMASH
QIGONGS	QUAFFER	QUANGOS
QINDARS	QUAGGAS	QUANNET
QINTARS	QUAICHS	QUANTAL
QUACKED	QUAIGHS	QUANTED
QUACKER	QUAILED	QUANTIC
QUACKLE	QUAKERS	QUANTUM
QUADDED	QUAKIER	QUAREST
QUADRAT	QUAKILY	QUARREL

QUARTAN	QUESTOR	QUININE
QUARTER	QUETZAL	QUININS
QUARTES	QUEUERS	QUINNAT
QUARTET	QUEUING	QUINOAS
QUARTIC	QUIBBLE	QUINOID
QUARTOS	QUICHED	QUINOLS
QUARTZY	QUICHES	QUINONE
QUASARS	QUICKEN	QUINTAL
QUASHED	QUICKER	QUINTAN
QUASHEE	QUICKIE	QUINTAR
QUASHER	QUICKLY	QUINTAS
QUASHES	QUIDAMS	QUINTES
QUASHIE	QUIDDIT	QUINTET
QUASSIA	QUIESCE	QUINTIC
QUASSIN	QUIETED	QUINTIN
QUATRES	QUIETEN	QUINZES
QUATTED	QUIETER	QUIPPED
QUAVERS	QUIETLY	QUIPPER
QUAVERY	QUIETUS	QUIPPUS
QUAYAGE	QUIFFED	QUIRING
QUEBECS	QUIGHTS	QUIRKED
QUEENED	QUILLAI	QUIRTED
QUEENIE	QUILLED	QUITING
QUEENLY	QUILLET	QUITTAL
QUEESTS	QUILLON	QUITTED
QUELLED	QUILLOW	QUITTER
QUELLER	QUILTED	QUITTOR
QUEMING	QUILTER	QUIVERS
QUERIDA	QUINARY	QUIVERY
QUERIED	QUINATE	QUIXOTE
QUERIER	QUINCES	QUIZZED
QUERIES	QUINCHE	QUIZZER
QUERIST	QUINELA	QUIZZES
QUESTED	QUINIES	QUODDED
QUESTER	QUININA	QUODLIN

Q

QUOHOGS QUOKKAS QUORUMS
QUOIFED QUOMODO QUOTERS
QUOINED QUONDAM QUOTING
QUOISTS QUONKED QUOTUMS
QUOITED QUOPPED QWERTYS
QUOITER QUORATE

Eight-letter words

QABALISM QUAINTER QUASHIES
QABALIST QUAINTLY QUASHING
QALAMDAN QUAKIEST QUASSIAS
QINDARKA QUALMIER QUATCHED
QINTARKA QUALMING QUATORZE
QUAALUDE QUALMISH QUATRAIN
QUACKERY QUANDANG QUATTING
QUACKIER QUANDARY QUAVERED
QUACKING QUANDONG QUAVERER
QUACKISH QUANTIFY QUAYLIKE
QUACKISM QUANTILE QUAYSIDE
QUACKLED QUANTING QUAZZIER
QUADDING QUANTISE QUEACHES
QUADPLAY QUANTITY QUEASIER
QUADPLEX QUANTIZE QUEASILY
QUADRANT QUANTONG QUEAZIER
QUADRATE QUANTUMS QUEENCUP
QUADRATI QUARRIAN QUEENITE
QUADRIGA QUARRIED QUEENLET
QUADROON QUARRIER QUELCHED
QUAESTOR QUARRIES QUELCHES
QUAFFING QUARRION QUELLING
QUAGGIER QUARTERN QUENCHED
QUAGMIRE QUARTETT QUENCHER
QUAGMIRY QUARTIER QUENCHES
QUAICHES QUARTILE QUENELLE
QUAILING QUARTZES QUERCINE

QUERYING	QUILLAIA	QUIRTING
QUESTANT	QUILLAJA	QUISLING
QUESTERS	QUILLING	QUITCHED
QUESTING	QUILLMAN	QUITCHES
QUESTION	QUILLMEN	QUITRENT
QUETCHED	QUILTING	QUITTALS
QUETCHES	QUINCHED	QUITTERS
QUETHING	QUINCHES	QUITTING
QUEUEING	QUINCUNX	QUIVERED
QUIBBLED	QUINELLA	QUIVERER
QUIBBLER	QUINIELA	QUIXOTES
QUIBBLES	QUININES	QUIXOTIC
QUICHING	QUINOIDS	QUIXOTRY
QUICKEST	QUINOLIN	QUIZZERY
QUICKIES	QUINONES	QUIZZIFY
QUICKSET	QUINSIED	QUIZZING
QUIDDANY	QUINSIES	QUODDING
QUIDDITY	QUINTAIN	QUODLINS
QUIDDLED	QUINTETS	QUOIFING
QUIDDLER	QUINTETT	QUOINING
QUIDNUNC	QUINTICS	QUOITERS
QUIESCED	QUINTILE	QUOITING
QUIESCES	QUIPPIER	QUONKING
QUIETEST	QUIPPING	QUOPPING
QUIETING	QUIPPISH	QUOTABLE
QUIETISM	QUIPSTER	QUOTABLY
QUIETIST	QUIRKIER	QUOTIENT
QUIETIVE	QUIRKILY	QWERTIES
QUIETUDE	QUIRKING	
QUIGHTED	QUIRKISH	

UNUSUAL WORDS FROM OVERSEAS ENGLISH

If you have an awkward combination of letters on your rack then words from overseas English may come in handy. Here are some beginning with Q.

Australian words

QUOKKA   small wallaby
QUOLL   native cat

Canadian words

QAJAQ   a kayak (original Inuit spelling)
QAMUTIK   a sled with wooden runners

Urdu word

QORMA   Indian dish of meat or vegetables
            braised with yoghurt or cream

Q

Handy Hint: QUIZ show

If you are lucky enough to have the letters Q, U, I and Z on your rack, or with one of them in a usable place on the board, the obvious choice would be to play QUIZ, an extremely useful and high-scoring word (22 points). Should your opponent be the lucky one to play QUIZ then perhaps you can then reap the benefits by playing a word with an S and front-hooking it to make SQUIZ (23 points).

Essential info
Value: 1 point
Number in set: 6

R is one of the most common consonants in Scrabble alongside N and T but, surprisingly, only begins one two-letter word: RE (2 points). Some useful three-letter words to remember include ROW and RAY (6 points each) and there are also more unusual words such as RAX (a Scots word for stretch or extend, 10 points) and REZ (a short informal word for reservation, 12 points) which use power tiles. R is one of the letters of the RETAIN set and is therefore a good letter to keep if trying to get a bonus word.

Two-letter word beginning with R

RE

Some three-letter words beginning with R

RAD	REH	RHO
RAH	REI	RHY
RAI	REM	RIF
RAJ	REN	RIN
RAS	REO	RIT
RAX	REP	RIZ
REB	RET	ROM
REC	REW	ROO
REE	REX	RYA
REG	REZ	RYU

HOOKS

Hooking requires a subtle change in a player's thought process, in that they must look at words already on the board without becoming distracted by their pronunciation.

Some front-hooks
Two letters to three

R-AD	R-AX	R-ET
R-AG	R-AY	R-EX
R-AH	R-ED	R-HO
R-AI	R-EE	R-ID
R-AM	R-EF	R-IF
R-AN	R-EH	R-IN
R-AS	R-EM	R-IT
R-AT	R-EN	R-OB
R-AW	R-ES	R-OD

R-OE	R-UG	R-YA
R-OM	R-UM	R-YE
R-OO	R-UN	R-YU
R-OW	R-UT	

Three letters to four

R-ACE	R-ATE	R-INK
R-AFF	R-AVE	R-OAR
R-AFT	R-AWN	R-OBE
R-AGE	R-EAR	R-ODE
R-AID	R-EEK	R-OIL
R-AIL	R-EEL	R-OLE
R-AIN	R-EFT	R-OOF
R-AKE	R-END	R-OOM
R-ALE	R-EST	R-OOT
R-AMP	R-ICE	R-OPE
R-AND	R-ICH	R-OSE
R-ANT	R-ICK	R-OUT
R-APT	R-ICY	R-ULE
R-ARE	R-IDE	R-UMP
R-ASH	R-IFF	R-USE
R-ASP	R-IGG	R-YES

Four letters to five

R-ABID	R-AVER	R-OAST
R-ACED	R-EACH	R-OILY
R-ACER	R-EAVE	R-OPED
R-AGED	R-EDDY	R-OUST
R-AGER	R-EGAL	R-OVEN
R-AKED	R-EMIT	R-OVER
R-ALLY	R-ENEW	R-OWED
R-AMEN	R-ETCH	R-OWER
R-ARED	R-ICED	
R-AVEL	R-OARY	

Five letters to six

R-ABIES
R-ACING
R-ADDER
R-ADIOS
R-AFTER
R-AGING
R-AIDED
R-AIDER
R-AILED
R-AKING
R-AMBLE
R-AMPED
R-ANGER
R-ANKER
R-ANKLE
R-ANTED
R-APPEL
R-APTLY
R-AREFY
R-ASHED
R-ASPER
R-AUGHT

R-AVINE
R-AZURE
R-EARED
R-EAVED
R-EBOOK
R-EDUCE
R-EFFED
R-EGRET
R-EJECT
R-ELATE
R-EMAIL
R-EMOTE
R-EMOVE
R-ENDED
R-ENTER
R-ESTER
R-ETAPE
R-EVERT
R-EVERY
R-EVOKE
R-ICIER
R-ICING

R-ICKLE
R-ICTAL
R-ICTUS
R-IGGED
R-INKED
R-OARED
R-OCKER
R-OILED
R-OLLER
R-OPING
R-OSIER
R-OTARY
R-OTTER
R-OUGHT
R-OUNCE
R-OUPED
R-OUTED
R-OUTER
R-OWING
R-UDDER
R-USHER
R-UTTER

R

Six letters to seven

R-ABIDER
R-ADDLED
R-AIDING
R-AILING
R-ALLIED
R-AMBLED
R-AMBLER
R-AMPING
R-ANKLED
R-ANTING
R-APPORT

R-ASHING
R-ASPISH
R-EARING
R-EAVING
R-EDDISH
R-EDUCED
R-EFFING
R-EGALLY
R-EGENCE
R-EGENCY
R-EGRESS

R-ELAPSE
R-ELATED
R-ELATER
R-EMERGE
R-EMOTER
R-EMOVED
R-ENDING
R-ENEWED
R-EPRISE
R-ESTATE
R-ETCHED

252

R-EVILER	R-IGGING	R-OUSTER
R-EVOKED	R-INKING	R-OUTING
R-EVOKER	R-OARING	R-OYSTER
R-EVOLVE	R-OILING	R-UGGING
R-ICHING	R-OUGHLY	R-UNLESS
R-ICIEST	R-OUSTED	

Seven letters to eight

R-ADDLING	R-ELATING	R-ENFORCE
R-ALLYING	R-ELATION	R-ENOUNCE
R-AMBLING	R-ELATIVE	R-ESTATED
R-ANKLING	R-EMAILED	R-ETCHING
R-APTNESS	R-EMAILER	R-EVERTED
R-AREFIED	R-EMERGED	R-EVOKING
R-ECLOSED	R-EMITTED	R-EVOLVED
R-EDUCING	R-EMITTER	R-EVOLVER
R-EGALITY	R-EMOTION	R-EVULSED
R-EJECTED	R-EMOVING	R-UNROUND
R-ELAPSED	R-ENEWING	R-URALITE

> ### Handy Hint: This way and that
>
> JAR (10 points) is an obvious word to spot on the rack.
> If it won't play then remember that JAR backwards
> makes the word RAJ which might fit in. RAJ is an
> Indian word for government and it also takes a useful
> A hook for RAJA, which then can take an H for RAJAH.
> Other short reversible words beginning with R are
> RAW/WAR (6 points) FIR/RIF (6 points) RAP/PAR
> (5 points) RIM/MIR (5 points).

R

Some end-hooks
Two letters to three

| AI-R | BO-R | EA-R |
| BA-R | DO-R | ER-R |

FA-R	LA-R	PA-R
FE-R	LO-R	PE-R
GO-R	MA-R	PI-R
GU-R	MI-R	SI-R
HE-R	MO-R	TA-R
JA-R	NO-R	TO-R
JO-R	NU-R	YA-R
KI-R	OO-R	YE-R
KO-R	OU-R	

Three letters to four

ACE-R	EYE-R	PEA-R
AGA-R	FEE-R	PIE-R
AGE-R	FIE-R	PUR-R
APE-R	FOU-R	SEA-R
AVE-R	GOE-R	SEE-R
BEE-R	HOA-R	SOU-R
BOA-R	HOE-R	SPA-R
BOO-R	HOO-R	SUE-R
BRR-R	HUE-R	TEA-R
BUR-R	ICE-R	TEE-R
CHA-R	JEE-R	TIE-R
CHE-R	LEA-R	USE-R
DEE-R	LEE-R	VEE-R
DOE-R	LIE-R	VIE-R
DOO-R	MEE-R	YEA-R
DYE-R	MOO-R	YOU-R
EVE-R	ONE-R	
EWE-R	OWE-R	

Four letters to five

ABLE-R	BIKE-R	CANE-R
BAKE-R	BITE-R	CAPE-R
BARE-R	BLUE-R	CARE-R
BASE-R	BORE-R	CATE-R
BIDE-R	CAGE-R	CAVE-R

CHAI-R	GONE-R	MATE-R
CIDE-R	HATE-R	MAYO-R
CITE-R	HAVE-R	METE-R
CODE-R	HAZE-R	MINE-R
COME-R	HIDE-R	MITE-R
COPE-R	HIKE-R	MOVE-R
COVE-R	HIRE-R	MUSE-R
CUBE-R	HOME-R	NAME-R
CURE-R	HOPE-R	NICE-R
CUTE-R	HOVE-R	NINE-R
DARE-R	HUGE-R	NOSE-R
DATE-R	HYPE-R	NOTE-R
DECO-R	IDLE-R	OCHE-R
DICE-R	JIVE-R	ONCE-R
DINE-R	JOKE-R	PACE-R
DIVE-R	LACE-R	PAGE-R
DONE-R	LAKE-R	PALE-R
DOPE-R	LAME-R	PATE-R
DOSE-R	LASE-R	PIKE-R
DOVE-R	LATE-R	PIPE-R
DOZE-R	LEVE-R	POKE-R
EASE-R	LIFE-R	POSE-R
EDGE-R	LIKE-R	PUKE-R
FACE-R	LINE-R	PURE-R
FADE-R	LIVE-R	RACE-R
FAKE-R	LONE-R	RARE-R
FILE-R	LOSE-R	RATE-R
FINE-R	LOVE-R	RAVE-R
FIRE-R	LUGE-R	RAZE-R
FIVE-R	LUNA-R	RICE-R
FREE-R	LURE-R	RIDE-R
FUME-R	LUTE-R	RIPE-R
GAME-R	LUXE-R	RISE-R
GATE-R	MACE-R	ROPE-R
GAZE-R	MAKE-R	ROTO-R
GIVE-R	MANO-R	ROVE-R

R

255

RUDE-R	SUPE-R	VILE-R
RULE-R	SURE-R	VINE-R
SABE-R	TAKE-R	VOTE-R
SAFE-R	TAME-R	WADE-R
SAGE-R	TAPE-R	WAGE-R
SANE-R	TIGE-R	WAKE-R
SAVE-R	TIME-R	WAVE-R
SHOE-R	TONE-R	WIDE-R
SIDE-R	TRUE-R	WIPE-R
SIZE-R	TUBE-R	WISE-R
SOLA-R	TUNE-R	ZONE-R
SORE-R	UNDE-R	

Five letters to six

ABIDE-R	CHAFE-R	EXILE-R
ACUTE-R	CHASE-R	FALSE-R
ADORE-R	CLEVE-R	FENCE-R
AGILE-R	CLONE-R	FLAKE-R
AMPLE-R	CLOSE-R	FLAME-R
AMUSE-R	CLOVE-R	FORCE-R
ANGLE-R	CONDO-R	GLAZE-R
ARGUE-R	CRATE-R	GLIDE-R
BADGE-R	CRUDE-R	GLOVE-R
BARBE-R	CURSE-R	GORGE-R
BATHE-R	CYCLE-R	GOUGE-R
BEIGE-R	DANCE-R	GRADE-R
BINGE-R	DENSE-R	GRAVE-R
BLAME-R	DODGE-R	GUIDE-R
BLAZE-R	DOUSE-R	GUISE-R
BOMBE-R	DRIVE-R	HEAVE-R
BOOZE-R	DRONE-R	HOUSE-R
BRAVE-R	DROVE-R	IRATE-R
BRIBE-R	EERIE-R	ISSUE-R
BULGE-R	ELATE-R	JUDGE-R
CARVE-R	ERASE-R	JUICE-R
CAUSE-R	EVADE-R	KNIFE-R

LANCE-R	QUAKE-R	SPARE-R
LARGE-R	REAVE-R	SPICE-R
LATHE-R	RECTO-R	STAKE-R
LATTE-R	RIFLE-R	STATE-R
LEASE-R	RINSE-R	STONE-R
LEAVE-R	ROGUE-R	SWIPE-R
LODGE-R	ROUTE-R	TASTE-R
LUNGE-R	SAUCE-R	TEASE-R
MERGE-R	SCALE-R	TITLE-R
MINCE-R	SCORE-R	TRACE-R
NOOSE-R	SERVE-R	TRADE-R
PARSE-R	SHAKE-R	TWICE-R
PASSE-R	SHAPE-R	UNITE-R
PHASE-R	SHARE-R	VAGUE-R
PIECE-R	SHAVE-R	VALUE-R
PLACE-R	SHINE-R	VERGE-R
PLANE-R	SINGE-R	WAIVE-R
PRIME-R	SLATE-R	WASTE-R
PROVE-R	SLIDE-R	WHITE-R

Six letters to seven

ACCUSE-R	COARSE-R	ESCAPE-R
ADMIRE-R	CREASE-R	EVOLVE-R
ADVISE-R	CRINGE-R	EXPOSE-R
AVENGE-R	CRUISE-R	FIERCE-R
BABBLE-R	DAMAGE-R	FLEECE-R
BAFFLE-R	DANGLE-R	FORAGE-R
BOTTLE-R	DEBASE-R	FREEZE-R
BOUNCE-R	DEBATE-R	GAMBLE-R
BROWSE-R	DECIDE-R	GENTLE-R
BUNDLE-R	DEFINE-R	GROOVE-R
CACKLE-R	DIVIDE-R	GROUSE-R
CHANGE-R	DOUBLE-R	HANDLE-R
CHARGE-R	ENABLE-R	HUDDLE-R
CHEQUE-R	ENCODE-R	HUMBLE-R
CLEAVE-R	ENDURE-R	HURDLE-R

R

257

HUSTLE-R	MUZZLE-R	RUSTLE-R
IGNITE-R	NEEDLE-R	SAMPLE-R
IMPALE-R	NOTICE-R	SAVAGE-R
IMPOSE-R	NUZZLE-R	SECURE-R
IMPURE-R	OBLIGE-R	SEDUCE-R
INCITE-R	OBTUSE-R	SNOOZE-R
INCOME-R	OFFICE-R	SPARSE-R
INHALE-R	OPPOSE-R	SQUARE-R
INSANE-R	PEOPLE-R	STRIKE-R
INSIDE-R	PERUSE-R	STRIPE-R
INSURE-R	PICKLE-R	TODDLE-R
INVADE-R	PIERCE-R	TROUSE-R
IONISE-R	PLEASE-R	TRUDGE-R
IONIZE-R	PLEDGE-R	TUMBLE-R
JUGGLE-R	POLITE-R	UNIQUE-R
KINDLE-R	PRAISE-R	UNSAFE-R
LADDIE-R	QUARTE-R	UNSURE-R
LOATHE-R	RAMBLE-R	UPDATE-R
LOCATE-R	RATTLE-R	VOYAGE-R
LOUNGE-R	REDUCE-R	WAFFLE-R
MANAGE-R	REFINE-R	WHEEZE-R
MARINE-R	REMOTE-R	WIGGLE-R
MENACE-R	RESCUE-R	WOBBLE-R
MINUTE-R	REVISE-R	

R

Seven letters to eight

ACHIEVE-R	CAPTURE-R	DIFFUSE-R
ADVANCE-R	CAROUSE-R	DISABLE-R
AIRLINE-R	CHUCKLE-R	DISPOSE-R
ARRANGE-R	COMBINE-R	ENDORSE-R
AVERAGE-R	COMMUTE-R	ENFORCE-R
BALANCE-R	COMPUTE-R	ENHANCE-R
BANDAGE-R	CONJURE-R	EXAMINE-R
BELIEVE-R	CONSUME-R	EXECUTE-R
BICYCLE-R	DECEIVE-R	EXPLORE-R
BREATHE-R	DECLINE-R	FORGIVE-R

FRAGILE-R	OBSERVE-R	REWRITE-R
GESTURE-R	OUTLINE-R	SERVICE-R
GRAPPLE-R	OUTSIDE-R	SHUTTLE-R
GRUMBLE-R	PERJURE-R	SILENCE-R
GUYLINE-R	PILLAGE-R	SINCERE-R
HOTLINE-R	POLLUTE-R	STICKLE-R
IMAGINE-R	PRECISE-R	STRANGE-R
IMMENSE-R	PREFACE-R	SURVIVE-R
IMPROVE-R	PREPARE-R	TEENAGE-R
INQUIRE-R	PRODUCE-R	TOASTIE-R
INTRUDE-R	PROFILE-R	TOPLINE-R
JOYRIDE-R	PROMOTE-R	TORTURE-R
JUSTICE-R	PROPOSE-R	TROUBLE-R
LECTURE-R	PROVIDE-R	TWINKLE-R
LICENCE-R	RECEIVE-R	UPGRADE-R
LICENSE-R	RECLINE-R	UPSTATE-R
MEASURE-R	RECYCLE-R	VENTURE-R
MISTAKE-R	REPLACE-R	VILLAGE-R
NARRATE-R	RESERVE-R	WARGAME-R
NEWCOME-R	RESTORE-R	WELCOME-R
NURTURE-R	REVERSE-R	WHISTLE-R
OBSCURE-R	REVOLVE-R	WHITTLE-R

BLOCKERS

It is useful to know which words are blockers and can't therefore be extended before or after. You may want to play a blocker that your opponent can't extend, or you may want to avoid playing a blocker because you want to keep the board open.

The three-letter blockers beginning with R

RAX   RHY

Some four-letter blockers beginning with R

RACA	RENK	ROUX
REFT	RIVO	RUBY
RELY	ROPY	RYFE

Some five-letter blockers beginning with R (except words ending in '-ED', '-J', '-S', '-X', '-Y' or '-Z')

RABID	REDID	RESAT
RADII	REJON	REWAN
RAREE	RELIT	RIFER
RARER	RENAL	RILEY
RASTA	RERAN	RUNIC

Some six-letter blockers beginning with R (except words ending in '-ED', '-J', '-S', '-X', '-Y' or '-Z')

RACIAL	RECHIE	RESEEN
RACIER	REDONE	RESHOD
RADDER	REDREW	RESHOT
RADGER	REFLEW	RETOOK
RADISH	REGAVE	RETORN
RAKISH	REGNAL	RETROD
RAMATE	REGREW	RICHER
RANCID	REHASH	RIDDEN
RAPPEN	REHUNG	RIFEST
RAREST	RELAID	RIPEST
RARING	RELISH	ROPIER
RATHER	REMOUD	RUEFUL
RAVISH	REPAND	RURBAN
RAWISH	RESAID	

R

BONUS WORDS

Bonus words on your rack can be hard to spot, especially for the less experienced player. One way to help find them is by using prefixes and suffixes.

Many larger words include a common prefix or suffix – remembering these and using them where you can is a good way to discover any longer words on your rack, including any potential bonus words. The key prefixes to remember beginning with R are RE- and RED-.

Some words beginning with RE-

Seven-letter words

RE-ACTED	RE-ELECT	RE-MORSE
RE-ADAPT	RE-ENACT	RE-MOVED
RE-AGENT	RE-ENTRY	RE-NEWER
RE-ALIGN	RE-FILLS	RE-ORDER
RE-APPLY	RE-FINED	RE-ORGED
RE-BASED	RE-FORMS	RE-PAINT
RE-BATED	RE-FRESH	RE-PASTS
RE-BIRTH	RE-FURBS	RE-PEALS
RE-BOOTS	RE-FUSED	RE-PEATS
RE-BOUND	RE-GIFTS	RE-PLACE
RE-BRAND	RE-GROUP	RE-PLAYS
RE-BUILD	RE-GROWN	RE-PLIES
RE-CALLS	RE-HOMED	RE-PORTS
RE-CEDED	RE-HOUSE	RE-PRESS
RE-CITAL	RE-INTER	RE-PRINT
RE-CITED	RE-ISSUE	RE-QUEST
RE-CLAIM	RE-JOINS	RE-READS
RE-COILS	RE-KEYED	RE-ROUTE
RE-CORDS	RE-LAPSE	RE-SEALS
RE-COUNT	RE-LAXER	RE-SERVE
RE-COVER	RE-LEASE	RE-SIGNS
RE-CYCLE	RE-LIVED	RE-SISTS
RE-DEEMS	RE-LOADS	RE-SOLVE
RE-DOUBT	RE-MARKS	RE-SOUND
RE-DRAFT	RE-MATCH	RE-SPIRE
RE-DRESS	RE-MINDS	RE-SPITE
RE-DUCES	RE-MIXED	RE-START

R

RE-STATE
RE-STORE
RE-TAILS
RE-TAPED
RE-TEACH
RE-THINK
RE-TIRED
RE-TOXED
RE-TRACT

RE-TREAD
RE-TREAT
RE-TWEET
RE-TURNS
RE-UNIFY
RE-UNION
RE-UNITE
RE-VENGE
RE-VERSE

RE-VISED
RE-VOLVE
RE-WATER
RE-WILDS
RE-WORKS
RE-WOUND
RE-WRITE

Eight-letter words

RE-ABSORB
RE-ACTION
RE-ADJUST
RE-APPEAR
RE-ASSESS
RE-BASING
RE-BOOTED
RE-BUFFED
RE-BUTTED
RE-CALLED
RE-CAPPED
RE-CEDING
RE-CHARGE
RE-CITING
RE-COILED
RE-COLOUR
RE-COMMIT
RE-CONNED
RE-CORDED
RE-COUPED
RE-COURSE
RE-CYCLED
RE-DEEMED
RE-DEFINE
RE-DEPLOY

RE-DESIGN
RE-DOUBLE
RE-DUBBED
RE-EMERGE
RE-ENGAGE
RE-ENLIST
RE-FILLED
RE-FINERY
RE-FITTED
RE-FLEXED
RE-FORMAT
RE-FORMED
RE-FUELED
RE-FUNDED
RE-GAINED
RE-GESTED
RE-GIFTED
RE-GROWTH
RE-HEARSE
RE-HEATED
RE-HOMING
RE-IGNITE
RE-INVENT
RE-ISSUED
RE-JOINED

RE-KINDLE
RE-LAPSED
RE-LAUNCH
RE-LAYING
RE-LEASED
RE-LOADED
RE-LOCATE
RE-MAILER
RE-MAKING
RE-MARKED
RE-MASTER
RE-MEMBER
RE-MINDED
RE-MOVING
RE-OCCUPY
RE-OFFEND
RE-ORGING
RE-PAIRED
RE-PEALED
RE-PHRASE
RE-PLACED
RE-PLOUGH
RE-PORTER
RE-PRISED
RE-QUITED

R

RE-RECORD	RE-STRICT	RE-VERSED
RE-ROUTED	RE-TAILED	RE-VIEWER
RE-SEALED	RE-TIRING	RE-VISING
RE-SEARCH	RE-TRACED	RE-VISION
RE-SECURE	RE-TURNED	RE-WARDED
RE-SOLVED	RE-UNITED	RE-WILDED
RE-SORTED	RE-USABLE	RE-WINDER
RE-STORED	RE-VALUED	RE-WRITER

Some words beginning with RED-

Seven-letter words

RED-BACK	RED-FOOT	RED-TAIL
RED-BIRD	RED-HEAD	RED-TOPS
RED-CAPS	RED-LINE	RED-WING
RED-COAT	RED-NECK	RED-WOOD
RED-EYES	RED-NESS	
RED-FISH	RED-ROOT	

Eight-letter words

RED-BELLY	RED-SHANK	RED-START
RED-BRICK	RED-SHIFT	RED-WATER
RED-HORSE	RED-SHIRE	
RED-LINED	RED-SHIRT	

R

UNUSUAL WORDS FROM OVERSEAS ENGLISH

If you have an awkward combination of letters on your rack then words from overseas English may come in handy. Here are some beginning with R.

Australian words

RAZOO	imaginary coin
REGO	registration of a motor vehicle

| RESTO | restored antique, vintage car, etc |
| ROUGHIE | something unfair, especially a trick |

Canadian words

REDEYE	drink incorporating beer and tomato juice
RODNEY	small fishing boat
RUBABOO	soup made by boiling pemmican
RUBBY	rubbing alcohol mixed with cheap wine for drinking

Hindi words

RAGGEE	cereal grass
RAITA	yoghurt-and-vegetable dish served with curry
RAJAH	ruler or landlord
RAMTIL	African plant grown in India
RANI	queen or princess
RATHA	four-wheeled carriage drawn by horses or bullocks
ROTI	type of unleavened bread
RUPEE	standard monetary unit of India
RUPIAH	standard monetary unit of Indonesia
RYOT	peasant or tenant farmer

R

New Zealand words

RAHUI	Maori prohibition
RATA	myrtaceous forest tree
RAUPATU	seizure of land
RAURIKI	sow thistle

South African word

| ROOIKAT | lynx |

Urdu word

| RABI | crop harvested at the end of winter |

Essential info
Value: 1 point
Number in set: 4

The **S** is such a valuable letter for making longer plays, especially a seven-letter bonus word, that it ought not to be squandered in a short word play. The four two-letter words that begin with S could assist in hooking your play onto an existing word: SH (a sound people make to request silence or quiet, 5 points) and SI, SO and ST (2 points each). Quite a few three-letter words which use no vowels begin with S (although you will need a Y), including: SHY (9 points), SKY (10 points) and SPY (8 points). S also forms various three-letter words using X and Z: SAX, SEX, SIX and SOX (10 points each) and SAZ, SEZ and SOZ (12 points each).

Two-letter words beginning with S

SH	SO
SI	ST

Some three-letter words beginning with S

SAB	SHA	SOL
SAE	SHH	SOM
SAI	SHO	SOT
SAL	SIB	SOU
SAM	SIC	SOV
SAN	SIF	SOX
SAR	SIG	SOY
SAX	SIK	SOZ
SAY	SIM	SUG
SAZ	SKA	SUQ
SED	SMA	SUR
SEL	SNY	SUS
SEN	SOC	SWY
SER	SOG	SYE
SEZ	SOH	

HOOKS

Examples of S as end hooks are not included in this book due to their ease of use as the simple plural form of the word originally played. We recommend checking the Collins Scrabble Dictionary (or the dictionary you are using) if you are in any doubt.

Some front-hooks
Two letters to three

S-AB	S-AE	S-AI
S-AD	S-AG	S-AL

S-AM	S-HE	S-OP
S-AN	S-HO	S-OS
S-AR	S-IF	S-OU
S-AT	S-IN	S-OW
S-AW	S-IS	S-OX
S-AX	S-IT	S-OY
S-AY	S-KA	S-PA
S-EA	S-KI	S-UG
S-ED	S-KY	S-UM
S-EE	S-MA	S-UN
S-EL	S-NY	S-UP
S-EN	S-OB	S-UR
S-ER	S-OD	S-US
S-ET	S-OH	S-YE
S-EX	S-OM	
S-HA	S-ON	

Three letters to four

S-ADO	S-AWN	S-HAM
S-AGA	S-CAB	S-HAW
S-AGE	S-CAG	S-HEN
S-AGO	S-CAM	S-HEW
S-AID	S-CAN	S-HIN
S-AIL	S-CAR	S-HIP
S-AIR	S-CAT	S-HOD
S-AKE	S-CRY	S-HOE
S-ALE	S-CUD	S-HOP
S-ALT	S-CUM	S-HOT
S-AND	S-EAR	S-HOW
S-ANE	S-EAT	S-HUN
S-ARK	S-EEK	S-HUT
S-ARS	S-EEN	S-ICK
S-ASH	S-ELF	S-IDE
S-ASS	S-ELL	S-ILK
S-ATE	S-END	S-ILL
S-AVE	S-HAH	S-INK

S

267

S-IRE	S-NIB	S-POT
S-KID	S-NIP	S-PRY
S-KIN	S-NOB	S-PUD
S-KIP	S-NOT	S-PUN
S-KIT	S-NOW	S-PUR
S-LAB	S-OAK	S-TAB
S-LAM	S-OAR	S-TAG
S-LAP	S-ODA	S-TAR
S-LAT	S-OFT	S-TAT
S-LAY	S-OIL	S-TAY
S-LED	S-OLD	S-TEN
S-LEW	S-OLE	S-TET
S-LID	S-OON	S-TEW
S-LIP	S-OOT	S-TOP
S-LIT	S-ORE	S-TOT
S-LOB	S-ORT	S-TOW
S-LOG	S-OUP	S-TUB
S-LOP	S-OUR	S-TUN
S-LOT	S-OWN	S-UMP
S-LOW	S-PAM	S-URE
S-LUG	S-PAN	S-WAB
S-LUM	S-PAR	S-WAG
S-LUR	S-PAT	S-WAN
S-MOG	S-PAY	S-WAP
S-MUG	S-PEC	S-WAT
S-MUT	S-PEW	S-WAY
S-NAG	S-PIN	S-WIG
S-NAP	S-PIT	S-WOP

Four letters to five

S-ABLE	S-CAMP	S-COLD
S-AGER	S-CANT	S-CONE
S-ALLY	S-CAPE	S-COOP
S-AUNT	S-CARE	S-COOT
S-AVER	S-CART	S-COPE
S-AWED	S-COFF	S-CORE

S-CORN	S-HOOT	S-MILE
S-COWL	S-HORN	S-MITE
S-CRAM	S-HOVE	S-MOCK
S-CRAN	S-HUCK	S-MOKE
S-CREW	S-HUNT	S-NAIL
S-CROW	S-HUSH	S-NIFF
S-CUFF	S-ICKY	S-OILY
S-CULL	S-IDLE	S-OWED
S-EDGE	S-IRED	S-PACE
S-EVEN	S-KELP	S-PAIN
S-EVER	S-KILL	S-PARE
S-EWER	S-KINK	S-PARK
S-EXED	S-LACK	S-PATE
S-HACK	S-LAIN	S-PAWN
S-HAFT	S-LAKE	S-PEAK
S-HAKE	S-LANG	S-PEAR
S-HALE	S-LASH	S-PECK
S-HALL	S-LATE	S-PELT
S-HALT	S-LEEK	S-PEND
S-HAME	S-LEET	S-PIKE
S-HANK	S-LICE	S-PILL
S-HARD	S-LICK	S-PINE
S-HARE	S-LIME	S-PLAY
S-HARK	S-LOAN	S-POKE
S-HARP	S-LOPE	S-POOL
S-HAVE	S-LOTH	S-PORE
S-HEAR	S-LUMP	S-PORK
S-HELL	S-LUNG	S-PORT
S-HERE	S-LUNK	S-POUT
S-HERO	S-LUSH	S-PRAY
S-HILL	S-MACK	S-PROG
S-HIRE	S-MALL	S-QUAD
S-HOCK	S-MART	S-QUID
S-HOED	S-MASH	S-TACK
S-HONE	S-MELL	S-TAKE
S-HOOK	S-MELT	S-TALE

S

S-TALK	S-TILL	S-WARM
S-TALL	S-TINT	S-WEAR
S-TANK	S-TOCK	S-WEEP
S-TART	S-TONE	S-WEER
S-TATE	S-TOOK	S-WELL
S-TEAK	S-TOOL	S-WELT
S-TEAL	S-TOUT	S-WEPT
S-TEAM	S-TOWN	S-WILL
S-TEED	S-TRAP	S-WINE
S-TEEL	S-TRAY	S-WING
S-TERN	S-TRIM	S-WIPE
S-TICK	S-TRIP	S-WISH
S-TIFF	S-TUCK	S-WORD
S-TILE	S-URGE	S-WORE

Five letters to six

S-ADDER	S-CURRY	S-IDLED
S-ADDLE	S-CURVY	S-INKER
S-AILED	S-EARED	S-INNER
S-ALLOW	S-EATER	S-KIDDY
S-ALTER	S-EDUCE	S-KITED
S-AMPLE	S-ELECT	S-LAKED
S-AVANT	S-ENDER	S-LATER
S-AWING	S-ENTRY	S-LAYER
S-AXMAN	S-EXIST	S-LEDGE
S-AXMEN	S-HANDY	S-LIGHT
S-CABBY	S-HARPY	S-LIMED
S-CARED	S-HAVEN	S-LOPED
S-CATTY	S-HAVER	S-LOWER
S-COPED	S-HEATH	S-LOWLY
S-CORED	S-HIRED	S-LURVE
S-CRAWL	S-HOVED	S-MIDGE
S-CREAM	S-HOVEL	S-MILER
S-CREED	S-HOVER	S-MITER
S-CRIED	S-ICKER	S-MOGGY
S-CRIMP	S-ICKLE	S-NAKED

S-NAPPY
S-NATCH
S-NIFFY
S-NITTY
S-NOOSE
S-OAKED
S-OARED
S-OFTEN
S-OILED
S-OLDER
S-OMBRE
S-OUGHT
S-OUPED
S-OWING
S-PACED
S-PARED
S-PARKY
S-PARSE

S-PAYED
S-PIKER
S-PINED
S-POKED
S-PORED
S-POTTY
S-PRINT
S-QUASH
S-TABLE
S-TARRY
S-TENCH
S-TICKY
S-TILED
S-TINGE
S-TITCH
S-TONED
S-TOWED
S-TRAIN

S-TRIKE
S-TRIPE
S-TROLL
S-TROVE
S-TRUCK
S-TUBBY
S-UNDER
S-UNLIT
S-UPPER
S-URGED
S-WAGER
S-WALLY
S-WAYED
S-WEARY
S-WEEPY
S-WIPED
S-WITCH
S-WOOSH

Six letters to seven

S-ADDLED
S-AILING
S-ALLIED
S-AMPLER
S-CABBED
S-CAMPER
S-CANNED
S-CANTER
S-CARING
S-CARPER
S-COFFER
S-COLDER
S-COOPER
S-COOTER
S-COPING
S-CORING

S-CORNED
S-CORNER
S-CRUMMY
S-CUDDLE
S-CUFFED
S-CUPPER
S-CUTTLE
S-EATING
S-EDUCED
S-ELFISH
S-ENDING
S-HACKED
S-HALLOW
S-HARING
S-HARKED
S-HARPER

S-HATTER
S-HAVING
S-HIPPED
S-HOOTER
S-HOPPED
S-HOVING
S-HUNTED
S-HUSHED
S-INKING
S-KIDDED
S-KILLED
S-KIPPED
S-KIPPER
S-KITING
S-LACKED
S-LAKING

S

S-LAMMED	S-MOCKED	S-TACKED
S-LANDER	S-MOLDER	S-TAGGER
S-LAPPED	S-MOTHER	S-TAKING
S-LASHED	S-MUGGER	S-TALKED
S-LASHER	S-NAGGED	S-TALKER
S-LAYING	S-NAILED	S-TAMPER
S-LEDGED	S-NAPPED	S-TEAMED
S-LEDGER	S-NIPPED	S-TICKER
S-LENDER	S-OILING	S-TICKLE
S-LICKED	S-PACING	S-TILTED
S-LIMIER	S-PANNER	S-TINGED
S-LINGER	S-PARING	S-TINKER
S-LINKED	S-PARKED	S-TONING
S-LITHER	S-PARSER	S-TOPPED
S-LOGGED	S-PATTER	S-TUMBLE
S-LOPING	S-PAWNED	S-UNLESS
S-LOWEST	S-PAYING	S-UNLIKE
S-LUGGED	S-PLAYED	S-URGING
S-LUMBER	S-PONGED	S-WAGGER
S-LUMPED	S-POOLED	S-WALLOW
S-LUSHED	S-PORTED	S-WARMED
S-MASHED	S-POTTED	S-WAYING
S-MATTER	S-PRAYED	S-WEEPER
S-MELLED	S-PURRED	S-WIPING
S-MELTED	S-TABBED	S-WITHER
S-MITTEN	S-TABLED	S-WORDED

Seven letters to eight

S-ADDLING	S-CRUMPLE	S-HARKING
S-ALLOWED	S-CRUNCHY	S-HEARING
S-ALLYING	S-CUFFING	S-HEATHER
S-CANNING	S-CURRIED	S-HILLING
S-CARLESS	S-EDITION	S-HIPPING
S-CRAMMED	S-ELECTED	S-HOCKING
S-CRAWLED	S-HACKING	S-HOOTING
S-CREAMED	S-HACKLED	S-HOPPING

S-HUNTING	S-PARKING	S-TICKLED
S-HUSHING	S-PAWNING	S-TILTING
S-HUTTING	S-PEAKING	S-TOPPING
S-KIDDING	S-PILLAGE	S-TOWAWAY
S-KILLING	S-PILLING	S-TRAINED
S-KINLESS	S-PINNING	S-TRAPPED
S-KIPPING	S-PITTING	S-TRESSED
S-LACKING	S-PLATTER	S-TRIDENT
S-LAPPING	S-PLAYING	S-TRIMMED
S-LASHING	S-POOLING	S-TRIPPED
S-LIGHTLY	S-PORTING	S-TRUMPET
S-LOWDOWN	S-POTTING	S-TUMBLED
S-LOWNESS	S-PRAYING	S-UNBAKED
S-LUGGING	S-PRINTED	S-UNBLOCK
S-MASHING	S-QUASHED	S-WADDLED
S-MELTING	S-TABBING	S-WARMING
S-MOOCHED	S-TABLING	S-WEARIER
S-MOULDER	S-TACKING	S-WEEPING
S-NAPPING	S-TAKEOUT	S-WILLING
S-NIPPING	S-TALKING	S-WINGING
S-OFTENER	S-TEAMING	S-WORDING
S-PANNING	S-TICKING	

Some end-hooks

Two letters to three

AA-S	AT-S	EA-S
AB-S	AY-S	ED-S
AD-S	BA-S	EF-S
AG-S	BE-S	EH-S
AH-S	BI-S	EL-S
AI-S	BO-S	EM-S
AL-S	BY-S	EN-S
AN-S	DA-S	ER-S
AR-S	DI-S	ES-S
AS-S	DPO-S	FA-S

S

FE-S	MI-S	PO-S
GI-S	MO-S	QI-S
GO-S	MU-S	RE-S
GU-S	NA-S	SI-S
HA-S	NO-S	SO-S
HE-S	NU-S	TA-S
HI-S	NY-S	TE-S
HO-S	OB-S	TI-S
ID-S	OD-S	UG-S
IF-S	OE-S	UM-S
IN-S	OH-S	UN-S
IO-S	OI-S	UP-S
IT-S	OM-S	UT-S
KA-S	ON-S	WO-S
KI-S	OO-S	XI-S
KO-S	OP-S	YA-S
LA-S	OR-S	YE-S
LI-S	OU-S	YO-S
LO-S	OY-S	YU-S
MA-S	PA-S	ZA-S
ME-S	PE-S	ZO-S
MI-S	PI-S	

S

BLOCKERS

It is useful to know which words are blockers and can't therefore be extended before or after. You may want to play a blocker that your opponent can't extend, or you may want to avoid playing a blocker because you want to keep the board open.

The three-letter blockers beginning with S

SAE	SIX	SOX
SAZ	SLY	SOZ
SEZ	SMA	SWY

Some four-letter blockers beginning with S

SAFT	SESH	SOON
SAGY	SEWN	SPED
SASH	SEXY	SPRY
SAWN	SHOD	SUCH
SCRY	SIZY	SUNG
SECO	SJOE	SUSS
SEEN	SOHO	SWUM
SEIK	SOME	

Some five-letter blockers beginning with S
(except words ending in '-ED', '-J', '-S', '-X', '-Y' or '-Z')

SAFER	SLAIN	STASH
SANER	SLASH	STEPT
SCAND	SLEPT	STOOD
SHALT	SLIPT	STUDE
SHAWN	SLUNG	STUNG
SHERE	SLUNK	STUNK
SHEWN	SLYER	SUPRA
SHOJO	SMASH	SWANG
SHONE	SMOTE	SWAPT
SHORN	SMUSH	SWARE
SHOWN	SNUCK	SWEPT
SHUSH	SOCKO	SWOPT
SIKER	SORBO	SWORE
SINCE	SORER	SWORN
SITKA	SPAKE	SWUNG
SKEEF	SPENT	SYKER
SKINT	STAID	

S

Some six-letter blockers ending with S
(except words ending in '-ED', '-J', '-S', '-X', '-Y' or '-Z')

SADDER	SAGEST	SAMIER
SAFEST	SAGIER	SANCTA
SAFING	SAIRER	SANEST

SANING	SHYISH	SPOILT
SAPEGO	SICKER	SPOKEN
SAPFUL	SINFUL	SPRUNG
SATING	SKEIGH	SPRYER
SAYEST	SKOOSH	STALER
SCOOCH	SKYING	STINKO
SCOOSH	SKYLIT	STITCH
SCORCH	SLIEST	STOBIE
SCOTCH	SLOWER	STOLEN
SEARCH	SLYEST	STREWN
SEARER	SLYISH	STRODE
SEDENT	SMOOSH	STRONG
SELDOM	SNIDER	STRUCK
SEMPER	SOAKEN	STRUNG
SEXIER	SOBFUL	SUABLE
SHAKEN	SOFTER	SUAVER
SHARON	SOLEMN	SUBSEA
SHAVEN	SOLGEL	SUNKEN
SHAZAM	SOLING	SUNLIT
SHOULD	SORDID	SUPERB
SHRANK	SOREST	SURBET
SHREWD	SOUGHT	SUREST
SHRUNK	SOURER	SWOOSH
SHYEST	SPEECH	
SHYING	SPLOSH	

S

Handy Hint: Saving the S for last

If you can earn at least 10 points more by playing the S
then do so, otherwise consider holding it back as an
investment for better scores later in the game. More
experienced players tend to save S tiles instead of
playing them immediately. This is because S is easy to
play at the end of a six-letter word, thus making it
much easier to score a 50-point bonus word by using
all your tiles in one go.

Some words beginning with SEA-

Seven-letter words

SEA-BANK	SEA-FOWL	SEA-PORT
SEA-BEDS	SEA-GULL	SEA-SICK
SEA-BIRD	SEA-HAWK	SEA-SIDE
SEA-DOGS	SEA-LIFT	SEA-WALL
SEA-FOAM	SEA-LINE	SEA-WARD
SEA-FOLK	SEA-MAID	SEA-WEED
SEA-FOOD	SEA-MING	

Eight-letter words

S

SEA-BEACH	SEA-GOING	SEA-SCOUT
SEA-BOARD	SEA-GRASS	SEA-SHELL
SEA-BORNE	SEA-HORSE	SEA-SHORE
SEA-COAST	SEA-HOUND	SEA-SPEAK
SEA-CRAFT	SEA-MANLY	SEA-TRAIN
SEA-DROME	SEA-MOUNT	SEA-TROUT
SEA-FARER	SEA-PLANE	SEA-WATER
SEA-FLOOR	SEA-QUAKE	SEA-WEEDY
SEA-FRONT	SEA-SCAPE	

Some words beginning with SUB-

Seven-letter words

SUB-AQUA	SUB-ITEM	SUB-TASK
SUB-ARID	SUB-JOIN	SUB-TEND
SUB-ATOM	SUB-LETS	SUB-TEXT
SUB-BASS	SUB-MISS	SUB-TONE
SUB-CELL	SUB-PLOT	SUB-TYPE
SUB-CODE	SUB-RENT	SUB-UNIT
SUB-CULT	SUB-RULE	SUB-URBS
SUB-DUCE	SUB-SECT	SUB-VERT
SUB-DUED	SUB-SETS	SUB-WAYS
SUB-DUES	SUB-SIDE	SUB-ZERO
SUB-EDIT	SUB-SIST	
SUB-FILE	SUB-SOIL	

Eight-letter words

SUB-ADULT	SUB-HUMAN	SUB-SPACE
SUB-AGENT	SUB-INDEX	SUB-STAGE
SUB-BASIN	SUB-LEASE	SUB-STATE
SUB-CHORD	SUB-LEVEL	SUB-TITLE
SUB-CLAIM	SUB-MERGE	SUB-TOPIC
SUB-CLASS	SUB-POLAR	SUB-TOTAL
SUB-DUING	SUB-PRIME	SUB-TRACT
SUB-DURAL	SUB-SCALE	SUB-TRADE
SUB-ENTRY	SUB-SENSE	SUB-URBAN
SUB-EQUAL	SUB-SERVE	SUB-URBIA
SUB-FLOOR	SUB-SIDED	SUB-VERSE
SUB-GENRE	SUB-SIDER	SUB-WAYED
SUB-GRADE	SUB-SKILL	SUB-WORLD
SUB-GROUP	SUB-SONIC	

Some words beginning with SUN-

Seven-letter words

SUN-BACK	SUN-BEAM	SUN-BELT
SUN-BAKE	SUN-BEDS	SUN-BURN

SUN-CARE	SUN-LESS	SUN-TANS
SUN-DIAL	SUN-RAYS	SUN-TRAP
SUN-DOWN	SUN-RISE	SUN-WARD
SUN-FISH	SUN-ROOF	SUN-WISE
SUN-HATS	SUN-SETS	
SUN-LAMP	SUN-SPOT	

Eight-letter words

SUN-BAKED	SUN-BURST	SUN-PROOF
SUN-BATHE	SUN-DRESS	SUN-SHADE
SUN-BERRY	SUN-GAZER	SUN-SHINE
SUN-BLOCK	SUN-GLASS	SUN-SHINY
SUN-BURNT	SUN-LIGHT	SUN-SPECS

Some words ending with -SET
Seven-letter words

BACK-SET	HARD-SET	OVER-SET
BONE-SET	HEAD-SET	TOOL-SET
CHIP-SET	LOCK-SET	TWIN-SET
FILM-SET	MIND-SET	TYPE-SET
HAND-SET	MOON-SET	

Eight-letter words

EARTH-SET	QUICK-SET	UNDER-SET
HEAVY-SET	THICK-SET	
PHOTO-SET	THORN-SET	

S

Some words ending with -SHIP
Seven-letter words

AIR-SHIP	KIN-SHIP	SON-SHIP
END-SHIP	MID-SHIP	WAR-SHIP
GOD-SHIP	PAL-SHIP	WOR-SHIP
GUN-SHIP	PRE-SHIP	

Eight-letter words

AMID-SHIP	HARD-SHIP	MOON-SHIP
BARD-SHIP	HEAD-SHIP	POET-SHIP
CLAN-SHIP	HEIR-SHIP	POPE-SHIP
DEAN-SHIP	HERO-SHIP	SERF-SHIP
DUKE-SHIP	KING-SHIP	STAR-SHIP
EARL-SHIP	LADY-SHIP	TANK-SHIP
FIRE-SHIP	LONG-SHIP	TOWN-SHIP
FLAG-SHIP	LORD-SHIP	TWIN-SHIP
FORE-SHIP	MATE-SHIP	WARD-SHIP

Some words ending with -SKIN
Seven-letter words

CAT-SKIN	DOG-SKIN	OIL-SKIN
COW-SKIN	FOX-SKIN	PIG-SKIN
DOE-SKIN	KID-SKIN	

Eight-letter words

BEAR-SKIN	FISH-SKIN	WINE-SKIN
BUCK-SKIN	GOAT-SKIN	WOLF-SKIN
CALF-SKIN	LAMB-SKIN	WOOL-SKIN
CAPE-SKIN	MOLE-SKIN	
DEER-SKIN	SEAL-SKIN	

S

Some words ending with -SOME
Seven-letter words

AIR-SOME	NOI-SOME	WAG-SOME
AWE-SOME	OWN-SOME	WIN-SOME
FUL-SOME	TOY-SOME	WOE-SOME
IRK-SOME	TRI-SOME	
LIS-SOME	TWO-SOME	

Eight-letter words

BORE-SOME	GRUE-SOME	PLAY-SOME
DARK-SOME	HAND-SOME	ROOM-SOME
DOLE-SOME	JOKE-SOME	TEDI-SOME
DUEL-SOME	LARK-SOME	TIRE-SOME
FEAR-SOME	LONE-SOME	TOIL-SOME
FOUR-SOME	LONG-SOME	WORK-SOME
FRET-SOME	LOTH-SOME	YAWN-SOME
GLAD-SOME	LOVE-SOME	
GLEE-SOME	MURK-SOME	

UNUSUAL WORDS FROM OVERSEAS ENGLISH

If you have an awkward combination of letters on your rack then words from overseas English may come in handy. Here are some beginning with S.

Australian words

SANGER	sandwich
SCOZZA	rowdy person
SCUNGY	miserable, sordid or dirty person
SHARPIE	a member of a teenage group with short hair and distinctive clothes
SHERANG	boss
SHYPOO	liquor of poor quality
SITELLA	small black-and-white bird
SMOKO	cigarette break
SPRUIK	speak in public
SWAGMAN	vagrant worker
SWY	a gambling game

S

Canadian words

SKOOKUM	strong or brave
SNYE	side channel of a river

| SPLAKE | hybrid trout bred by Canadian zoologists |
| SWILER | seal hunter |

Hindi words

SAKTI	the wife of a god
SAMBAR	deer with three-tined antlers
SAMITI	polictical association
SAMOSA	triangular pastry containing spiced vegetables or meat
SARANGI	stringed instrument played with a bow
SARDAR	Sikh title
SAROD	Indian stringed instrument
SATSANG	sacred gathering
SWAMI	title for a Hindu saint or religious teacher

New Zealand word

| SHEEPO | person who brings sheep to the catching pen for shearing |

South African words

SCAMTO	argot of South African Blacks
SKOLLY	hooligan
SNOEK	edible marine fish
SPEK	bacon, fat or fatty pork
STEEN	variety of white grape
STOKVEL	savings pool or syndicate

Urdu words

SAHIB	title placed after a man's name
SARPANCH	head of a village council
SHALWAR	loose-fitting trousers
SHIKAR	hunting
SICE	servant who looks after horses

S

Essential info
Value: 1 point
Number in set: 6

T is one of the most common consonants in Scrabble alongside N and R. Four two-letter words begin with T (all scoring 2 points), but they are easy to remember as there is one for every vowel except U. Various useful three-letter words begin with T. Some that you may not know include TAI (a type of sea bream, 3 points), TAO (in Confucian philosophy, the correct course of action, 3 points) and TEF (African grass grown for its grain, 6 points). T is one of the letters of the RETAIN set and is therefore a good letter to keep if trying to get a bonus word.

Two-letter words beginning with T

TA	TI
TE	TO

Some three-letter words beginning with T

TAD	TEE	TIZ
TAE	TEF	TOC
TAI	TEG	TOD
TAJ	TEL	TOG
TAK	TET	TOM
TAM	TEW	TOR
TAO	TEX	TUM
TAT	THO	TUN
TAU	TIC	TUP
TAV	TID	TUT
TAW	TIG	TUX
TAY	TIK	TWP
TEC	TIL	TYE
TED	TIX	

HOOKS

Hooking requires a subtle change in a player's thought process, in that they must look at words already on the board without becoming distracted by their pronunciation. Simple hooking solutions may be overlooked by a player, but things become easier with T as it is one of the most versatile letters when it comes to combining words.

When it comes to end-hooking, players often concentrate on S, as it can be easy to convert a singular word to a plural. However, T can also be

T

highly effective and by learning a few of the hooks below, many more options present themselves to the player.

> **Handy Hint: Consonantitis**
>
> If you are stuck with very few vowels in your rack but you also have a letter T, it is useful to remember that T can form several words using only consonants. These are TSK (a sound uttered in disapproval, 7 points), TWP (a Welsh word meaning stupid, 8 points), TYG (a cup with more than one handle, 7 points), NTH (of an unspecified number), 6 points, and PHT (expression of irritation), 8 points.

Some front-hooks

Two letters to three

T-AB	T-ED	T-OE
T-AD	T-EE	T-OM
T-AE	T-EF	T-ON
T-AG	T-EL	T-OO
T-AI	T-EN	T-OP
T-AM	T-ES	T-OR
T-AN	T-ET	T-OW
T-AP	T-EX	T-OY
T-AR	T-HE	T-UG
T-AS	T-HO	T-UM
T-AT	T-ID	T-UN
T-AW	T-IN	T-UP
T-AX	T-IS	T-UT
T-AY	T-IT	T-WO
T-EA	T-OD	T-YE

T

Three letters to four

T-ABS	T-HAW	T-OWN
T-ACT	T-HEM	T-RAD
T-AIL	T-HEN	T-RAM
T-AKE	T-HEY	T-RAP
T-ALE	T-HIN	T-RAY
T-ALL	T-HIS	T-REM
T-APE	T-HUG	T-RIM
T-ARE	T-ICK	T-RIP
T-ART	T-IDE	T-ROD
T-ASK	T-ILL	T-ROT
T-ATE	T-IRE	T-RUE
T-EAR	T-OFF	T-URN
T-EAT	T-OIL	T-WEE
T-ELL	T-OLD	T-WIG
T-END	T-ONE	T-WIN
T-EST	T-OOT	T-WIT
T-HAN	T-OUR	
T-HAT	T-OUT	

Four letters to five

T-ABLE	T-EPEE	T-IRED
T-ACHE	T-HALE	T-IRES
T-ALKY	T-HANG	T-ITCH
T-ALLY	T-HANK	T-OAST
T-APED	T-HEFT	T-ONER
T-APER	T-HEIR	T-OUCH
T-AUNT	T-HERE	T-OWED
T-AWNY	T-HICK	T-OWER
T-AXED	T-HIGH	T-RACE
T-AXES	T-HING	T-RACK
T-EACH	T-HORN	T-RADE
T-EASE	T-HOSE	T-RAIL
T-EDDY	T-HUMP	T-RAIN
T-EMPT	T-IMID	T-RAIT

T

T-RAMP	T-ROOP	T-WEED
T-RASH	T-ROUT	T-WEEP
T-READ	T-RUCK	T-WEET
T-REES	T-RUER	T-WICE
T-REND	T-RULY	T-WINE
T-RIAL	T-RUST	T-WINY
T-RICK	T-RUTH	T-WIST
T-RIPS	T-WANG	
T-ROLL	T-WEAK	

Five letters to six

T-ABBED	T-ERROR	T-OUTER
T-ABLED	T-ESTER	T-OWING
T-ABLET	T-ETHER	T-RACED
T-AILED	T-HANKS	T-RACER
T-ANGLE	T-HATCH	T-RACES
T-ANNOY	T-HAWED	T-RANCE
T-APING	T-HENCE	T-RAVEL
T-ASKED	T-HORNY	T-RIFLE
T-ASTER	T-HOUGH	T-ROUGH
T-AUGHT	T-ICKLE	T-ROWEL
T-AXING	T-INGLE	T-RUSTY
T-AXMAN	T-INNER	T-UMBLE
T-EARED	T-IRADE	T-URBAN
T-EASED	T-IRING	T-URNED
T-EASER	T-ISSUE	T-WEEDY
T-EASES	T-OASTS	T-WIGGY
T-ENDED	T-OILED	T-WINGE
T-ENDER	T-OTTER	T-WIRED
T-ENURE	T-OUTED	T-WITCH

T

Six letters to seven

T-ABLING	T-ANGLER	T-EASING
T-AILING	T-ASKING	T-EDDIES
T-ALLIED	T-EARFUL	T-ENABLE

287

T-ENDING	T-RACKED	T-ROTTER
T-ENFOLD	T-RAILER	T-ROUBLE
T-ENURED	T-RAINED	T-RUCKED
T-ESTATE	T-RAMPED	T-RUFFLE
T-HANKER	T-RANKED	T-RUSTED
T-HAWING	T-RAPPER	T-UNABLE
T-HEREBY	T-RASHES	T-WEAKER
T-HEREIN	T-RAVELS	T-WIGGED
T-HUMPED	T-REASON	T-WINGED
T-INNING	T-RIFLES	T-WINKLE
T-ISSUED	T-RIGGER	T-WITCHY
T-OILING	T-RILLED	T-WITTER
T-OUTING	T-RIMMED	
T-RACING	T-RIPPED	

Seven letters to eight

T-ALLOWED	T-ISSUING	T-RIPPING
T-ALLYING	T-RACKING	T-ROTTING
T-ANGLING	T-RAILING	T-RUCKING
T-ANNOYED	T-RAINING	T-RUSTING
T-APELIKE	T-RAMMING	T-WEEDIER
T-EARDROP	T-RAMPING	T-WIGLESS
T-EARLIKE	T-RAPPING	T-WINGING
T-ENFOLDS	T-RASHING	T-WINKLED
T-ENTERED	T-RAVELER	T-WINNING
T-HATCHED	T-READING	T-WITCHES
T-HICKIES	T-RIFLING	
T-HUMPING	T-RIMMING	

Some end-hooks
Two letters to three

AI-T	AR-T	BE-T
AL-T	AT-T	BI-T
AN-T	BA-T	BO-T

DI-T	KI-T	OW-T
DO-T	LA-T	PA-T
EA-T	LI-T	PE-T
EF-T	LO-T	PI-T
EL-T	MA-T	PO-T
ES-T	ME-T	RE-T
FA-T	MO-T	SI-T
FE-T	MU-T	SO-T
GI-T	NA-T	TA-T
GO-T	NE-T	TE-T
GU-T	NO-T	TI-T
HA-T	NU-T	TO-T
HE-T	OF-T	WE-T
HI-T	OO-T	WO-T
HO-T	OP-T	YE-T
JO-T	OR-T	
KA-T	OU-T	

Three letters to four

BEE-T	DIE-T	JOL-T
BEN-T	DOL-T	JUS-T
BOA-T	DUE-T	KEP-T
BOO-T	EAS-T	LAS-T
CAN-T	FAS-T	LIN-T
CAR-T	FEE-T	LIS-T
CEL-T	FON-T	LOS-T
CHA-T	FOR-T	LOU-T
CHI-T	GEN-T	MAL-T
COL-T	GIF-T	MAS-T
COO-T	GIS-T	MEL-T
COS-T	GOA-T	MIS-T
CUR-T	GUS-T	MOA-T
DEB-T	HIN-T	MOO-T
DEF-T	HOO-T	MOS-T
DEN-T	HUN-T	MUS-T

T

NEW-T	ROO-T	TIN-T
PAC-T	RUN-T	TOO-T
PAR-T	SAL-T	UNI-T
PAS-T	SEA-T	VAS-T
PES-T	SEN-T	VOL-T
PIN-T	SKI-T	WAI-T
POS-T	SPA-T	WAN-T
RAN-T	SUI-T	WAT-T
RAP-T	TAR-T	WEN-T
REN-T	TAU-T	WHA-T
RES-T	TEN-T	WIS-T
RIF-T	TES-T	ZOO-T

Four letters to five

AVER-T	FEAR-T	OVER-T
BEAU-T	FILE-T	PLAN-T
BLUR-T	FIRS-T	PLEA-T
BOAS-T	FLEE-T	ROOS-T
BOOS-T	GOES-T	SHIR-T
BURN-T	GRAN-T	SHOO-T
CADE-T	GUES-T	SIGH-T
CHAR-T	HEAR-T	SPEC-T
CLEF-T	ISLE-T	SPUR-T
COME-T	JOIN-T	STAR-T
COVE-T	LEAN-T	STUN-T
DEAL-T	LEAP-T	TEMP-T
EVEN-T	MEAN-T	TWEE-T
FACE-T	NIGH-T	VALE-T

Five letters to six

BARES-T	BOUGH-T	DIVER-T
BASAL-T	BUDGE-T	DRIES-T
BASES-T	CACHE-T	FABLE-T
BLUES-T	CLOSE-T	FILLE-T
BONNE-T	COVER-T	FINES-T

FORES-T   LOCUS-T   SAFES-T
FORGE-T   MIDGE-T   SAGES-T
FORGO-T   MODES-T   SHIES-T
GADGE-T   MUTES-T   SONNE-T
GAMES-T   PALES-T   SORES-T
HONES-T   PLANE-T   SPOIL-T
IDLES-T   PURES-T   TURBO-T
LANCE-T   RABBI-T   WEIGH-T
LAXES-T   RARES-T
LEARN-T   RIPES-T

Six letters to seven

ARCHES-T   DEARES-T   ROSIES-T
ARTIES-T   EASIES-T   SINGLE-T
BRAVES-T   FALSES-T   STALES-T
BROUGH-T   GRAVES-T   TENSES-T
BRUTES-T   HOLIES-T   THOUGH-T
BUSIES-T   INANES-T   TIDIES-T
CLOSES-T   LAZIES-T   TINIES-T
CONSUL-T   LUSHES-T   TRITES-T
COSIES-T   NAIVES-T   UGLIES-T
COUPLE-T   NOBLES-T   WARRAN-T
COZIES-T   PERCEN-T   WAVIES-T
CRUDES-T   POSIES-T
CURRAN-T   RICHES-T

Seven letters to eight

ANGRIES-T   CROSSES-T   FEEBLES-T
APPLIES-T   DIPLOMA-T   FLAKIES-T
BAGGIES-T   DIVINES-T   FLASHES-T
BLONDES-T   DIVVIES-T   FRESHES-T
BULLIES-T   DIZZIES-T   FUNNIES-T
CHOICES-T   EARLIES-T   GENTLES-T
CONTRAS-T   EMPTIES-T   HARDIES-T
CRAZIES-T   FAIRIES-T   HEAVIES-T

INTERNE-T	REGIMEN-T	SQUARES-T
JOLLIES-T	REMOTES-T	STABLES-T
LITTLES-T	ROOMIES-T	SUNBURN-T
LUCKIES-T	ROWDIES-T	SUNNIES-T
MATURES-T	SAVAGES-T	TALKIES-T
MUDDIES-T	SECURES-T	TELETEX-T
NASTIES-T	SHIPMEN-T	TINNIES-T
READIES-T	SILLIES-T	UNLEARN-T
REDREAM-T	SIMPLES-T	WEARIES-T

BLOCKERS

It is useful to know which words are blockers and can't therefore be extended before or after. You may want to play a blocker that your opponent can't extend, or you may want to avoid playing a blocker because you want to keep the board open.

The three-letter blockers beginning with T

TAJ	TIX	TWP
THY	TUX	

Some four-letter blockers beginning with T

TALI	THIS	TOED
THAE	THUS	TOHO
THAT	TIDY	TOLD
THEY	TINY	TORN

Some five-letter blockers beginning with T
(except words ending in '-ED', '-J', '-S', '-X', '-Y' or '-Z')

TACIT	TEACH	THAIM
TAKEN	TEUCH	THIEF
TAULD	TEUGH	THINE

T

| THOSE | TIDAL | TONKA |
| THRAE | TIMID | TRUER |

Some six-letter blockers beginning with T
(except words ending in '-ED', '-J', '-S', '-X', '-Y' or '-Z')

TAIHOA	TERGAL	TOMPOT
TALLER	THRESH	TREIFA
TAMEST	THRICE	TRENCH
TAUGHT	THROWN	TRUEST
TENSER	TINIER	TUBATE
TERAPH	TOMATO	

BONUS WORDS

Bonus words on your rack can be hard to spot, especially for the less experienced player. One way to help find them is by using prefixes and suffixes.

Many larger words include a common prefix or suffix – remembering these and using them where you can is a good way to discover any longer words on your rack, including any potential bonus words. The key prefix to remember beginning with T is TRI- and the key suffixes are -TION and -TIME.

T

Some words beginning with TRI-
Seven-letter words

TRI-ABLE	TRI-CEPS	TRI-DENT
TRI-ACID	TRI-CITY	TRI-DUAN
TRI-ACTS	TRI-CLAD	TRI-FOLD
TRI-ARCH	TRI-CORN	TRI-FORM
TRI-AXON	TRI-COTS	TRI-GAMY
TRI-CARS	TRI-DARN	TRI-GONS

TRI-GRAM   TRI-ODES   TRI-SEME
TRI-JETS   TRI-OXID   TRI-SHAW
TRI-LITH   TRI-PACK   TRI-SOME
TRI-LOBE   TRI-PART   TRI-SOMY
TRI-LOGY   TRI-PODS   TRI-TONE
TRI-NARY   TRI-SECT   TRI-ZONE

Eight-letter words

TRI-ACIDS   TRI-FOCAL   TRI-PEDAL
TRI-ACTOR   TRI-GLYPH   TRI-PHASE
TRI-ANGLE   TRI-GRAMS   TRI-PHONE
TRI-AXIAL   TRI-GRAPH   TRI-PLANE
TRI-AXONS   TRI-LEMMA   TRI-PODAL
TRI-AZINE   TRI-LITHS   TRI-POSES
TRI-AZOLE   TRI-LOBED   TRI-SECTS
TRI-BASIC   TRI-LOBES   TRI-SEMES
TRI-BRACH   TRI-METER   TRI-SHAWS
TRI-CHORD   TRI-MIXES   TRI-STATE
TRI-CLADS   TRI-MORPH   TRI-STICH
TRI-COLOR   TRI-MOTOR   TRI-TONES
TRI-CORNS   TRI-NODAL   TRI-UNITY
TRI-CYCLE   TRI-OLEIN   TRI-VALVE
TRI-DARNS   TRI-OXIDE   TRI-ZONAL
TRI-DENTS   TRI-OXIDS   TRI-ZONES
TRI-ETHYL   TRI-PACKS

T

Some words ending with -TIME
Seven-letter words

AIR-TIME   DAY-TIME   PAS-TIME
ANY-TIME   LAY-TIME   RAG-TIME
BED-TIME   MIS-TIME   TEA-TIME
BIG-TIME   ONE-TIME   WAR-TIME

Eight-letter words

CALL-TIME	LIFE-TIME	REAL-TIME
CHOW-TIME	LONG-TIME	SEED-TIME
DOWN-TIME	MARI-TIME	SHIP-TIME
FACE-TIME	MEAL-TIME	SHOW-TIME
FLEX-TIME	MEAN-TIME	SOME-TIME
FORE-TIME	NOON-TIME	TALK-TIME
GOOD-TIME	OVER-TIME	TERM-TIME
HALF-TIME	PLAY-TIME	ZONE-TIME

Some words ending with -TION

Seven-letter words

ALA-TION	ELU-TION	PAC-TION
AMA-TION	EMO-TION	POR-TION
AMO-TION	EMP-TION	REC-TION
AUC-TION	ENA-TION	RUC-TION
CAN-TION	FAC-TION	SEC-TION
CAP-TION	FIC-TION	STA-TION
CAU-TION	LEC-TION	SUC-TION
COC-TION	MEN-TION	TAC-TION
COI-TION	MIC-TION	TUI-TION
DIC-TION	MIX-TION	UNC-TION
EDI-TION	ORA-TION	UNI-TION
ELA-TION	OVA-TION	

Eight-letter words

ABLA-TION	AERA-TION	CITA-TION
ABLU-TION	AGNA-TION	COAC-TION
ABOR-TION	AMBI-TION	CONA-TION
ADAP-TION	AUDI-TION	COOP-TION
ADDI-TION	AVIA-TION	CREA-TION
ADNA-TION	BIBA-TION	CURA-TION
ADOP-TION	CIBA-TION	DELA-TION

T

DELE-TION	HIMA-TION	OBLA-TION
DEMO-TION	IDEA-TION	PACA-TION
DERA-TION	IGNI-TION	PETI-TION
DEVO-TION	ILLA-TION	POSI-TION
DILA-TION	INAC-TION	POTA-TION
DILU-TION	INUS-TION	PUNI-TION
DONA-TION	IODA-TION	PUPA-TION
DOTA-TION	JOBA-TION	QUES-TION
DURA-TION	JUNC-TION	REAC-TION
EDUC-TION	LAVA-TION	RELA-TION
EGES-TION	LEGA-TION	REMO-TION
EJEC-TION	LENI-TION	ROGA-TION
ELEC-TION	LIBA-TION	ROTA-TION
EMIC-TION	LIGA-TION	SANC-TION
ENAC-TION	LIMA-TION	SCON-TION
EQUA-TION	LOBA-TION	SEDA-TION
EREC-TION	LOCA-TION	SEDI-TION
ERUP-TION	LOCU-TION	SOLA-TION
EVEC-TION	LUNA-TION	SOLU-TION
EVIC-TION	LUXA-TION	SORP-TION
EXAC-TION	MONI-TION	STIC-TION
EXER-TION	MUNI-TION	SUDA-TION
FETA-TION	MUTA-TION	SWAP-TION
FIXA-TION	NATA-TION	TAXA-TION
FLEC-TION	NEGA-TION	TRAC-TION
FRAC-TION	NIDA-TION	VACA-TION
FRIC-TION	NIVA-TION	VENA-TION
FRUI-TION	NODA-TION	VEXA-TION
FUNC-TION	NOLI-TION	VOCA-TION
GELA-TION	NOTA-TION	VOLI-TION
GUMP-TION	NOVA-TION	VOLU-TION
HALA-TION	NUTA-TION	ZONA-TION

T

UNUSUAL WORDS FROM OVERSEAS ENGLISH

If you have an awkward combination of letters on your rack then words from overseas English may come in handy. Here are some beginning with T.

Australian words

TOOSHIE	angry or upset
TRIELLA	three horse races nominated for a bet
TROPPO	mentally affected by a tropical climate
TRUCKIE	truck driver
TRUGO	game similar to croquet
TUAN	flying phalanger
TUART	type of eucalyptus tree

Canadian words

TILLICUM	friend
TOONIE	Canadian two-dollar coin
TULLIBEE	whitefish found in the Great Lakes
TUPEK	Inuit tent of animal skins
TURR	the guillemot

Hindi words

TABLA	pair of drums whose pitches can be varied
THALI	meal consisting of several small dishes
TOLA	unit of weight
TONGA	light two-wheeled vehicle
TOPEE	pith helmet

New Zealand words

TAIAHA	ceremonial fighting staff
TAIHOA	hold on!

TAKAHE	rare flightless bird
TANGI	Maori funeral ceremony
TANIWHA	legendary monster
TAONGA	treasure
TAPU	sacred or forbidden
TAUIWI	non-Maori people of New Zealand
TIKANGA	Maori customs
TOETOE	type of tall grass
TOITOI	type of tall grass
TWINK	white correction fluid

Urdu words

TAHSIL	administrative division
TALOOKA	subdivision of a district
TAMASHA	show or entertainment

T

Essential info
Value: 1 point
Number in set: 4

U can be a difficult tile to play as it doesn't go well with most other letters and there are very few good-scoring short words which start with U. In order to make the best of your tiles, some handy words to remember are UH (5 points), UM (4 points), UP (4 points) and UG (3 points). It is worth noting the three-letter words that enable you to dump two Us in one play: ULU, UMU and UTU.

Two-letter words beginning with U

UG	UN	US
UH	UP	UT
UM	UR	

Some three-letter words beginning with U

UDO	UMU	URE
UGH	UNI	URP
ULU	UPO	UTA
UMM	URB	UTE
UMP	URD	UTU

HOOKS

Hooking requires a subtle change in a player's thought process, in that they must look at words already on the board without becoming distracted by their pronunciation.

Some front-hooks

Two letters to three

U-DO	U-PO	U-TE
U-MM	U-RE	
U-MU	U-TA	

Three letters to four

U-DAL	U-NIS	U-SER
U-DON	U-NIT	U-TIS
U-LES	U-PAS	U-VAE
U-LEX	U-SED	U-VAS

U

Four letters to five

U-LAMA	U-RASE	U-RITE
U-NARY	U-RATE	U-SAGE
U-NITE	U-REAL	U-SING
U-PEND	U-REDO	U-SURE
U-PLAY	U-RENT	U-TILE
U-PLED	U-RIAL	U-VEAL
U-RARE	U-RINE	

Five letters to six

U-LEXES	U-PLEAD	U-REDIA
U-LOSES	U-PLINK	U-SABLE
U-NEATH	U-PLOOK	U-SAGER
U-NITER	U-PRATE	U-SAGES
U-NOWED	U-PREST	U-SURED
U-PASES	U-PRISE	U-SURER
U-PHANG	U-PROLL	U-SWARD
U-PLAID	U-PROSE	

Six letters to seven

U-NEARED	U-PLINKS	U-PREACH
U-NEATEN	U-PLYING	U-PRISER
U-PENDED	U-PRAISE	U-REDIAL
U-PLIGHT	U-PRATED	U-SURING

Seven letters to eight

U-PENDING	U-PRAISED	U-PRISING
U-PLAYING	U-PRAISER	U-PROLLED
U-PLINKED	U-PRATING	

U

301

Some end-hooks
Two letters to three

AL-U	KY-U	TA-U
AM-U	LO-U	UM-U
AY-U	ME-U	UT-U
EA-U	MO-U	YO-U
EM-U	PI-U	
FE-U	SO-U	

Three letters to four

AIT-U	KOR-U	RAG-U
BAH-U	LAT-U	RAT-U
BAL-U	LEK-U	RIM-U
BAP-U	LIE-U	SUS-U
BED-U	LIT-U	TAB-U
BUB-U	MAS-U	TAP-U
DOC-U	MEN-U	TAT-U
EME-U	MOT-U	TEG-U
FRA-U	MUM-U	THO-U
FUG-U	NAM-U	TUT-U
GEN-U	PAT-U	VAT-U
GUR-U	PUD-U	WUD-U
HAP-U	PUL-U	
HUH-U	PUP-U	

Four letters to five

U

BANT-U	CORN-U	PARE-U
BATT-U	FOND-U	PEND-U
BITO-U	HAIK-U	PIKA-U
BUCK-U	JAMB-U	PILA-U
BUND-U	KAWA-U	QUIP-U
BUSS-U	LASS-U	TEND-U
CENT-U	MUNT-U	VERT-U

Five letters to six

CONGO-U	HALER-U	MANAT-U

Six letters to seven

MANITO-U	TAMARA-U
SUBMEN-U	TURACO-U

> **Handy Hint: You can use these U words**
>
> UKE (7 points) is a short form of UKULELE (11 points).
> There are not many short high-scoring words
> beginning with U: UKE and UGH (a sound people make
> when they dislike or are disgusted by something) are
> the highest-scoring three-letter words at 7 points
> each, along with UMM and UMP.

BLOCKERS

It is useful to know which words are blockers and can't
therefore be extended before or after. You may want to
play a blocker that your opponent can't extend, or you
may want to avoid playing a blocker because you want
to keep the board open.

The four-letter blockers beginning with U

UPGO	UPSY	UVAE

U

Some five-letter blockers beginning with U
(except words ending in '-ED', '-J', '-S', '-X', '-Y' or '-Z')

ULPAN	UNDEE	UNDUG
UNAPT	UNDID	UNGOT
UNBID	UNDUE	UNHIP

UNMET	UPLIT	URNAL
UNRID	UPTER	UTERI
UNWET	URDEE	
UPBYE	UREAL	

Some six-letter blockers beginning with U
(except words ending in '-ED', '-J', '-S', '-X', '-Y' or '-Z')

UBIQUE	UNLAID	UNWELL
ULNARE	UNLASH	UNWISH
ULTIMO	UNLOST	UNWORN
UMBRAL	UNMADE	UPBLEW
UNBENT	UNMEEK	UPDREW
UNBORE	UNMEET	UPGONE
UNCHIC	UNMESH	UPGREW
UNCLAD	UNMIXT	UPGUSH
UNCOOL	UNMOWN	UPHAND
UNCUTE	UNOPEN	UPHELD
UNDEAD	UNPAID	UPHILD
UNDEAR	UNPENT	UPHOVE
UNDONE	UNPURE	UPHUNG
UNDREW	UNREAL	UPLAID
UNEVEN	UNRENT	UPMOST
UNFELT	UNSAID	UPPISH
UNFIRM	UNSAWN	UPROSE
UNFOND	UNSENT	UPRUSH
UNGAIN	UNSEWN	UPSENT
UNHEWN	UNSHOD	UPTOOK
UNHUNG	UNSOLD	UPTORE
UNHURT	UNSPUN	UPTORN
UNIFIC	UNSUNG	UPWENT
UNITAL	UNSUNK	URETIC
UNJUST	UNTOLD	URSINE
UNKEPT	UNTORN	USABLE
UNKIND	UNTROD	

U

Some words beginning with UN-

Seven-letter words

UN-ACTED	UN-BURNT	UN-CORKS
UN-ADDED	UN-CAGED	UN-COUTH
UN-AGING	UN-CANNY	UN-COVER
UN-AIDED	UN-CARED	UN-CUFFS
UN-AIMED	UN-CASED	UN-CURED
UN-AIRED	UN-CHAIN	UN-CURLS
UN-ARMED	UN-CHECK	UN-DATED
UN-AWARE	UN-CITED	UN-DEALT
UN-BAKED	UN-CIVIL	UN-DOERS
UN-BEGUN	UN-CLASP	UN-DOING
UN-BENDS	UN-CLEAN	UN-DRAWN
UN-BINDS	UN-CLEAR	UN-DRESS
UN-BLOCK	UN-CLING	UN-DRUNK
UN-BLOWN	UN-CLIPS	UN-DYING
UN-BOLTS	UN-CLOAK	UN-EAGER
UN-BONED	UN-CLOGS	UN-EARTH
UN-BOUND	UN-CODED	UN-EATEN
UN-BOWED	UN-COILS	UN-ENDED
UN-BOXED	UN-COMFY	UN-EQUAL

U

UN-FAIRS	UN-KNOWN	UN-ROBED
UN-FAKED	UN-LACED	UN-ROLLS
UN-FAZED	UN-LADED	UN-SAFER
UN-FENCE	UN-LATCH	UN-SATED
UN-FILED	UN-LEARN	UN-SAVED
UN-FIRED	UN-LEASH	UN-SCARY
UN-FLUSH	UN-LINED	UN-SCREW
UN-FOLDS	UN-LIVED	UN-SEATS
UN-FORMS	UN-LOADS	UN-SEWED
UN-FOUND	UN-LOCKS	UN-SHELL
UN-FROCK	UN-LOVED	UN-SHOED
UN-FROZE	UN-LUCKY	UN-SHORN
UN-FUNNY	UN-MAKER	UN-SHOWN
UN-FUSSY	UN-MANLY	UN-SIGHT
UN-GAZED	UN-MASKS	UN-SIZED
UN-GLUED	UN-MIXED	UN-SLAIN
UN-GODLY	UN-MORAL	UN-SLUNG
UN-GORED	UN-MOUNT	UN-SNAGS
UN-GREEN	UN-MOVED	UN-SOLID
UN-GROUP	UN-NAMED	UN-SOUND
UN-GROWN	UN-NERVE	UN-SPENT
UN-GUARD	UN-OAKED	UN-SPILT
UN-GULAR	UN-OILED	UN-SPLIT
UN-HANDS	UN-PACKS	UN-SPOOL
UN-HAPPY	UN-PAVED	UN-STACK
UN-HASTY	UN-PICKS	UN-STICK
UN-HEALS	UN-PLACE	UN-STRAP
UN-HEARD	UN-PLUGS	UN-STUCK
UN-HELMS	UN-POSED	UN-STUNG
UN-HINGE	UN-QUIET	UN-SURER
UN-HITCH	UN-QUOTE	UN-TAKEN
UN-HOOKS	UN-RATED	UN-TAMED
UN-HORSE	UN-RAVEL	UN-TAXED
UN-HUMAN	UN-READY	UN-THAWS
UN-KEMPT	UN-RESTS	UN-TILED

U

UN-TIMED	UN-TRUST	UN-WAGED
UN-TIRED	UN-TRUTH	UN-WINDS
UN-TONED	UN-TWIST	UN-WIRED
UN-TRACE	UN-TYING	UN-WISER
UN-TRIED	UN-USUAL	UN-WOUND
UN-TRUER	UN-VEILS	UN-WRAPS

Eight-letter words

UN-ABATED	UN-BUTTON	UN-EARNED
UN-ACTIVE	UN-CALLED	UN-EASIER
UN-AFRAID	UN-CANNED	UN-EASILY
UN-AGEING	UN-CAPPED	UN-EDIBLE
UN-AMUSED	UN-CARING	UN-EDITED
UN-ARGUED	UN-CASTED	UN-ENDING
UN-ARMING	UN-CAUGHT	UN-ENVIED
UN-AVOWED	UN-CHOSEN	UN-ERRING
UN-BAITED	UN-CLENCH	UN-EVENLY
UN-BEARED	UN-CLOTHE	UN-FALLEN
UN-BEATEN	UN-CLUTCH	UN-FAMOUS
UN-BEGGED	UN-COATED	UN-FASTEN
UN-BELIEF	UN-COCKED	UN-FENCED
UN-BIASED	UN-COILED	UN-FILLED
UN-BIDDEN	UN-COMMON	UN-FILMED
UN-BILLED	UN-COOKED	UN-FOLDED
UN-BITTEN	UN-CORKED	UN-FOLLOW
UN-BOLTED	UN-COUPLE	UN-FORCED
UN-BONDED	UN-CUFFED	UN-FORMED
UN-BOOKED	UN-CURLED	UN-FROZEN
UN-BOUGHT	UN-DARING	UN-FURLED
UN-BOWING	UN-DECENT	UN-GAINLY
UN-BRIDLE	UN-DELETE	UN-GENTLE
UN-BROKEN	UN-DENIED	UN-GIVING
UN-BURDEN	UN-DINTED	UN-GUIDED
UN-BURIED	UN-DOCILE	UN-HANDED
UN-BUSIED	UN-DRIVEN	UN-HAPPEN

U

307

UN-HARMED	UN-MENDED	UN-SHAVEN
UN-HEEDED	UN-MOVING	UN-SIGNED
UN-HELPED	UN-NERVED	UN-SOILED
UN-HINGED	UN-OPENED	UN-SOLVED
UN-HOLIER	UN-PACKED	UN-SPOILT
UN-HOOKED	UN-PAIRED	UN-SUBTLE
UN-HORSED	UN-PLAYED	UN-SURELY
UN-IRONED	UN-PRICED	UN-TAPPED
UN-ISSUED	UN-PROVED	UN-THRONE
UN-JAMMED	UN-QUOTED	UN-TIDILY
UN-JOINED	UN-REALLY	UN-TIEING
UN-KINDER	UN-REASON	UN-TITLED
UN-LAWFUL	UN-RESTED	UN-TOWARD
UN-LEADED	UN-RINSED	UN-USABLE
UN-LEARNT	UN-ROLLED	UN-VERSED
UN-LIKELY	UN-SAFELY	UN-VIABLE
UN-LISTED	UN-SALTED	UN-WANTED
UN-LOADED	UN-SAVORY	UN-WARILY
UN-LOCKED	UN-SEATED	UN-WASHED
UN-LOVING	UN-SEEING	UN-WIELDY
UN-MANNED	UN-SEEMLY	UN-WISELY
UN-MARKED	UN-SETTLE	UN-WORTHY
UN-MASKED	UN-SHAKEN	

Some words beginning with UP-

Seven-letter words

UP-ALONG	UP-CYCLE	UP-GROWN
UP-BEATS	UP-DATED	UP-HEAVE
UP-BRAID	UP-DRAFT	UP-HOLDS
UP-BRING	UP-ENDED	UP-LIFTS
UP-CHUCK	UP-FIELD	UP-LOADS
UP-CLOSE	UP-FLUNG	UP-LYING
UP-COMES	UP-FRONT	UP-PINGS
UP-CURVE	UP-GOING	UP-RAISE

UP-RATED	UP-SLOPE	UP-SWELL
UP-REACH	UP-STAGE	UP-SWING
UP-RIGHT	UP-STAIR	UP-TAKEN
UP-RISEN	UP-STAND	UP-TEMPO
UP-RIVER	UP-START	UP-TIGHT
UP-ROOTS	UP-STATE	UP-TOWNS
UP-SCALE	UP-SURGE	UP-TURNS
UP-SKIRT	UP-SWARM	UP-WARDS

Eight-letter words

UP-COMING	UP-LANDER	UP-SIZING
UP-DATING	UP-LIFTED	UP-SPOKEN
UP-DIVING	UP-LINKED	UP-SPRUNG
UP-DOMING	UP-LOADED	UP-STAGED
UP-ENDING	UP-LOOKED	UP-STREAM
UP-FLOWED	UP-MARKET	UP-STROKE
UP-FURLED	UP-RATING	UP-SURGED
UP-GAZING	UP-RISING	UP-TAKING
UP-GRADED	UP-ROARED	UP-THROWN
UP-GROWTH	UP-ROOTED	UP-TURNED
UP-HEAPED	UP-SCALED	
UP-HEAVED	UP-SETTER	

Some words ending with -URE
Seven-letter words

BRAV-URE	FAIL-URE	MEAS-URE
CAPT-URE	FEAT-URE	MIXT-URE
CENS-URE	FISS-URE	NURT-URE
CLOS-URE	FIXT-URE	ORAT-URE
COUT-URE	FLEX-URE	PAST-URE
CULT-URE	GEST-URE	PICT-URE
DENT-URE	LEAS-URE	RAPT-URE
ERAS-URE	LECT-URE	RUPT-URE
FACT-URE	LEIS-URE	SEIS-URE

U

SEIZ-URE	TONS-URE	VERD-URE
STAT-URE	TORT-URE	VULT-URE
TEXT-URE	VENT-URE	

Eight-letter words

ANNEX-URE	DOUBL-URE	MOIST-URE
APERT-URE	EXPOS-URE	PLEAS-URE
ARMAT-URE	FIXAT-URE	PRESS-URE
AVENT-URE	FRACT-URE	PUNCT-URE
BROCH-URE	INSEC-URE	REPOS-URE
COIFF-URE	JUNCT-URE	TAINT-URE
CREAT-URE	LIGAT-URE	TINCT-URE

UNUSUAL WORDS FROM OVERSEAS ENGLISH

If you have an awkward combination of letters on your rack then words from overseas English may come in handy. Here are some beginning with U.

Australian words

UMPIE	umpire
UNCO	awkward or clumsy
UPTA	of poor quality

Hindi word

| URD | bean plant |

U

V
4

Essential info
Value: 4 points
Number in set: 2

It is important to note that there are no two-letter
words with the **V** which can make it a natural blocker,
preventing parallel plays. Generally it is easier to play
the V with vowels, but watch out for some good scoring
in combination with other high-scoring consonants such
as VEX and VOX (13 points), VLY and VOW (9 points),
VUM (8 points). You may be surprised to learn there is
one three-letter word that enables you to use both Vs:
VAV (a Hebrew letter).

Three-letter words beginning with V

VAC	VEE	VOM
VAE	VID	VOR
VAG	VIM	VOX
VAR	VIN	VUG
VAS	VIS	VUM
VAV	VLY	
VAW	VOE	

HOOKS

Hooking requires a subtle change in a player's thought process, in that they must look at words already on the board without becoming distracted by their pronunciation.

Some front-hooks
Two letters to three

V-AE	V-EE	V-OM
V-AG	V-ET	V-OR
V-AN	V-EX	V-OW
V-AR	V-ID	V-OX
V-AS	V-IN	V-UG
V-AT	V-IS	V-UM
V-AW	V-OE	

Three letters to four

V-AIL	V-ANT	V-ELL
V-AIN	V-APE	V-END
V-AIR	V-ARE	V-ERA
V-ALE	V-ARY	V-ERS
V-AMP	V-EGO	V-EST
V-ANE	V-ELD	V-ICE

V

V-IDE	V-ITA	V-OLE
V-IFF	V-LEI	V-ROT
V-ILL	V-LOG	V-ROW
V-IRE	V-OAR	V-UGH

Four letters to five

V-AGUE	V-ERST	V-OARS
V-AIRY	V-ETCH	V-OLES
V-ALES	V-EXED	V-OMER
V-APED	V-EXES	V-OMIT
V-APER	V-IBEX	V-OUCH
V-ARIA	V-ICED	V-OWED
V-ARNA	V-IRED	V-OWER
V-AUNT	V-IRID	V-ROOM
V-EALE	V-ISIT	
V-EERY	V-LIES	

Five letters to six

V-AGILE	V-AUNTY	V-ERVEN
V-AGUED	V-AWARD	V-EXING
V-AILED	V-EALES	V-ICING
V-ALINE	V-EGGED	V-IDIOT
V-ALLEY	V-ELATE	V-IRING
V-AMPED	V-ENDED	V-IZARD
V-APING	V-ENDER	V-ORANT
V-ASTER	V-ENDUE	V-OTARY
V-ATMAN	V-ENTER	V-OWING

Six letters to seven

V-ACUATE	V-ASSAIL	V-ENDING
V-ACUITY	V-AUNTER	V-ENTAIL
V-AILING	V-AUNTIE	V-ESTRAL
V-AIRIER	V-EGGING	V-OCULAR
V-ALGOID	V-ELATED	V-OUCHED
V-AMPING	V-ENATIC	V-ROOMED

V

Seven letters to eight

V-AGILITY	V-ENTAYLE	V-IRIDIAN
V-AIRIEST	V-ERISTIC	V-OTARIES
V-ALLEYED	V-ERMINED	V-OUCHING
V-ENATION	V-ICELESS	V-ROOMING
V-ENOLOGY	V-ICELIKE	

Some end-hooks
Two letters to three

DE-V	LA-V	SO-V
DI-V	NA-V	TA-V
GO-V	PA-V	
GU-V	RE-V	

Three letters to four

CHA-V	DEE-V	MIR-V
CHI-V	ERE-V	PER-V

Four letters to five

GANE-V	OLLA-V	PARE-V

BLOCKERS

It is useful to know which words are blockers and can't therefore be extended before or after. You may want to play a blocker that your opponent can't extend, or you may want to avoid playing a blocker because you want to keep the board open.

V

The three-letter blockers beginning with V

VLY   VOX

The four-letter blockers beginning with V

VAGI	VETO	VIVO
VAIN	VEXT	VIZY
VERA	VIAE	VROT
VERD	VIBS	

> ### Handy Hint: V is for vowels
>
> If you have a V and the board is quite blocked then it is more likely that vowels on your rack, or on the board, will help you out. Look out for plays involving AVA, AVE, OVA, UVA, VAE, VAU (all 6 points). Even if you have two Vs the vowels could rescue you with VIVA VIVE VIVO (all 10 points). There is also VAV (A Hebrew letter, 9 points).

Some five-letter blockers beginning with V
(except words ending in '-ED', '-J', '-S', '-X', '-Y' or '-Z')

VACUA	VENAE	VITAE
VAGAL	VENAL	VIVID
VAIRE	VERRA	VOILA
VALID	VILDE	VOLTA
VAPID	VILLI	VOLTI
VASAL	VIMEN	VOULU
VATIC	VINIC	VULGO
VEHME	VIOLD	
VELUM	VIRID	

Some six-letter blockers beginning with V
(except words ending in '-ED', '-J', '-S', '-X', '-Y' or '-Z')

VACANT	VAINER	VARSAL
VAGILE	VALIUM	VASTER
VAGROM	VALVAL	VEDUTA
VAGUER	VALVAR	VEDUTE

V

315

VENIAL	VILLAE	VISIVE
VERIER	VILLAR	VISTAL
VERMAL	VINEAL	VOLAGE
VERNAL	VINIER	VOLING
VIABLE	VINING	VORANT
VIBIER	VIRENT	VORPAL
VICING	VIRILE	VOSTRO
VIDUAL	VIRING	
VIENNA	VISCID	

UNUSUAL WORDS FROM OVERSEAS ENGLISH

If you have an awkward combination of letters on your rack then words from overseas English may come in handy. Here are some beginning with V.

Australian words

| VEGO | vegetarian |
| VIGORO | women's game similar to cricket |

Hindi words

VAHANA	vehicle in Indian myth
VANDA	type of orchid
VINA	stringed musical instrument

South African words

VLEI	area of marshy ground
VOEMA	vigour or energy
VROU	woman or wife

V

W₄

Essential info
Value: 4 points
Number in set: 2

There are only two two-letter words beginning with **W**:
WE (5 points) and WO (an old-fashioned spelling of
woe, also 5). There are, however, many short,
common-usage words which can return good scores
such as WAX (13 points), WHO (9 points) and WOK
(10 points). The highest-scoring three-letter word
beginning with W is WIZ (short form of wizard, 15 points).

Two-letter words beginning with W

WE   WO

Some three-letter words beginning with W

WAB	WEN	WOP
WAE	WEX	WOT
WAI	WEY	WOW
WAN	WHA	WOX
WAP	WIS	WUS
WAT	WIZ	WUZ
WAW	WOF	WYE
WAZ	WOG	WYN
WEM	WOK	

HOOKS

Hooking requires a subtle change in a player's thought process, in that they must look at words already on the board without becoming distracted by their pronunciation.

Some front-hooks
Two letters to three

W-AB	W-AW	W-HA
W-AD	W-AX	W-HO
W-AE	W-AY	W-IN
W-AG	W-ED	W-IS
W-AI	W-EE	W-IT
W-AN	W-EM	W-OE
W-AR	W-EN	W-OF
W-AS	W-ET	W-ON
W-AT	W-EX	W-OO

W

| W-OP | W-OW | W-US |
| W-OS | W-OX | W-YE |

Three letters to four

W-AAH	W-AVE	W-HIP
W-ADD	W-AWA	W-HIT
W-AFF	W-AWE	W-HOA
W-AFT	W-AWL	W-HOM
W-AGE	W-EAN	W-HOP
W-AID	W-EAR	W-HOT
W-AIL	W-EEK	W-HOW
W-AIN	W-EEL	W-HUP
W-AIR	W-EEN	W-ICE
W-AIT	W-EFT	W-ICH
W-AKE	W-ELD	W-ICK
W-ALE	W-ELK	W-IDE
W-ALL	W-ELL	W-ILL
W-AND	W-ELT	W-IMP
W-ANE	W-END	W-INK
W-ANT	W-ERE	W-INN
W-ANY	W-EST	W-IRE
W-ARB	W-ETA	W-ISH
W-ARD	W-HAE	W-OKE
W-ARE	W-HAM	W-OLD
W-ARK	W-HAP	W-OOF
W-ARM	W-HAT	W-OON
W-ART	W-HEN	W-OOT
W-ARY	W-HET	W-ORD
W-ASH	W-HEW	W-ORE
W-ASP	W-HEY	W-ORT
W-ATE	W-HID	W-RAP
W-ATT	W-HIM	W-REN
W-AUK	W-HIN	W-RIT

W

Four letters to five

W-ADDY	W-HEAT	W-OMEN
W-AGED	W-HEEL	W-OOFY
W-AGER	W-HEFT	W-OOSE
W-AGON	W-HELM	W-OOZY
W-AIDE	W-HELP	W-OULD
W-AKED	W-HERE	W-OVEN
W-ALLY	W-HIPT	W-OWED
W-ANNA	W-HISH	W-OXEN
W-ARED	W-HISS	W-RACK
W-ARTY	W-HIST	W-RANG
W-ASHY	W-HIZZ	W-RAPT
W-ATAP	W-HOLE	W-RAST
W-AVER	W-HOOF	W-RATE
W-AXED	W-HOOP	W-RATH
W-EAVE	W-HOOT	W-REAK
W-ECHT	W-HOPS	W-RECK
W-EDGE	W-HORE	W-REST
W-EDGY	W-HOSE	W-RICK
W-EXED	W-HUMP	W-RING
W-EXES	W-HUPS	W-RITE
W-HACK	W-ICKY	W-ROKE
W-HALE	W-IDES	W-RONG
W-HANG	W-ILLY	W-ROOT
W-HARE	W-INCH	W-ROTE
W-HEAL	W-IRED	W-RUNG
W-HEAR	W-ITCH	

Five letters to six

W-ACKER	W-AGGER	W-AKING
W-ADDED	W-AGING	W-ALLEY
W-ADDER	W-AILED	W-ALLOW
W-ADDLE	W-AIRED	W-AMBLE
W-AFTER	W-AIVER	W-ANGLE

320

W-ANION	W-ENDED	W-IMPED
W-ANKER	W-ESTER	W-INDOW
W-ANKLE	W-ETHER	W-INKED
W-ANTED	W-EXING	W-INKER
W-ARKED	W-HALED	W-INKLE
W-ARMED	W-HALER	W-INNED
W-ARMER	W-HAMMY	W-INNER
W-ARRAY	W-HEELS	W-INTER
W-ASHED	W-HEEZE	W-IRING
W-ASHEN	W-HENCE	W-ISHES
W-ASHES	W-HERRY	W-ITCHY
W-ASTER	W-HEUGH	W-ITHER
W-AUGHT	W-HEWED	W-IZARD
W-AXING	W-HILLY	W-ONNED
W-EANED	W-HINGE	W-ORMER
W-EARED	W-HINNY	W-OUBIT
W-EASEL	W-HIPPY	W-OUNDY
W-EAVED	W-HOLLY	W-OWING
W-EAVES	W-HOOSH	W-RASSE
W-EBBED	W-ICHES	W-RETCH
W-EDGED	W-ICKER	W-RIGHT
W-EIGHT	W-IGGED	
W-ELDER	W-ILLER	

Six letters to seven

W-ADDING	W-ARLING	W-AXLIKE
W-ADDLED	W-ARMING	W-EANING
W-AILING	W-ARRANT	W-EARING
W-AIRING	W-ARTIER	W-EAVING
W-AMBLED	W-ASHERY	W-EBBING
W-ANGLED	W-ASHIER	W-EDGIER
W-ANGLER	W-ASHING	W-EDGING
W-ANTING	W-ASPISH	W-EIGHTY
W-APPEND	W-ASSAIL	W-ELDING
W-ARKING	W-ATTEST	W-ENDING

W

321

W-HACKED	W-HISSED	W-INKING
W-HACKER	W-HISTED	W-INKLED
W-HALING	W-HITHER	W-INNING
W-HAMMED	W-HITTER	W-ITCHED
W-HANGED	W-HIZZED	W-ITCHES
W-HAPPED	W-HOLISM	W-ONNING
W-HEELED	W-HOLIST	W-OOZIER
W-HEELER	W-HOOFED	W-OOZILY
W-HEEZED	W-HOOPED	W-RACKED
W-HELMED	W-HOOPER	W-RANGED
W-HELPED	W-HOOPLA	W-RAPPED
W-HEREAT	W-HOOTED	W-RAPPER
W-HEREBY	W-HOPPED	W-RASSES
W-HEREIN	W-HOPPER	W-RASSLE
W-HEREOF	W-HUMPED	W-REAKED
W-HEREON	W-HUPPED	W-RECKED
W-HERETO	W-IGGING	W-RESTED
W-HETHER	W-ILLEST	W-RESTER
W-HEWING	W-IMPING	W-RICKED
W-HIDDER	W-IMPISH	W-RINGED
W-HINGED	W-IMPLED	W-RINGER
W-HINGER	W-INCHED	W-ROOTED
W-HIPPED	W-INCHER	W-ROUGHT
W-HIPPER	W-INCHES	
W-HISHED	W-INDIGO	

Seven letters to eight

W-ADDLING	W-ARTIEST	W-HAMMING
W-AGELESS	W-ARTLESS	W-HANGING
W-ALLEYED	W-ASHIEST	W-HAPPING
W-ALLOWED	W-ASTABLE	W-HEELING
W-AMBLING	W-EANLING	W-HEEZING
W-ANGLING	W-EASELED	W-HELMING
W-ANTHILL	W-EDGIEST	W-HELPING
W-ARRAYED	W-HACKING	W-HERRIED

W

W-HINGING	W-HOOSHED	W-OULDEST
W-HINNIED	W-HOOSHES	W-RACKFUL
W-HINNIES	W-HOOTING	W-RACKING
W-HIPLIKE	W-HOPPING	W-RANGING
W-HIPPIER	W-HUMPING	W-RAPPING
W-HIPPING	W-HUPPING	W-RASSLED
W-HIPSTER	W-INCHING	W-REAKING
W-HIRLING	W-INDOWED	W-RECKING
W-HISHING	W-INKLING	W-RESTING
W-HISSING	W-IRELESS	W-RETCHED
W-HISTING	W-ITCHIER	W-RICKING
W-HIZZING	W-ITCHING	W-RINGING
W-HOOFING	W-OOFIEST	W-ROOTING
W-HOOPING	W-OOZIEST	

Some end-hooks

Two letters to three

BO-W	KA-W	PO-W
DA-W	KO-W	RE-W
DE-W	LA-W	SO-W
DO-W	LO-W	TA-W
EE-W	MA-W	TE-W
FA-W	ME-W	TO-W
FE-W	MO-W	WO-W
HA-W	NA-W	YA-W
HE-W	NE-W	YE-W
HO-W	NO-W	YO-W
JA-W	PA-W	
JO-W	PE-W	

Three letters to four

ALE-W	AVO-W	CHA-W
ANE-W	BRA-W	CHE-W
ARE-W	BRO-W	ENE-W

FRO-W	SHE-W	THE-W
PRO-W	SKA-W	VIE-W
SHA-W	SPA-W	WHO-W

Four letters to five

BEDE-W	PAWA-W	THRO-W
KOTO-W	PILA-W	VINE-W
NAVE-W	SINE-W	VROU-W
PAPA-W	SYBO-W	

Five letters to six

BARRO-W	MATLO-W	PURSE-W
BURRO-W	MISSA-W	REVIE-W
HALLO-W	MORRO-W	UNCLE-W
HOLLO-W	OUTRO-W	

Six letters to seven

DAYGLO-W

Seven letters to eight

| BUDGERO-W | RICKSHA-W |

> **Handy Hint: Wild words**
>
> Some of the more unusual words beginning with W
> are WAKIKI (Melanesian shell currency, 12 points),
> WAMBLE (move unsteadily, 13 points), WUXIA (genre
> of Chinese fiction and film, concerning the adventures
> of sword-wielding chivalrous heroes, 15 points) and
> WYVERN (heraldic beast having a serpent's tail, a dragon's
> head and a body with wings and two legs, 15 points).

W

BLOCKERS

It is useful to know which words are blockers and can't therefore be extended before or after. You may want to play a blocker that your opponent can't extend, or you may want to avoid playing a blocker because you want to keep the board open.

The three-letter blockers beginning with W

WOX WUZ

The four-letter blockers beginning with W

WAAH	WERE	WIRY
WADY	WERT	WOAH
WANY	WHAE	WOST
WARY	WHOA	WOWF
WAVY	WHOT	WYCH
WAXY	WICH	
WENA	WILY	

Some five-letter blockers beginning with W
(except words ending in '-ED', '-J', '-S', '-X', '-Y' or '-Z')

WANLE	WHIPT	WOWEE
WANNA	WHOSE	WOXEN
WAXEN	WHOSO	WRAPT
WELCH	WIDER	WRATE
WELSH	WILCO	WROTE
WENCH	WINCH	WROTH
WHAMO	WISER	WRUNG
WHICH	WISHT	WRYER
WHILK	WOMEN	

Some six-letter blockers beginning with W
(except words ending in '-ED', '-J', '-S', '-X', '-Y' or '-Z')

WANIER	WHILST	WITHAL
WANKLE	WHITER	WITING
WANNEL	WHOMSO	WOEFUL
WANNER	WHOOSH	WORSER
WARIER	WIDEST	WOWFER
WARING	WIDISH	WOWING
WASHEN	WIFING	WRENCH
WASSUP	WILFUL	WRETCH
WAVIER	WILIER	WROKEN
WAXIER	WIMMIN	WRYEST
WEYARD	WIRIER	WRYING
WHATSO	WISEST	
WHILOM	WISING	

BONUS WORDS

Bonus words on your rack can be hard to spot,
especially for the less experienced player. One way to
help find them is by using prefixes and suffixes.

Many larger words include a common prefix or suffix
– remembering these and using them where you can
is a good way to discover any longer words on your
rack, including any potential bonus words. The key
prefix to remember is WAR- and the key suffixes are
-WARD, -WARDS, -WAY, -WISE, -WOOD, -WORK,
-WORM and -WORT.

Some words beginning with WAR-
Seven-letter words

WAR-BIRD	WAR-DOGS	WAR-GAME
WAR-BOTS	WAR-FARE	WAR-HEAD

WAR-LESS   WAR-PATH   WAR-WORK
WAR-LIKE   WAR-PING   WAR-WORN
WAR-LING   WAR-SHIP   WAR-ZONE
WAR-LOCK   WAR-TIME
WAR-LORD   WAR-WOLF

Eight-letter words

WAR-CRAFT   WAR-GAMED   WAR-MOUTH
WAR-DRESS   WAR-GAMER   WAR-PAINT
WAR-FARED   WAR-HORSE   WAR-PLANE
WAR-FARER   WAR-MAKER   WAR-POWER

Some words ending with -WARD
Seven-letter words

AIR-WARD   LEE-WARD   SKY-WARD
AWK-WARD   NAY-WARD   SUN-WARD
BED-WARD   NOR-WARD   VAN-WARD
FOR-WARD   OUT-WARD   WAY-WARD
HAY-WARD   SEA-WARD   WEY-WARD

Eight-letter words

BACK-WARD   HIND-WARD   REAR-WARD
CITY-WARD   HIVE-WARD   SELF-WARD
DOWN-WARD   HOME-WARD   SIDE-WARD
EAST-WARD   KIRK-WARD   TOWN-WARD
FORE-WARD   LAKE-WARD   WEST-WARD
GOAL-WARD   LAND-WARD   WIND-WARD
HEAD-WARD   LEFT-WARD   WOOD-WARD
HELL-WARD   MOON-WARD   WOOL-WARD

W

Some words ending with -WAY
Seven-letter words

ARCH-WAY   AREA-WAY   BELT-WAY

BIKE-WAY	HALL-WAY	RUNA-WAY
CART-WAY	HEAD-WAY	SHIP-WAY
CUTA-WAY	HIGH-WAY	SIDE-WAY
DOOR-WAY	LANE-WAY	SKID-WAY
DRAG-WAY	LAYA-WAY	SLIP-WAY
FAIR-WAY	LIFE-WAY	SOME-WAY
FARA-WAY	PACK-WAY	TAXI-WAY
FISH-WAY	PARK-WAY	THRU-WAY
FLYA-WAY	PART-WAY	TIDE-WAY
FOLK-WAY	PATH-WAY	TOLL-WAY
FOOT-WAY	RACE-WAY	TOWA-WAY
FREE-WAY	RAIL-WAY	TRAM-WAY
GANG-WAY	RING-WAY	WALK-WAY
GATE-WAY	ROAD-WAY	WIND-WAY
GETA-WAY	RODE-WAY	WIRE-WAY
HADA-WAY	ROLL-WAY	
HALF-WAY	ROPE-WAY	

Eight-letter words

AISLE-WAY	GIVEA-WAY	STAIR-WAY
ALLEY-WAY	GREEN-WAY	STAYA-WAY
BROAD-WAY	GUIDE-WAY	STOWA-WAY
CABLE-WAY	HIDEA-WAY	TAKEA-WAY
CASTA-WAY	HORSE-WAY	TEARA-WAY
CAUSE-WAY	MOTOR-WAY	THATA-WAY
CLEAR-WAY	MULTI-WAY	THISA-WAY
CRAWL-WAY	RIDGE-WAY	TRACK-WAY
CROSS-WAY	RIVER-WAY	TRAIN-WAY
CYCLE-WAY	ROCKA-WAY	UNDER-WAY
DRIVE-WAY	ROLLA-WAY	WALKA-WAY
ENTRY-WAY	ROUTE-WAY	WANTA-WAY
EVERY-WAY	SLIDE-WAY	WASHA-WAY
FADEA-WAY	SOARA-WAY	WASTE-WAY
FLOOD-WAY	SPEED-WAY	WATER-WAY
FOLDA-WAY	SPILL-WAY	

W

Some words ending with -WISE

Seven-letter words

AIR-WISE	END-WISE	MAP-WISE
ANY-WISE	FAN-WISE	SUN-WISE
BIT-WISE	MAN-WISE	TAX-WISE

Eight-letter words

ARCH-WISE	LIKE-WISE	SOME-WISE
BEND-WISE	LONG-WISE	STEP-WISE
CRAB-WISE	PAIR-WISE	SUCH-WISE
DROP-WISE	PLOW-WISE	TEAM-WISE
EDGE-WISE	RING-WISE	TENT-WISE
FLAT-WISE	SIDE-WISE	

Some words ending with -WOOD

Seven-letter words

BAR-WOOD	DOG-WOOD	OAK-WOOD
BAY-WOOD	ELM-WOOD	PLY-WOOD
BOG-WOOD	FUR-WOOD	RED-WOOD
BOW-WOOD	INK-WOOD	SAP-WOOD
BOX-WOOD	LOG-WOOD	
BUD-WOOD	NUT-WOOD	

Eight-letter words

AGAR-WOOD	CORK-WOOD	PINE-WOOD
BACK-WOOD	DEAD-WOOD	ROSE-WOOD
BARN-WOOD	FIRE-WOOD	SOFT-WOOD
BASS-WOOD	FUEL-WOOD	SOUR-WOOD
BEAR-WOOD	HARD-WOOD	TEAK-WOOD
BENT-WOOD	IRON-WOOD	WILD-WOOD
BLUE-WOOD	KING-WOOD	WORM-WOOD
COLT-WOOD	MILK-WOOD	
CORD-WOOD	PEAR-WOOD	

W

Some words ending with -WORK

Seven-letter words

ART-WORK
CUT-WORK
DAY-WORK
LEG-WORK
NET-WORK
NON-WORK

OUT-WORK
PIN-WORK
PRE-WORK
RAG-WORK
RIB-WORK
TIN-WORK

TOP-WORK
TUT-WORK
WAR-WORK
WAX-WORK
WEB-WORK

Eight-letter words

BACK-WORK
BEAD-WORK
BODY-WORK
BOOK-WORK
BUSY-WORK
CAGE-WORK
CASE-WORK
FARM-WORK
FIRE-WORK
FOOT-WORK
FRET-WORK
GOLD-WORK
HACK-WORK

HAIR-WORK
HAND-WORK
HEAD-WORK
HOME-WORK
IRON-WORK
LACE-WORK
LEAD-WORK
LIFE-WORK
MESH-WORK
OPEN-WORK
OVER-WORK
PART-WORK
PILE-WORK

PIPE-WORK
RACK-WORK
ROAD-WORK
ROPE-WORK
SEAT-WORK
STUD-WORK
TASK-WORK
TEAM-WORK
TELE-WORK
TIME-WORK
WIRE-WORK
WOOD-WORK
YARD-WORK

Some words ending with -WORM

Seven-letter words

BAG-WORM
BUD-WORM
CAT-WORM
CUT-WORM
EAR-WORM

EEL-WORM
ICE-WORM
LOB-WORM
LUG-WORM
PIN-WORM

RAG-WORM
SEA-WORM
WAX-WORM
WEB-WORM

Eight-letter words

ARMY-WORM
BOLL-WORM
BOOK-WORM
CASE-WORM
CORN-WORM
FIRE-WORM
FISH-WORM
FLAT-WORM
GLOW-WORM
GRUB-WORM

HAIR-WORM
HOOK-WORM
HORN-WORM
INCH-WORM
LEAF-WORM
LONG-WORM
LUNG-WORM
MEAL-WORM
PILL-WORM
RING-WORM

SAND-WORM
SHIP-WORM
SILK-WORM
SLOW-WORM
TAPE-WORM
TUBE-WORM
WHIP-WORM
WIRE-WORM
WOOD-WORM

Some words ending with -WORT

Seven-letter words

AWL-WORT
BLA-WORT
BUG-WORT
FAN-WORT

FEL-WORT
FIG-WORT
MAD-WORT
MUD-WORT

MUG-WORT
RAG-WORT
RIB-WORT

Eight-letter words

BELL-WORT
COLE-WORT
DAME-WORT
DANE-WORT
DROP-WORT
FLEA-WORT
GOUT-WORT
HONE-WORT

HORN-WORT
LEAD-WORT
LUNG-WORT
MILK-WORT
MODI-WORT
MOON-WORT
MOOR-WORT
PILE-WORT

PILL-WORT
PIPE-WORT
SALT-WORT
SAND-WORT
SOAP-WORT
STAR-WORT
WALL-WORT
WART-WORT

UNUSUAL WORDS FROM OVERSEAS ENGLISH

If you have an awkward combination of letters on your rack then words from overseas English may come in handy. Here are some beginning with W.

Australian words

WADDY	heavy wooden club used by native Australians
WAGGA	blanket made of sacks stitched together
WALLABY	marsupial resembling a small kangaroo
WANDOO	eucalyptus tree with white bark
WARATAH	shrub with dark green leaves and crimson flowers
WARB	dirty or insignificant person
WHARFIE	wharf labourer
WILGA	small drought-resistant tree
WIRILDA	acacia tree with edible seeds
WIRRAH	saltwater fish with bright blue spots
WOOMERA	spear-throwing stick
WURLEY	Aboriginal hut

Canadian words

WAWA	speech or language
WENDIGO	evil spirit or cannibal

Hindi word

WALLAH	person in charge of a specific thing

New Zealand words

WAKA	Maori canoe
WEKA	flightless bird
WERO	warrior's challenge
WETA	long-legged wingless insect
WHANAU	family
WHENAU	native land

W

Essential info
Value: 8 points
Number in set: 1

POWER TILE

X may be the most versatile of the power tiles. It is extremely useful when it comes to parallel plays as it forms a two-letter word with every vowel. The only two valid two-letter words starting with X are XI (14th letter in the Greek alphabet, 9 points) and XU (the Vietnamese unit of currency, also 9 points) and, apart from XIS (plural of XI), the only three-letter word starting with X is XED (crossed out, 11 points). Therefore, you are more likely to be playing the X in words that embed or end in X. There are plenty of examples of three-letter words ending in X listed below.

Two-letter words beginning with X

XI   XU

Three-letter word beginning with X

XED

Some three-letter words using X

AXE	LUX	SIX
BOX	MAX	SOX
COX	MIX	TAX
DEX	MUX	TEX
DUX	NIX	TIX
EXO	NOX	TUX
FAX	OXO	VEX
FIX	OXY	VOX
FOX	PAX	WAX
GOX	PIX	WEX
HEX	POX	WOX
HOX	PYX	YEX
KEX	RAX	ZAX
LAX	REX	ZEX
LEX	SAX	
LOX	SEX	

Some four-letter words using X

Some useful four-letter words you may not know include BRUX (to grind one's teeth, 13 points), NIXY (a female water sprite, 14 points) and WEXE (obsolete form of wax, 14 points).

APEX	BRUX	EAUX
AXED	COAX	EXAM
AXEL	COXA	EXEC
AXIS	CRUX	EXED
AXLE	DEXY	EXIT
AXON	DIXY	EXON
BOXY	DOUX	EXPO

X

FAUX	LANX	PLEX
FIXT	LYNX	POXY
FLAX	MAXI	PREX
FLEX	MINX	ROUX
FLOX	MIXT	SEXT
FLUX	MYXO	SEXY
FOXY	NEXT	TAXA
GREX	NIXY	TAXI
HOAX	ONYX	TEXT
IBEX	ORYX	ULEX
ILEX	OXEN	VEXT
IXIA	OXER	WAXY
JAXY	OXIC	WEXE
JEUX	OXID	XRAY
JINX	OXIM	XYST
JYNX	PIXY	YUNX

HOOKS

Hooking requires a subtle change in a player's thought process, in that they must look at words already on the board without becoming distracted by their pronunciation.

Some front-hooks
Two letters to three

X-ED   X-IS

Three letters to four

X-RAY

Four letters to five

X-ERIC   X-YLEM

Five letters to six

X-YLEMS

X

Six letters to seven

X-EROSES   X-EROTIC

Some end-hooks
Two letters to three

BO-X	MI-X	TA-X
DE-X	MU-X	TE-X
FA-X	NO-X	TI-X
GO-X	PA-X	WE-X
HE-X	PI-X	WO-X
HO-X	PO-X	YE-X
LA-X	RE-X	ZA-X
LO-X	SI-X	
MA-X	SO-X	

Three letters to four

APE-X	FLU-X	ONY-X
BRU-X	HOA-X	PRE-X
CRU-X	JEU-X	ULE-X
EAU-X	JIN-X	

Four letters to five

BEAU-X	LATE-X	SILE-X
BORA-X	LIMA-X	SORE-X
CAPE-X	LURE-X	TELE-X
CARE-X	MALA-X	THAN-X
CHOU-X	MIRE-X	VIBE-X
CODE-X	MURE-X	VITE-X
FORE-X	PYRE-X	
GALA-X	REDO-X	

X

Five letters to six

ADIEU-X	BOYAU-X	DUPLE-X
BIJOU-X	CARNY-X	NITRO-X

Six letters to seven

BATEAU-X	GATEAU-X	SIMPLE-X
BUREAU-X	MILIEU-X	TRIPLE-X
CADEAU-X	MINIMA-X	
COTEAU-X	RESEAU-X	

Seven letters to eight

BANDEAU-X	FABLIAU-X	PONCEAU-X
BATTEAU-X	JAMBEAU-X	RONDEAU-X
BERCEAU-X	MANTEAU-X	ROULEAU-X
CAMAIEU-X	MORCEAU-X	TABLEAU-X
CHAPEAU-X	NOUVEAU-X	TONNEAU-X
CHATEAU-X	OCTUPLE-X	TRUMEAU-X
COUTEAU-X	PLATEAU-X	

BLOCKERS

It is useful to know which words are blockers and can't therefore be extended before or after. You may want to play a blocker that your opponent can't extend, or you may want to avoid playing a blocker because you want to keep the board open.

Two-letter blocker beginning with X

XU

The five-letter blockers beginning with X

XERIC	XYLIC
XOANA	XYSTI

The six-letter blockers beginning with X

X

XENIAL	XOANON	XYSTOI
XENIUM	XYLOID	

Bonus words

Seven-letter words

XANTHAM	XEROSES	XYLENOL
XANTHAN	XEROSIS	XYLIDIN
XANTHIC	XEROTES	XYLITOL
XANTHIN	XEROTIC	XYLOGEN
XENOPUS	XEROXED	XYLOMAS
XERAFIN	XEROXES	XYLONIC
XERARCH	XERUSES	XYLOSES
XERASIA	XIPHOID	XYSTERS
XEROMAS	XYLENES	

Eight-letter words

XANTHAMS	XENOGAMY	XEROMATA
XANTHANS	XENOGENY	XEROSERE
XANTHATE	XENOLITH	XEROXING
XANTHEIN	XENOPHYA	XYLIDINE
XANTHENE	XENOTIME	XYLITOLS
XANTHINE	XENURINE	XYLOCARP
XANTHINS	XERANSES	XYLOIDIN
XANTHISM	XERANSIS	XYLOLOGY
XANTHOMA	XERANTIC	XYLOMATA
XANTHONE	XERAPHIM	XYLONITE
XANTHOUS	XERAPHIN	XYLOTOMY

X

Essential info
Value: 4 points
Number in set: 2

Y is worth 4 points on its own, making it a tile with good scoring potential. There are four two-letter words beginning with Y using each of the vowels except for I: YA, YE, YO and YU (5 points each). High-scoring three-letter words beginning with Y include YAK (10 points), YEW (9 points) and YOB (8 points). Y is also excellent for end hooking onto nouns for use as adjectives.

Two-letter words beginning with Y

YA	YO
YE	YU

Some three-letter words beginning with Y

YAD	YEH	YOK
YAE	YEP	YOM
YAG	YER	YON
YAH	YEX	YOW
YAM	YEZ	YUG
YAR	YGO	YUK
YAW	YID	YUM
YAY	YIN	YUP
YEA	YOD	

HOOKS

Hooking requires a subtle change in a player's thought process, in that they must look at words already on the board without becoming distracted by their pronunciation.

Some front-hooks
Two letters to three

Y-AD	Y-EH	Y-OD
Y-AE	Y-EN	Y-OM
Y-AG	Y-ER	Y-ON
Y-AH	Y-ES	Y-OS
Y-AM	Y-ET	Y-OU
Y-AR	Y-EX	Y-OW
Y-AS	Y-GO	Y-UG
Y-AW	Y-ID	Y-UM
Y-AY	Y-IN	Y-UP
Y-EA	Y-OB	Y-US

Y

Three letters to four

Y-AFF	Y-EAR	Y-OLD
Y-AGE	Y-EGG	Y-OOF
Y-ALE	Y-ELK	Y-OOP
Y-APP	Y-ELL	Y-ORE
Y-ARD	Y-ELM	Y-OUK
Y-ARE	Y-EST	Y-OUR
Y-ARK	Y-EVE	Y-OWE
Y-ATE	Y-ILL	Y-OWL
Y-AWL	Y-IRK	Y-UKE
Y-AWN	Y-ODE	Y-ULE
Y-EAN	Y-OKE	Y-UMP

Four letters to five

Y-ABBA	Y-CLAD	Y-LIKE
Y-ACCA	Y-COND	Y-MOLT
Y-AGER	Y-DRAD	Y-OGEE
Y-AMEN	Y-EARD	Y-OURN
Y-ARCO	Y-EARN	Y-OWED
Y-AULD	Y-EAST	Y-ULAN
Y-AWED	Y-EVEN	Y-UPON
Y-AWNY	Y-EXED	
Y-BORE	Y-FERE	

Five letters to six

Y-ACKER	Y-BLENT	Y-ESTER
Y-AGGER	Y-BOUND	Y-EUKED
Y-ANKER	Y-BRENT	Y-EXING
Y-ANTRA	Y-CLEPT	Y-ICKER
Y-ARKED	Y-EANED	Y-IRKED
Y-ARROW	Y-EARDS	Y-OWING
Y-AWING	Y-EARLY	Y-OWLED
Y-AWNED	Y-EMMER	Y-OWLER
Y-AWNER	Y-ESSES	Y-PIGHT

Y

| Y-PLAST | Y-SHENT | Y-UMPIE |
| Y-SHEND | Y-UMPED | Y-WROKE |

Six letters to seven

Y-ARKING	Y-EARDED	Y-MOLTEN
Y-AWNERS	Y-EARNED	Y-OWLING
Y-AWNIER	Y-EARNER	Y-PLIGHT
Y-AWNING	Y-EASTED	Y-SLAKED
Y-CLEPED	Y-EUKING	Y-UMPIES
Y-EANING	Y-IRKING	Y-UMPING

Seven letters to eight

Y-ATAGHAN	Y-EANLING	Y-EASTING
Y-AWNIEST	Y-EARDING	Y-OURSELF
Y-BOUNDEN	Y-EARLIES	
Y-CLEEPED	Y-EARNING	

> **Handy Hint: Wise words**
>
> Some useful short high-scoring words beginning with
> Y are YEX (Scots word for hiccup or cough, 13 points),
> YOK (a noisy laugh, 10 points) and YUK (a noise used
> to express disgust or dislike, also 10 points), as well
> as more common words such as YAK and YEW.

Some end-hooks
Two letters to three

AB-Y	DA-Y	GU-Y
AN-Y	DE-Y	HA-Y
AR-Y	DO-Y	HE-Y
BA-Y	FA-Y	HO-Y
BE-Y	FE-Y	JA-Y
BO-Y	GO-Y	JO-Y

Y

KA-Y	NO-Y	ST-Y
LA-Y	ON-Y	TA-Y
LO-Y	OX-Y	TO-Y
MA-Y	PA-Y	WE-Y
MO-Y	SH-Y	YA-Y
NA-Y	SO-Y	

Three letters to four

ACH-Y	COW-Y	GOR-Y
ADD-Y	COX-Y	GUL-Y
AFF-Y	COZ-Y	HER-Y
AIR-Y	DEF-Y	HOM-Y
ALA-Y	DEN-Y	HUG-Y
ALL-Y	DEW-Y	ICK-Y
ARM-Y	DEX-Y	IFF-Y
ARS-Y	DID-Y	ILL-Y
ART-Y	DOG-Y	INK-Y
ASH-Y	DOM-Y	JOE-Y
AWA-Y	DOP-Y	JUD-Y
AWN-Y	DOR-Y	LAC-Y
BOD-Y	DOT-Y	LAD-Y
BOG-Y	EAS-Y	LEV-Y
BON-Y	EEL-Y	LIN-Y
BOX-Y	EGG-Y	LOG-Y
BRA-Y	ELM-Y	MAN-Y
BUR-Y	FAD-Y	MAR-Y
BUS-Y	FOG-Y	MAT-Y
CAG-Y	FOX-Y	MIX-Y
CAN-Y	FRA-Y	MOB-Y
CHA-Y	FUM-Y	MOL-Y
CIT-Y	FUR-Y	MON-Y
COL-Y	GAB-Y	MOP-Y
CON-Y	GAM-Y	NIX-Y
COP-Y	GAP-Y	NOS-Y
COR-Y	GOB-Y	NOW-Y
COS-Y	GOE-Y	OAK-Y

Y

OAR-Y	POS-Y	TIN-Y
OAT-Y	POX-Y	TOD-Y
OBE-Y	PRE-Y	TOE-Y
OFF-Y	PUL-Y	TON-Y
OIL-Y	PUN-Y	TOR-Y
OKA-Y	QUA-Y	TOW-Y
OLD-Y	RIM-Y	TUN-Y
ORB-Y	RUB-Y	TWA-Y
OWL-Y	RUD-Y	UPS-Y
PAC-Y	SAG-Y	VAR-Y
PAL-Y	SHA-Y	VIN-Y
PAT-Y	SPA-Y	WAD-Y
PIN-Y	SUM-Y	WAN-Y
PIP-Y	TAK-Y	WAR-Y
PIT-Y	TED-Y	WAX-Y
PIX-Y	THE-Y	WIN-Y
POL-Y	TID-Y	YUK-Y

Four letters to five

ACID-Y	BEAK-Y	BOTH-Y
AGON-Y	BEAN-Y	BRIN-Y
ANNO-Y	BEEF-Y	BUFF-Y
ANTS-Y	BEER-Y	BULK-Y
ARTS-Y	BELL-Y	BULL-Y
AUNT-Y	BEND-Y	BUMP-Y
BALD-Y	BIFF-Y	BUNG-Y
BALM-Y	BILL-Y	BUNN-Y
BAND-Y	BING-Y	BUNT-Y
BARB-Y	BITS-Y	BURL-Y
BARK-Y	BLOW-Y	BURR-Y
BARM-Y	BLUE-Y	BUSH-Y
BARN-Y	BONE-Y	BUSK-Y
BASS-Y	BOOK-Y	BUST-Y
BATT-Y	BOOM-Y	BUTT-Y
BAWD-Y	BOOT-Y	BUZZ-Y
BEAD-Y	BOSS-Y	CAGE-Y

CAKE-Y	DICK-Y	FOAM-Y
CALM-Y	DILL-Y	FOLK-Y
CAMP-Y	DING-Y	FOOD-Y
CARB-Y	DINK-Y	FOOT-Y
CARN-Y	DIRT-Y	FORA-Y
CARR-Y	DISH-Y	FORK-Y
CASK-Y	DITT-Y	FORT-Y
CHEW-Y	DITZ-Y	FULL-Y
CLUE-Y	DOLL-Y	FUNK-Y
COAL-Y	DOOM-Y	FUSS-Y
COCK-Y	DOPE-Y	FUZZ-Y
CONE-Y	DORK-Y	GAME-Y
CONK-Y	DOWD-Y	GASP-Y
COOK-Y	DOWN-Y	GAUD-Y
COPS-Y	DUCK-Y	GAWK-Y
CORE-Y	DUMP-Y	GEEK-Y
CORK-Y	DUNG-Y	GERM-Y
CORN-Y	DUSK-Y	GILL-Y
COSE-Y	DUST-Y	GIMP-Y
COVE-Y	EARL-Y	GINN-Y
COZE-Y	EBON-Y	GIPS-Y
CULT-Y	EMPT-Y	GIRL-Y
CURL-Y	EVER-Y	GLUE-Y
CURR-Y	FAIR-Y	GOLD-Y
CUSH-Y	FAWN-Y	GOOD-Y
CUSP-Y	FELT-Y	GOOF-Y
CUTE-Y	FIER-Y	GOOS-Y
DAFF-Y	FILL-Y	GOTH-Y
DAIS-Y	FILM-Y	GOUT-Y
DAMP-Y	FISH-Y	GRAV-Y
DEAR-Y	FIST-Y	GRIM-Y
DECO-Y	FIZZ-Y	GRIP-Y
DEED-Y	FLAK-Y	GULL-Y
DEIF-Y	FLAM-Y	GUNG-Y
DELL-Y	FLAX-Y	GUNK-Y
DICE-Y	FLUE-Y	GUSH-Y

Y

GUST-Y	JIVE-Y	MEAN-Y
GUTS-Y	JOCK-Y	MEAT-Y
GYPS-Y	JOKE-Y	MELT-Y
HAIL-Y	JOLL-Y	MERC-Y
HAIR-Y	JOWL-Y	MESS-Y
HAND-Y	JUMP-Y	MIFF-Y
HANK-Y	JUNK-Y	MILK-Y
HARD-Y	KELP-Y	MINT-Y
HARP-Y	KICK-Y	MISS-Y
HAST-Y	KISS-Y	MIST-Y
HEAD-Y	KOOK-Y	MOLD-Y
HEFT-Y	LACE-Y	MOOD-Y
HERB-Y	LAIR-Y	MORA-Y
HILL-Y	LARD-Y	MOSS-Y
HISS-Y	LEAF-Y	MUCK-Y
HOAR-Y	LEAK-Y	MUMM-Y
HOKE-Y	LEER-Y	MUMS-Y
HOLE-Y	LEFT-Y	MURK-Y
HOME-Y	LIME-Y	MUSH-Y
HONE-Y	LOAM-Y	MUSK-Y
HONK-Y	LOFT-Y	NARK-Y
HOOD-Y	LOLL-Y	NEED-Y
HOOK-Y	LOOK-Y	NERD-Y
HORN-Y	LOON-Y	NIFF-Y
HUFF-Y	LOOP-Y	NOSE-Y
HULK-Y	LORD-Y	PACE-Y
HUNK-Y	LOUS-Y	PALL-Y
HUSK-Y	LOVE-Y	PALM-Y
HUSS-Y	LUCK-Y	PANS-Y
IRON-Y	LUMP-Y	PARK-Y
ITCH-Y	LUST-Y	PART-Y
JAKE-Y	MALT-Y	PAST-Y
JAZZ-Y	MANG-Y	PATS-Y
JELL-Y	MASH-Y	PEAK-Y
JERK-Y	MATE-Y	PEAT-Y
JIFF-Y	MEAL-Y	PERK-Y

Y

346

PHON-Y	ROPE-Y	TEEN-Y
PICK-Y	RUST-Y	TELL-Y
PINE-Y	SALT-Y	TEST-Y
PINK-Y	SAME-Y	TILL-Y
PITH-Y	SAND-Y	TIPS-Y
PLUM-Y	SASS-Y	TOAD-Y
POKE-Y	SCAR-Y	TOFF-Y
POLL-Y	SEAM-Y	TOWN-Y
PONG-Y	SEED-Y	TWIN-Y
POOP-Y	SHAD-Y	UNIT-Y
PORK-Y	SHIN-Y	VAMP-Y
POSE-Y	SHOW-Y	VEIN-Y
PROS-Y	SICK-Y	VIBE-Y
PUFF-Y	SILK-Y	VIEW-Y
PUKE-Y	SILL-Y	WACK-Y
PULL-Y	SISS-Y	WALL-Y
PULP-Y	SLIM-Y	WART-Y
PUNK-Y	SLOP-Y	WAVE-Y
PUSH-Y	SNOW-Y	WEAR-Y
RAIN-Y	SOAP-Y	WEED-Y
RANG-Y	SOFT-Y	WELL-Y
RAVE-Y	SONS-Y	WHIN-Y
READ-Y	SOOT-Y	WHIT-Y
REED-Y	SOUP-Y	WIFE-Y
REEK-Y	SPIN-Y	WIMP-Y
REST-Y	STAG-Y	WIND-Y
RICE-Y	STUD-Y	WISP-Y
RILE-Y	SULK-Y	WOMB-Y
RISK-Y	TACK-Y	WOOD-Y
RITZ-Y	TALK-Y	WOOL-Y
ROCK-Y	TALL-Y	WORD-Y
ROOK-Y	TANG-Y	ZEST-Y
ROOM-Y	TATT-Y	
ROOT-Y	TEAR-Y	

Y

347

Five letters to six

ANGST-Y	CHIRP-Y	FINER-Y
ARMOR-Y	CHOKE-Y	FLAKE-Y
AUGUR-Y	CHUFF-Y	FLESH-Y
BAKER-Y	CHUNK-Y	FLINT-Y
BARON-Y	CLASS-Y	FLOAT-Y
BEACH-Y	CLOUD-Y	FLOSS-Y
BEARD-Y	CLUCK-Y	FLOUR-Y
BEAUT-Y	CLUNK-Y	FLUFF-Y
BEECH-Y	COLON-Y	FLUNK-Y
BLANK-Y	COUNT-Y	FOLKS-Y
BLEAR-Y	CRAFT-Y	FOOTS-Y
BLING-Y	CRANK-Y	FREAK-Y
BLOCK-Y	CRAWL-Y	FRIAR-Y
BLOKE-Y	CREAK-Y	FRILL-Y
BLOOD-Y	CREAM-Y	FRISK-Y
BLOOP-Y	CREEP-Y	FRIZZ-Y
BLOWS-Y	CRISP-Y	FROST-Y
BLUES-Y	CROAK-Y	FROTH-Y
BOOZE-Y	CRUST-Y	FRUIT-Y
BOWER-Y	CURVE-Y	FRUMP-Y
BRAIN-Y	CUTES-Y	GLASS-Y
BRAND-Y	DRAFT-Y	GLITZ-Y
BRASS-Y	DRAWL-Y	GLOOM-Y
BRAWN-Y	DREAM-Y	GLOSS-Y
BRICK-Y	DREAR-Y	GNARL-Y
BROOD-Y	DRESS-Y	GRAIN-Y
BROTH-Y	DROOP-Y	GRASS-Y
BROWN-Y	DROPS-Y	GREED-Y
BRUSH-Y	EARTH-Y	GROWL-Y
BURST-Y	EATER-Y	GRUMP-Y
CHALK-Y	EIGHT-Y	GUILT-Y
CHEAP-Y	FAULT-Y	HEART-Y
CHEEK-Y	FEIST-Y	HERES-Y
CHEER-Y	FELON-Y	HORSE-Y
CHILL-Y	FILTH-Y	HOUSE-Y

Y

348

HURRA-Y	SAVOR-Y	SPORT-Y
JAPER-Y	SCARE-Y	STEAD-Y
LEMON-Y	SCREW-Y	STEAM-Y
LIVER-Y	SCUZZ-Y	STEEL-Y
MARSH-Y	SHACK-Y	STICK-Y
MEDLE-Y	SHAND-Y	STING-Y
MELON-Y	SHARP-Y	STINK-Y
MEREL-Y	SHELL-Y	STOCK-Y
MIGHT-Y	SHIFT-Y	STOMP-Y
MISER-Y	SHIRT-Y	STONE-Y
MOULD-Y	SHORT-Y	STOOL-Y
MOUTH-Y	SHOUT-Y	STORE-Y
MUNCH-Y	SINEW-Y	STORM-Y
MYRRH-Y	SKANK-Y	STRIP-Y
NIGHT-Y	SKIMP-Y	STUFF-Y
ONION-Y	SLANG-Y	STUMP-Y
PAPER-Y	SLEEP-Y	SUGAR-Y
PARLE-Y	SLINK-Y	SWAMP-Y
PATCH-Y	SLURP-Y	SWEAR-Y
PEACH-Y	SLUSH-Y	SWEAT-Y
PEARL-Y	SMART-Y	SWEET-Y
PHONE-Y	SMELL-Y	SWIRL-Y
PLUCK-Y	SMILE-Y	SYRUP-Y
POINT-Y	SMITH-Y	TEENS-Y
PRESS-Y	SMOKE-Y	THICK-Y
PRICE-Y	SNACK-Y	THING-Y
PRIOR-Y	SNAKE-Y	THONG-Y
PRUNE-Y	SNEAK-Y	THORN-Y
PUNCH-Y	SNIFF-Y	TITCH-Y
QUACK-Y	SNOOP-Y	TOAST-Y
QUICK-Y	SPACE-Y	TOOTH-Y
QUIRK-Y	SPARK-Y	TOOTS-Y
RIGHT-Y	SPEED-Y	TOUCH-Y
ROOTS-Y	SPICE-Y	TRASH-Y
ROUGH-Y	SPIKE-Y	TREAT-Y
RUDER-Y	SPOOK-Y	TREND-Y

Y

TRICK-Y   VINER-Y   WHINE-Y
TRUST-Y   VOMIT-Y   WHIRL-Y
TWANG-Y   WAFER-Y   WHIRR-Y
TWEED-Y   WATER-Y   WHISK-Y
TWEEN-Y   WEIRD-Y   WHITE-Y
TWIRL-Y   WHIFF-Y   WIELD-Y
TWIST-Y   WHIMS-Y   WORTH-Y

Six letters to seven

ALMOND-Y   CRUISE-Y   GRUNGE-Y
ANALOG-Y   CRUNCH-Y   GUNNER-Y
ANARCH-Y   CURSOR-Y   HACKER-Y
ARCHER-Y   CUTLER-Y   HAUGHT-Y
ARMOUR-Y   DODDER-Y   HEALTH-Y
AUTUMN-Y   DRAPER-Y   HICCUP-Y
BALSAM-Y   DROUTH-Y   HONEST-Y
BATTER-Y   DYNAST-Y   HOSIER-Y
BILLOW-Y   EPONYM-Y   IMAGER-Y
BLIGHT-Y   FACTOR-Y   INDEED-Y
BLOTCH-Y   FARMER-Y   JARGON-Y
BOFFIN-Y   FIBBER-Y   JITTER-Y
BRAVER-Y   FIDDLE-Y   JOINER-Y
BREATH-Y   FIDGET-Y   JUDDER-Y
BREWER-Y   FISHER-Y   KITSCH-Y
BRIBER-Y   FLAVOR-Y   LATHER-Y
BURSAR-Y   FLIGHT-Y   LECHER-Y
BUTTER-Y   FLOWER-Y   LENGTH-Y
CARVER-Y   FORGER-Y   LIQUID-Y
CHINTZ-Y   GADGET-Y   LOTTER-Y
CHOOSE-Y   GARAGE-Y   MARTYR-Y
CITRUS-Y   GINGER-Y   MASTER-Y
CLIQUE-Y   GLITCH-Y   MISTER-Y
CLOVER-Y   GOSSIP-Y   MOCKER-Y
COOKER-Y   GRAVEL-Y   MODEST-Y
COPPER-Y   GROCER-Y   MONGER-Y
COTTON-Y   GROUCH-Y   MUMMER-Y

Y

MUSCLE-Y   RUBBER-Y   STRING-Y
NAUGHT-Y   SALMON-Y   STRIPE-Y
NURSER-Y   SAVOUR-Y   SURGER-Y
ORANGE-Y   SCARED-Y   TANNER-Y
ORATOR-Y   SCRUFF-Y   THIRST-Y
PANICK-Y   SENSOR-Y   THRASH-Y
PAUNCH-Y   SERVER-Y   THRIFT-Y
PEDLAR-Y   SHADOW-Y   TIMBER-Y
PEPPER-Y   SHIVER-Y   TINSEL-Y
PEWTER-Y   SHLOCK-Y   TORQUE-Y
PHLEGM-Y   SHOWER-Y   TRANCE-Y
PILFER-Y   SHRILL-Y   TRICKS-Y
PILLOW-Y   SILVER-Y   TURNIP-Y
POTTER-Y   SKETCH-Y   TWITCH-Y
POWDER-Y   SLAVER-Y   UNREAD-Y
PREACH-Y   SMOOTH-Y   VELVET-Y
QUIVER-Y   SNIVEL-Y   VICTOR-Y
RAGGED-Y   SPIDER-Y   WASHER-Y
RAISIN-Y   SPLASH-Y   WEALTH-Y
RAUNCH-Y   SPRING-Y   WEASEL-Y
RECTOR-Y   SQUASH-Y   WEIGHT-Y
RIFLER-Y   SQUEAK-Y   WILLOW-Y
ROBBER-Y   STARCH-Y   WINTER-Y
ROCKER-Y   STREAK-Y

Seven letters to eight

ADVISOR-Y   CAJOLER-Y   COLLIER-Y
AUDITOR-Y   CALAMAR-Y   CREAMER-Y
BISCUIT-Y   CARTOON-Y   CRYOGEN-Y
BLADDER-Y   CHANCER-Y   CURATOR-Y
BLOSSOM-Y   CHEATER-Y   CUSTARD-Y
BLUSTER-Y   CHIFFON-Y   DASTARD-Y
BOULDER-Y   CHIRRUP-Y   DELIVER-Y
BURGLAR-Y   CITATOR-Y   DRAUGHT-Y
BUTCHER-Y   CLATTER-Y   DRUDGER-Y
CABBAGE-Y   COBBLER-Y   ENTREAT-Y

Y

FEATHER-Y	MONITOR-Y	SHMALTZ-Y
FLATTER-Y	MUSTARD-Y	SLIPPER-Y
FLICKER-Y	NEGATOR-Y	SLOBBER-Y
FLUSTER-Y	NITPICK-Y	SLUMBER-Y
FRILLER-Y	ORDINAR-Y	SMOTHER-Y
FRIPPER-Y	PARADOX-Y	SOLDIER-Y
FRUITER-Y	PEDAGOG-Y	SPINNER-Y
GIMMICK-Y	PLASTER-Y	SPUTTER-Y
GLITTER-Y	POLYGAM-Y	SQUELCH-Y
GLUTTON-Y	POLYMER-Y	STEALTH-Y
GREENER-Y	PUDDING-Y	STUDENT-Y
GRINDER-Y	QUIZZER-Y	SYNONYM-Y
GYRATOR-Y	RECOVER-Y	TABLOID-Y
HATCHER-Y	REFINER-Y	THUNDER-Y
HEATHER-Y	RINGLET-Y	TITULAR-Y
HOMONYM-Y	RUBBISH-Y	TOURIST-Y
INCISOR-Y	SADDLER-Y	TRICKER-Y
JEALOUS-Y	SAVAGER-Y	TWITTER-Y
JEOPARD-Y	SCHLOCK-Y	UNTRUST-Y
KETCHUP-Y	SCRATCH-Y	UNWORTH-Y
KNACKER-Y	SCREECH-Y	VILLAGE-Y
LAMINAR-Y	SCRUNCH-Y	VILLAIN-Y
LEATHER-Y	SEAWEED-Y	WARRANT-Y
MILITAR-Y	SEMINAR-Y	WHISKER-Y
MONARCH-Y	SHIMMER-Y	

BLOCKERS

It is useful to know which words are blockers and can't therefore be extended before or after. You may want to play a blocker that your opponent can't extend, or you may want to avoid playing a blocker because you want to keep the board open.

352

The three-letter blockers beginning with Y

YAE	YEH	YEX

Some four-letter blockers beginning with Y

YALD	YEOW	YUCH
YEBO	YOND	YUTZ

Some five-letter blockers beginning with Y
(except words ending in '-ED', '-J', '-S', '-X', '-Y' or '-Z')

YAULD	YOKUL	YUCKO
YEWEN	YOURN	YUMMO
YINCE	YOUSE	
YOGIC	YUCCH	

Some six-letter blockers beginning with Y
(except words ending in '-ED', '-J', '-S', '-X', '-Y' or '-Z')

YAKUZA	YIKING	YITTEN
YAWING	YIPPEE	

BONUS WORDS

Bonus words on your rack can be hard to spot, especially for the less experienced player. One way to help find them is by using prefixes and suffixes.

Many larger words include a common prefix or suffix – remembering these and using them where you can is a good way to discover any longer words on your rack, including any potential bonus words. The key suffix to remember beginning with Y is -YARD.

Some words ending with -YARD

Seven-letter words

BEE-YARD	INN-YARD	TAN-YARD
HAL-YARD	LAN-YARD	

Eight-letter words

BACK-YARD	FEED-YARD	SALE-YARD
BALL-YARD	FORE-YARD	SAVO-YARD
BARN-YARD	HAUL-YARD	SHIP-YARD
BOAT-YARD	JUNK-YARD	SHOW-YARD
BONE-YARD	KAIL-YARD	TILT-YARD
COAL-YARD	KALE-YARD	VINE-YARD
DEER-YARD	KIRK-YARD	WHIN-YARD
DOCK-YARD	MAIN-YARD	WILL-YARD
DOOR-YARD	METE-YARD	WOOD-YARD
FARM-YARD	RICK-YARD	

UNUSUAL WORDS FROM OVERSEAS ENGLISH

If you have an awkward combination of letters on your rack then words from overseas English may come in handy. Here are some beginning with Y.

Australian words

YABBER	talk or jabber
YABBY	small freshwater crayfish
YACCA	grass tree
YARRAN	small hardy tree
YIKE	argument, squabble or fight
YUCKO	disgusting
YUMMO	delicious

South African word

YEBO	yes

Y

Essential info
Value: 10 points
Number in set: 1

POWER TILE

Z is one of the most valuable tiles in the Scrabble set.
It is easier to use than the J or Q and is nearly as flexible
as the X. Various three-letter words using Z can be
remembered easily as sets of two, with another fixed
consonant and alternating vowels, for example ZIG and
ZAG, ZEP and ZIP, BIZ and BEZ, and especially ZAX and
ZEX (using two power tiles and thus potentially
achieving huge scores).

Two-letter words beginning with Z

ZA	ZO

Some three-letter words beginning with Z

ZAG	ZEK	ZIN
ZAP	ZEL	ZIP
ZAX	ZEP	ZIT
ZEA	ZEX	ZOA
ZED	ZHO	ZOL
ZEE	ZIG	ZOO

Some three-letter words using Z

ADZ	FEZ	RIZ
AZO	FIZ	SAZ
BEZ	LUZ	SEZ
CAZ	MIZ	TIZ
COZ	MOZ	WIZ
CUZ	POZ	YEZ
DZO	REZ	

Some four-letter words using Z

Some interesting four-letter words using the letter Z are AZYM (unleavened bread, 18 points) and NAZE (marshy headland, 13 points). Words beginning with Z which may be unfamiliar include ZATI (a type of macaque, 13 points) and ZOEA (larva of a crab or crustacean, 13 points). Don't forget words such as JAZY (wig, 23 points) and QUIZ (22 points) as they use more than one power tile and can return relatively high scores considering their length.

ADZE	BIZE	CHEZ
AZAN	BOZO	CHIZ
AZON	BUZZ	COZE
AZYM	CAZH	COZY

CZAR	OOZY	ZEDA
DAZE	ORZO	ZEIN
DITZ	OUZO	ZERK
DOZE	OYEZ	ZEST
DOZY	PHIZ	ZETA
DZHO	PIZE	ZIFF
FAZE	PREZ	ZILA
FIZZ	PUTZ	ZILL
FOZY	QUIZ	ZIMB
FUTZ	RAZE	ZINC
FUZE	RAZZ	ZING
FUZZ	RITZ	ZIPS
GAZE	RIZA	ZITE
HAZE	SITZ	ZITI
HAZY	SIZE	ZOBO
IZAR	SIZY	ZOBU
JAZZ	SWIZ	ZOEA
KUZU	TIZZ	ZOIC
LAZE	TOZE	ZONA
LAZO	TREZ	ZONE
LAZY	TZAR	ZONK
LOLZ	VIZY	ZOOM
LUTZ	WHIZ	ZOON
MAZE	YUTZ	ZOOT
MAZY	YUZU	ZORI
MEZE	ZACK	ZOUK
MOZE	ZANY	ZULU
MOZO	ZARF	ZUPA
MZEE	ZARI	ZURF
NAZE	ZATI	ZYGA
NAZI	ZEAL	ZYME
OOZE	ZEBU	

Some front-hooks

Two letters to three

Z-AG	Z-EE	Z-IT
Z-AS	Z-EL	Z-OO
Z-AX	Z-EX	Z-OS
Z-EA	Z-HO	
Z-ED	Z-IN	

Three letters to four

Z-ARF	Z-IFF	Z-OON
Z-ERK	Z-ILL	Z-OOT
Z-ETA	Z-OBO	Z-OUK

Four letters to five

Z-AMIA	Z-HOMO	Z-OPPO
Z-ANTE	Z-INKY	Z-UPAS
Z-AYIN	Z-LOTE	

Five letters to six

Z-ANANA	Z-INKED	Z-ONERS
Z-ESTER	Z-ITHER	

Z

358

Six letters to seven

Z-INCITE   Z-OOGENY   Z-OOLITH
Z-INKIER   Z-OOIDAL   Z-ORBING
Z-OOGAMY   Z-OOLITE

Seven letters to eight

Z-OOLITIC   Z-OOPHYTE   Z-OOSPORE
Z-OOLOGIC   Z-OOSPERM

> **Handy Hint: IdealiZED opportunities**
>
> Power tile letters may be less common than others
> in the set but there are many simple and easy-to-
> remember words that use them. Some examples for Z
> include: LAZY (16 points), QUIZ (22), ZERO (13), ZAP
> (14), ZOOM (15) and ZONE (13).

Some end-hooks
Two letters to three

AD-Z   MI-Z   SO-Z
BE-Z   MO-Z   TI-Z
BI-Z   PO-Z   YE-Z
FE-Z   RE-Z

Three letters to four

CHI-Z   MOZ-Z   SIT-Z
GEE-Z   PHI-Z
MIZ-Z   POZ-Z

Four letters to five

BORT-Z   GREN-Z   SPIT-Z
CAPI-Z   MILT-Z   WARE-Z
CHIZ-Z   PLOT-Z   WOOT-Z

Z

Five letters to six

QUART-Z   SPELT-Z   SPRIT-Z

Six letters to seven

SCHNOZ-Z

BLOCKERS

It is useful to know which words are blockers and can't therefore be extended before or after. You may want to play a blocker that your opponent can't extend, or you may want to avoid playing a blocker because you want to keep the board open.

The three-letter blockers beginning with Z

ZAS   ZEX   ZUZ
ZAX   ZOA

The four-letter blockers beginning with Z

ZANY   ZITE

Some five-letter blockers beginning with Z

ZLOTE   ZOPPO   ZOWIE
ZOPPA   ZOWEE   ZYGON

Some six-letter blockers beginning with Z

ZAFTIG   ZEROTH   ZOFTIG
ZAPATA   ZIPTOP   ZUFOLI

Z

Seven-letter words

ZABTIEH	ZAPTIEH	ZESTIER
ZACATON	ZAREEBA	ZESTING
ZADDICK	ZARNICH	ZETETIC
ZAIDEHS	ZEALANT	ZEUXITE
ZAIDIES	ZEALFUL	ZIFFIUS
ZAITECH	ZEALOUS	ZIGANKA
ZAKUSKA	ZEBRAIC	ZIKURAT
ZAKUSKI	ZEBRINA	ZILLION
ZAMARRA	ZEBRINE	ZIMOCCA
ZAMARRO	ZEBROID	ZINCATE
ZAMBUCK	ZEBRULA	ZINCIER
ZAMOUSE	ZEBRULE	ZINCIFY
ZAMPONE	ZECCHIN	ZINCING
ZAMPONI	ZEDOARY	ZINCITE
ZANELLA	ZELATOR	ZINCKED
ZANIEST	ZELKOVA	ZINCODE
ZANJERO	ZEMSTVA	ZINCOID
ZAPATEO	ZEMSTVO	ZINCOUS
ZAPPIER	ZENAIDA	ZINGANI
ZAPPING	ZEOLITE	ZINGANO
ZAPTIAH	ZESTFUL	ZINGARA

Z

ZINGARE   ZONATED   ZOOTOMY
ZINGARI   ZONKING   ZOOTYPE
ZINGARO   ZONOIDS   ZORBING
ZINKIER   ZONULAE   ZORGITE
ZINKIFY   ZONULAR   ZORILLA
ZINKING   ZONULES   ZORILLE
ZIPLINE   ZONULET   ZORILLO
ZIPOLAS   ZOOECIA   ZOYSIAS
ZIPPILY   ZOOGAMY   ZUFFOLI
ZIPWIRE   ZOOGENY   ZUFFOLO
ZITHERN   ZOOGLEA   ZUFOLOS
ZLOTYCH   ZOOGONY   ZYGOSIS
ZOARIAL   ZOOIDAL   ZYGOTIC
ZOARIUM   ZOOLITE   ZYMOGEN
ZOCCOLO   ZOOLITH   ZYMOSAN
ZOECIUM   ZOOLOGY   ZYMOSIS
ZOEFORM   ZOONITE   ZYMOTIC
ZOISITE   ZOONOMY   ZYMURGY
ZOMBIFY   ZOOPERY
ZONALLY   ZOOTAXY

Eight-letter words

ZABAIONE   ZASTRUGA   ZEPPELIN
ZABAJONE   ZASTRUGI   ZERUMBET
ZADDIKIM   ZEALLESS   ZESTIEST
ZAIBATSU   ZEALOTRY   ZESTLESS
ZAKOUSKA   ZEBRINNY   ZHOOSHED
ZAKOUSKI   ZECCHINE   ZHOOSHES
ZAMBOMBA   ZECCHINI   ZIBELINE
ZAMINDAR   ZECCHINO   ZIGGURAT
ZAMPOGNA   ZELATRIX   ZIGZAGGY
ZAMZAWED   ZEMINDAR   ZIKKURAT
ZAPPIEST   ZEMSTVOS   ZIMOCCAS
ZARATITE   ZENITHAL   ZINCIEST
ZARZUELA   ZEOLITIC   ZINCKIER

Z

ZINCKIFY	ZOOGENIC	ZOOSPORE
ZINCKING	ZOOGLEAE	ZOOTHOME
ZINCODES	ZOOGLEAL	ZOOTIEST
ZINDABAD	ZOOGLOEA	ZOOTOMIC
ZINGIBER	ZOOGRAFT	ZOOTOXIC
ZINGIEST	ZOOLATER	ZOOTOXIN
ZINKIEST	ZOOLATRY	ZOOTROPE
ZIPLOCKS	ZOOLITIC	ZOOTYPIC
ZIPLINES	ZOOLOGIC	ZOPILOTE
ZIPWIRES	ZOOMABLE	ZUCCHINI
ZIRCALOY	ZOOMANCY	ZUCHETTA
ZIRCONIA	ZOOMANIA	ZUCHETTO
ZIRCONIC	ZOOMETRY	ZWIEBACK
ZODIACAL	ZOOMORPH	ZYGAENID
ZOETROPE	ZOONITIC	ZYGANTRA
ZOIATRIA	ZOONOMIA	ZYGODONT
ZOMBIISM	ZOONOMIC	ZYGOMATA
ZOMBORUK	ZOONOSIS	ZYGOSITY
ZONATION	ZOONOTIC	ZYGOTENE
ZONELESS	ZOOPATHY	ZYLONITE
ZONETIME	ZOOPERAL	ZYMOGENE
ZOOBLAST	ZOOPHOBE	ZYMOGENS
ZOOCHORE	ZOOPHORI	ZYMOGRAM
ZOOCHORY	ZOOPHYTE	ZYMOLOGY
ZOOCYTIA	ZOOSCOPY	ZYMOTICS
ZOOECIUM	ZOOSPERM	

Z

UNUSUAL WORDS FROM OVERSEAS ENGLISH

If you have an awkward combination of letters on your rack then words from overseas English may come in handy. Here are some beginning with Z.

Australian words

ZAMBUCK   St John ambulance attendant
ZIFF   beard

Hindi words

ZENANA   part of a house reserved for women
ZILA   administrative district in India

Handy Hint: ZHO many words

There are various alternative spellings for ZHO (a Tibetan breed of cattle, developed by crossing the yak with common cattle). These are DSO, DZO, DZHO and ZO, all of which it is worth remembering in order to form short, high-scoring words (ZHO scores 15 points and DZO is worth 13).

Z

Two-letter words (with definitions)

AA   *noun* volcanic rock

AB   *noun* abdominal muscle

AD   *noun* advertisement

AE   *determiner* one

AG   *noun* agriculture

AH   *exclamation* expression surprise, joy; *verb* say ah

AI   *noun* shaggy-coated slow-moving animal of South America

AL   *noun* Asian shrub or tree

AM   first person singular present tense of *be*

AN   *determiner* form of *a* used before vowels; *noun* additional condition

AR   *noun* letter R

AS   *adverb* used to indicate amount or extent in comparisons; *noun* ancient Roman unit of weight

AT   *noun* Laotian monetary unit worth one hundredth of a kip

AW   variant of *all*

AX   same as *axe*

AY   *adverb* ever; *noun* expression of agreement

BA   *noun* symbol for the soul in ancient Egyptian religion

BE   *verb* exist or live

BI   short for *bisexual*

BO   *exclamation* uttered to startle or surprise someone; *noun* fellow, buddy

BY   *preposition* indicating the doer of an action, nearness, movement past, time before or during which, etc; *noun* pass to the next round (of a competition, etc)

CH	obsolete form of *I*
DA	*noun* Burmese knife
DE	*preposition* of or from
DI	plural of *deus*, god.
DO	*verb* perform or complete (a deed or action); *noun* party, celebration
EA	*noun* river
ED	*noun* education
EE	Scots word for *eye* (plural **EEN**)
EF	*noun* letter F
EH	*exclamation* of surprise or inquiry; *verb* say eh
EL	*noun* American elevated railway
EM	*noun* square of a body of any size of type, used as a unit of measurement
EN	*noun* unit of measurement, half the width of an em
ER	interjection made when hesitating in speech
ES	*noun* letter S
ET	dialect past tense of *ate*
EX	*prepositions* not including; *noun* former husband, wife, etc; *verb* cross out or delete
FA	*noun* (in tonic sol-fa) fourth degree of any major scale
FE	*noun* variant of Hebrew letter *pe*, transliterated as *f*
FY	*exclamation* of disapproval
GI	*noun* white suit worn in martial arts
GO	*verb* move to or from a place; *noun* attempt
GU	*noun* type of violin used in Shetland
HA	*exclamation* of triumph, surprise, or scorn
HE	*pronoun* male person or animal; *noun* male person or animal; expression of amusement or derision

HI	*interjection* hello
HM	sound made to express hesitation or doubt
HO	*noun* derogatory term for a woman; *interjection* imitation or representation of the sound of a deep laugh; *verb* halt
ID	*noun* mind's instinctive unconscious energies
IF	*noun* uncertainty or doubt
IN	*preposition* indicating position inside, state, or situation, etc; *adverb* indicating position inside, entry into, etc.; *adjective* fashionable; *noun* way of approaching or befriending a person; *verb* take in
IO	*exclamation* of trimph; *noun* cry of io
IS	third person singular present tense of *be*
IT	*pronoun* refers to a nonhuman, animal, plant, or inanimate object; *noun* player whose turn it is to catch the others in children's games
JA	*interjection and sentence substitute* yes
JO	*noun* Scots word for sweetheart (plural **JOES**)
KA	*noun* (in ancient Egypt) type of spirit; *verb* help
KI	*noun* vital energy
KO	*noun* (in New Zealand) traditional digging tool
KY	*plural noun* Scots word for cows
LA	*exclamation* of surprise or emphasis; *noun* the sixth note of the musical scale
LI	*noun* Chinese measurement of distance
LO	*interjection* look!
MA	*noun* mother
ME	*pronoun* refers to the speaker or writer
MI	*noun* (in tonic sol-fa) third degree of any major scale
MM	expression of enjoyment of taste or smell
MO	*noun* moment

MU	*noun* twelveth letter in the Greek alphabet
MY	*adjective* belonging to me; *interjection exclamation* of surprise or awe
NA	Scots word for *no*
NE	*conjunction* nor
NO	*interjection* expresses denial, disagreement, refusal; *adjective/adverb* not any, not a, not at all; *noun* answer or vote of no
NU	*noun* thirteenth letter in the Greek alphabet
NY	nigh
OB	*noun* expression of opposition
OD	*noun* hypothetical force
OE	*noun* grandchild
OF	*preposition* belonging to
OH	*exclamation* of surprise, pain, etc; *verb* say oh
OI	shout to attract attention; *noun* grey-faced petrel
OM	*noun* sacred syllable in Hinduism
ON	*prepositon* indicating position above, attachment, closeness, etc; *adjective/adverb* in operation; *noun* side of the field on which the batsman stands (in cricket); *verb* go on
OO	*noun* Scots word for *wool*
OP	*noun* operation
OR	*preposition* before; *adjective* of the metal gold; *noun* gold
OS	*noun* mouth or mouthlike part or opening
OU	*interjection* expressing concession; *noun* man, bloke, or chap
OW	*exclamation* of pain
OX	*noun* castrated bull
OY	*noun* grandchild

PA	*noun* (formerly) fortified Māori settlement
PE	*noun* seventeenth letter of the Hebrew alphabet, transliterated as *p*
PI	*noun* sixteenth letter in the Greek alphabet; *verb* spill and mix (set type) indiscriminately
PO	*noun* chamber pot
QI	*noun* vital force
RE	*preposition* concerning; *noun* the second note of the musical scale
SH	*interjection* hush
SI	*noun* (in tonic sol-fa) seventh degree of any major scale
SO	*adverb* to such an extent; *exclamation* of surprise, triumph, or realization; *noun* the fifth note of the musical scale
ST	*exclamation* to attract attention
TA	*interjection* thank you
TE	*noun* (in tonic sol-fa) seventh degree of any major scale
TI	*noun* (in tonic sol-fa) seventh degree of any major scale
TO	*preposition* indicating movement towards, equality, or comparison, etc; *adverb* a closed position
UG	*verb* hate
UH	*interjection* used to express hesitation
UM	representation of a common sound made when hesitating in speech; *verb* hesitate while speaking
UN	*pronoun* spelling of *one* to reflect dialectal or informal pronunciation
UP	*adverb* indicating movement to or position at a higher place; *adjective* of a high or higher position; *verb* increase or raise

UR	hestitant utterance used to fill gaps in talking
US	*pronoun* refers to the speaker or writer and another person or other people
UT	syllable used in the fixed system of solmization for the note C
WE	*pronoun* speaker or writer and one or more others
WO	archaic spelling of *woe*
XI	*noun* fourteenth letter in the Greek alphabet
XU	*noun* Vietnamese currency unit
YA	*noun* a type of Asian pear
YE	*pronoun* you; *determiner* the
YO	expression used as a greeting
YU	*noun* jade
ZA	*noun* pizza
ZO	*noun* Tibetan breed of cattle

Three-letter words (with definitions)

AAH   *verb* exclaim in pleasure

AAL   *noun* Asian shrub or tree

AAS   inflected form of *aa*

ABA   *noun* type of Syrian cloth

ABB   *noun* yarn used in weaving

ABO   *noun* offensive word for an Aborigine

ABS   inflected form of *ab*

ABY   *verb* pay the penalty for

ACE   *noun* playing card with one symbol on it; *adjective* excellent; *verb* serve an ace in racquet sports

ACH   Scots expression of surprise

ACT   *noun* thing done; *verb* do something

ADD   *verb* combine (numbers or quantities)

ADO   *noun* fuss, trouble

ADS   inflected form of *ad*

ADZ   *noun* (US) woodworking tool; *verb* use an adz

AFF   same as *off*

AFT   *adjective/adverb* at or towards the rear of a ship or aircraft

AGA   *noun* title of respect

AGE   *noun* length of time a person or thing has existed; *verb* make or grow old

AGO   *adverb* in the past

AGS   inflected form of *ag*

AHA   exclamation

AHI   *noun* yellowfin tuna

AHS   inflected form of *ah*

AIA   *noun* female servant in East

AID   *noun* (give) assistance or support; *verb* help financially or in other ways

AIL   *verb* trouble, afflict

AIM   *verb* point (a weapon or missile) or direct (a blow or remark) at a target; noun aiming

AIN   *noun* sixteenth letter in the Hebrew alphabet

AIR   *noun* mixture of gases forming the earth's atmosphere; verb make known publicly

AIS   inflected form of ai

AIT   *noun* islet, esp in a river

AJI   *noun* type of spicy pepper

AKA   *noun* type of New Zealand vine

AKE   *verb* old spelling of ache

ALA   *noun* winglike structure

ALB   *noun* long white robe worn by a Christian priest

ALE   *noun* kind of beer

ALF   *noun* uncultivated Australian

ALL   *adjective* whole quantity or number (of); *adverb* wholly, entirely; *noun* entire being, effort, or property

ALP   *noun* high mountain

ALS   inflected form of al

ALT   *noun* octave directly above the treble staff

ALU   *noun* (in Indian cookery) potato

AMA   *noun* vessel for water

AME   *noun* soul

AMI   *noun* male friend

AMP   *noun* ampere; verb excite or become excited

AMU   *noun* unit of mass

ANA   *adverb* in equal quantities; noun collection of reminiscences

AND	*noun* additional matter or problem
ANE	Scots word for one
ANI	*noun* tropical bird
ANN	*noun* old Scots word for a widow's pension
ANS	*plural noun* as in ifs and ans things that might have happened, but which did not
ANT	*noun* small insect living in highly-organized colonies
ANY	*adjective* one or some, no matter which; *adverb* at all
APE	*noun* tailless monkey such as the chimpanzee or gorilla; *verb* imitate
APO	*noun* type of protein
APP	*noun* application program
APT	*adjective* having a specified tendency; *verb* be fitting
ARB	*noun* arbitrage: purchase of currencies, securities, or commodities in one market for immediate resale in others in order to profit from unequal prices
ARC	*noun* part of a circle or other curve; *verb* form an arc
ARD	*noun* primitive plough
ARE	*noun* unit of measure, 100 square metres; *verb* used as the singular form with you
ARF	*noun* barking sound
ARK	*noun* boat built by Noah, which survived the Flood; *verb* place in an ark
ARM	*noun* limbs from the shoulder to the wrist; *verb* supply with weapons
ARS	inflected form of ar
ART	*noun* creation of works of beauty, esp paintings or sculpture
ARY	dialect form of any
ASH	*noun* powdery substance left when something is burnt; *verb* reduce to ashes

ASK	*verb* say (something) in a form that requires an answer
ASP	*noun* small poisonous snake
ASS	*noun* donkey
ATE	past tense of eat
ATS	inflected form of at
ATT	*noun* old Siamese coin
AUA	*noun* yellow-eye mullet
AUE	Māori exclamation
AUF	old word for oaf
AUK	*noun* sea bird with short wings
AVA	*adverb* at all; *noun* Polynesian shrub
AVE	*noun* expression of welcome or farewell
AVO	*noun* Macao currency unit
AWA	same as away
AWE	*noun* wonder and respect mixed with dread; *verb* fill with awe
AWK	*noun* type of programming language
AWL	*noun* pointed tool for piercing wood, leather, etc
AWN	*noun* bristles on grasses
AXE	*noun* tool with a sharp blade for felling trees or chopping wood; *verb* dismiss (employees), restrict (expenditure), or terminate (a project)
AYE	*noun* affirmative vote or voter; *adverb* always
AYS	inflected form of ay
AYU	*noun* small Japanese fish
AZO	*adjective* of the divalent group -N:N-
BAA	*verb* the characteristic bleating sound of a sheep; *noun* cry made by a sheep
BAC	*noun* baccalaureate

BAD *adjective* not good; *noun* unfortunate or unpleasant events collectively; *adverb* badly

BAG *noun* flexible container with an opening at one end; *verb* put into a bag

BAH expression of contempt or disgust

BAL *noun* balmoral: laced walking shoe

BAM *verb* cheat

BAN *verb* prohibit or forbid officially; *noun* official prohibition

BAP *noun* large soft bread roll

BAR *noun* rigid usually straight length of metal, wood, etc, longer than it is wide or thick; *verb* fasten or secure with a bar

BAS inflected form of ba

BAT *noun* any of various types of club used to hit the ball in certain sports; *verb* strike with or as if with a bat

BAY *noun* wide semicircular indentation of a shoreline; *verb* howl in deep tones

BED *noun* piece of furniture on which to sleep; *verb* plant in a bed

BEE *noun* insect that makes wax and honey

BEG *verb* solicit (money, food, etc), esp in the street

BEL *noun* unit for comparing two power levels or measuring the intensity of a sound

BEN *noun* mountain peak; *adverb* in; *adjective* inner

BES *noun* second letter of the Hebrew alphabet, transliterated as b

BET *noun* wager between two parties predicting different outcomes of an event; *verb* make or place a bet with (a person or persons)

BEY *noun* (in the Ottoman empire) a title given to senior officers, provincial governors, and certain other officials

BEZ	*noun* part of deer's horn
BIB	*noun* bibcock: tap with a nozzle bent downwards
BID	*verb* offer (an amount) in attempting to buy something; *noun* offer of a specified amount, as at an auction
BIG	*adjective* of considerable size, height, number, or capacity; *adverb* on a grand scale; *verb* build
BIN	*noun* container for rubbish or for storing grain, coal, etc; *verb* put in a rubbish bin
BIO	short for biography
BIS	*adverb* twice; *sentence substitute* encore! again!
BIT	*noun* small piece, portion, or quantity
BIZ	*noun* business
BOA	*noun* large nonvenomous snake
BOB	*verb* move or cause to move up and down repeatedly; *noun* short abrupt movement, as of the head
BOD	*noun* person
BOG	*noun* wet spongy ground; *verb* mire or delay
BOH	same as bo
BOI	*noun* lesbian who dresses like a boy
BOK	*noun* S African antelope
BON	*adjective* good
BOO	shout of disapproval; *verb* shout "boo" to show disapproval
BOP	*verb* dance to pop music; *noun* form of jazz with complex rhythms and harmonies
BOR	*noun* neighbour
BOS	inflected form of bo
BOT	*noun* larva of a botfly
BOW	*verb* lower (one's head) or bend (one's knee or body) as a sign of respect or shame; *noun* movement made when bowing

BOX	*noun* container with a firm flat base and sides; *verb* put into a box
BOY	*noun* male child; *verb* act the part of a boy in a play
BRA	*noun* woman's undergarment
BRO	*noun* family member
BRR	interjection used to suggest shivering
BRU	South African word for friend
BUB	*noun* youngster
BUD	*noun* swelling on a plant that develops into a leaf or flower; *verb* produce buds
BUG	*noun* insect; *verb* irritate
BUM	*noun* buttocks or anus; *verb* get by begging; *adjective* of poor quality
BUN	*noun* small sweet bread roll or cake
BUR	*noun* small rotary file; *verb* form a rough edge on (a workpiece)
BUS	*noun* large motor vehicle for carrying passengers between stops; *verb* travel by bus
BUT	*preposition* except; *adverb* only; *noun* outer room of a two-roomed cottage: usually the kitchen
BUY	*verb* acquire by paying money for; *noun* thing acquired through payment
BYE	*noun* situation where a player or team wins a round by having no opponent; interjection goodbye
BYS	inflected form of by
CAA	a Scot word for call
CAB	*noun* taxi; *verb* take a taxi
CAD	*noun* dishonourable man
CAF	short for cafeteria
CAG	*noun* cagoule: lightweight hooded waterproof jacket
CAL	short for calorie

CAM	*noun* device that converts a circular motion to a to-and-fro motion; *verb* furnish (a machine) with a cam
CAN	*verb* be able to; *noun* metal container for food or liquids
CAP	*noun* soft close-fitting covering for the head; *verb* cover or top with something
CAR	*noun* motor vehicle designed to carry a small number of people
CAT	*noun* small domesticated furry mammal; *verb* flog with a cat-'o-nine-tails
CAW	*noun* cry of a crow, rook, or raven; *verb* make this cry
CAY	*noun* low island or bank composed of sand and coral fragments
CAZ	short for casual
CEE	*noun* third letter of the alphabet
CEL	short for celluloid
CEP	*noun* edible woodland fungus
CHA	*noun* tea
CHE	*pronoun* dialectal form of I
CHI	*noun* twenty-second letter of the Greek alphabet
CID	*noun* leader
CIG	same as cigarette
CIS	*adjective* having two groups of atoms on the same side of a double bond
CIT	*noun* pejorative term for a town dweller
CLY	*verb* to steal or seize
COB	*noun* stalk of an ear of maize; *verb* beat, esp on the buttocks
COD	*noun* large food fish of the North Atlantic; *adjective* having the character of an imitation or parody; *verb* make fun of

COG *noun* one of the teeth on the rim of a gearwheel; *verb* roll (cast-steel ingots) to convert them into blooms

COL *noun* high mountain pass

CON *verb* deceive, swindle; *noun* convict; *preposition* with

COO *verb* (of a dove or pigeon) make a soft murmuring sound; *noun* sound of cooing; exclamation of surprise, awe, etc

COP same as copper

COR exclamation of surprise, amazement, or admiration

COS *noun* cosine: trigonometric function

COT *noun* baby's bed with high sides; *verb* entangle or become entangled

COW *noun* mature female of certain mammals; *verb* intimidate, subdue

COX *noun* coxswain; *verb* act as cox of (a boat)

COY *adjective* affectedly shy or modest; *verb* to caress

COZ archaic word for cousin

CRU *noun* (in France) a vineyard, group of vineyards, or wine-producing region

CRY *verb* shed tears; *noun* fit of weeping

CUB *noun* young wild animal such as a bear or fox; *adjective* young or inexperienced; *verb* give birth to cubs

CUD *noun* partially digested food chewed by a ruminant

CUE *noun* signal to an actor or musician to begin speaking or playing; *verb* give a cue to

CUM *preposition* with; *noun* vulgar and offensive word for semen; *verb* vulgar and offensive word for ejaculate

CUP *noun* small bowl-shaped drinking container with a handle; *verb* form (one's hands) into the shape of a cup

CUR	*noun* mongrel dog
CUT	*verb* open up, penetrate, wound, or divide with a sharp instrument
CUZ	*noun* cousin
CWM	*noun* steep-sided semicircular hollow found in mountainous areas
DAB	*verb* pat lightly; *noun* small amount of something soft or moist
DAD	*noun* father; *verb* act or treat as a father
DAE	a Scot word for do
DAG	*noun* character; *verb* cut daglocks from sheep
DAH	*noun* long sound used in combination with the short sound in the spoken representation of Morse and other telegraphic codes
DAK	*noun* system of mail delivery or passenger transport
DAL	*noun* decalitre: ten litres
DAM	*noun* barrier built across a river to create a lake; *verb* build a dam across (a river)
DAN	*noun* in judo, any of the ten black-belt grades of proficiency
DAP	*verb* engage in a type of fly fishing
DAS	inflected form of da
DAW	*noun* archaic, dialect, or poetic name for a jackdaw; *verb* old word for dawn
DAY	*noun* period of 24 hours
DEB	*noun* debutante
DEE	a Scot word for die
DEF	*adjective* very good
DEG	*verb* water (a plant, etc)
DEI	plural of deus (god)
DEL	*noun* differential operator

DEN	*noun* home of a wild animal; *verb* live in or as if in a den
DEP	*noun* small shop where newspapers, sweets, soft drinks, etc are sold
DEV	*noun* deva: (in Hinduism and Buddhism) divine being or god
DEW	*noun* drops of water that form on the ground at night from vapour in the air; *verb* moisten with or as with dew
DEX	*noun* dextroamphetamine
DEY	*noun* title given to commanders or governors of the Janissaries of Algiers
DIB	*verb* fish by allowing the bait to bob and dip on the surface
DID	inflected form of do
DIE	*verb* cease all biological activity permanently; *noun* shaped block used to cut or form metal
DIF	*noun* (slang) difference
DIG	*verb* cut into, break up, and turn over or remove (earth), esp with a spade; *noun* digging
DIM	*adjective* badly lit; *verb* make or become dim
DIN	*noun* loud unpleasant confused noise; *verb* instil (something) into someone by constant repetition
DIP	*verb* plunge quickly or briefly into a liquid; *noun* dipping
DIS	*verb* treat (a person) with contempt
DIT	*verb* stop something happening; *noun* short sound used in the spoken representation of telegraphic codes
DIV	*noun* stupid or foolish person
DOB	*verb* as in dob in inform against or report
DOC	same as doctor

DOD	*verb* clip
DOE	*noun* female deer, hare, or rabbit
DOF	informal South African word for stupid
DOG	*noun* domesticated four-legged mammal; *verb* follow (someone) closely
DOH	*noun* in tonic sol-fa, first degree of any major scale; exclamation of annoyance when something goes wrong
DOL	*noun* unit of pain intensity, as measured by dolorimetry
DOM	*noun* title given to various monks and to certain of the canons regular
DON	*verb* put on (clothing); *noun* member of the teaching staff at a university or college
DOO	a Scot word for dove
DOP	*verb* curtsy; *noun* tot or small drink, usually alcoholic; *verb* fail to reach the required standard in (an examination, course, etc)
DOR	*noun* European dung beetle
DOS	inflected form of do
DOT	*noun* small round mark; *verb* mark with a dot
DOW	*verb* archaic word meaning to be of worth
DOY	*noun* beloved person: used esp as an endearment
DRY	*adjective* lacking moisture; *verb* make or become dry
DSO	same as zho
DUB	*verb* give (a person or place) a name or nickname; *noun* style of reggae record production
DUD	*noun* ineffectual person or thing; *adjective* bad or useless
DUE	*verb* supply with; *adjective* expected or scheduled to be present or arrive; *noun* something that is owed or required; *adverb* directly or exactly
DUG	inflected form of dig

DUH	ironic response to a question or statement
DUI	inflected form of duo
DUM	*adjective* steamed
DUN	*adjective* brownish-grey; *verb* demand payment from (a debtor); *noun* demand for payment
DUO	same as duet
DUP	*verb* open
DUX	*noun* (in Scottish and certain other schools) the top pupil in a class or school
DYE	*noun* colouring substance; *verb* colour (hair or fabric) by applying a dye
DZO	a variant spelling of zo
EAN	*verb* give birth
EAR	*noun* organ of hearing, esp the external part of it; *verb* (of cereal plants) to develop parts that contain seeds, grains, or kernels
EAS	inflected form of ea
EAT	*verb* take (food) into the mouth and swallow it
EAU	same as ea
EBB	*verb* (of tide water) flow back; *noun* flowing back of the tide
ECH	*verb* eke out
ECO	*noun* ecology activist
ECU	*noun* any of various former French gold or silver coins
EDH	*noun* character of the runic alphabet
EDS	inflected form of ed
EEK	indicating shock or fright
EEL	*noun* snakelike fish
EEN	inflected form of ee
EEW	exclamation of disgust

EFF	*verb* euphemistic substitute for a certain offensive word
EFS	inflected form of ef
EFT	*noun* dialect or archaic name for a newt; *adverb* again
EGG	*noun* object laid by birds and other creatures, containing a developing embryo; *verb* urge or incite, esp to daring or foolish acts
EGO	*noun* conscious mind of an individual
EHS	inflected form of eh
EIK	variant form of eke
EKE	*verb* increase, enlarge, or lengthen
ELD	*noun* old age
ELF	*noun* (in folklore) small mischievous fairy; *verb* entangle (esp hair)
ELK	*noun* large deer of N Europe and Asia
ELL	*noun* obsolete unit of length
ELM	*noun* tree with serrated leaves
ELS	inflected form of el
ELT	*noun* young female pig
EME	*noun* uncle
EMO	*noun* type of music
EMS	inflected form of em
EMU	*noun* large Australian flightless bird with long legs
END	*noun* furthest point or part; *verb* bring or come to a finish
ENE	variant of even
ENG	*noun* symbol used to represent a velar nasal consonant
ENS	*noun* being or existence in the most general abstract sense

EON	*noun* two or more eras
ERA	*noun* period of time considered as distinctive
ERE	*preposition* before; *verb* plough
ERF	*noun* plot of land marked off for building purposes
ERG	*noun* ergometer: instrument measuring power or force
ERK	*noun* aircraftman or naval rating
ERM	expression of hesitation
ERN	archaic variant of earn
ERR	*verb* make a mistake
ERS	*noun* type of vetch (leguminous climbing plant)
ESS	*noun* letter S
EST	*noun* treatment intended to help people towards psychological growth
ETA	*noun* seventh letter in the Greek alphabet
ETH	same as edh
EUK	*verb* itch
EVE	*noun* evening or day before some special event
EVO	informal word for evening
EWE	*noun* female sheep
EWK	*verb* itch
EWT	archaic form of newt
EXO	informal word for excellent
EYE	*noun* organ of sight; *verb* look at carefully or warily
FAA	Scot word for fall
FAB	*adjective* excellent; *noun* fabrication
FAD	*noun* short-lived fashion
FAE	Scot word for from
FAG	*noun* boring or wearisome task; *verb* become exhausted by work

FAH	*noun* (in tonic sol-fa) fourth degree of any major scale
FAN	*noun* object used to create a current of air; *verb* blow or cool with a fan
FAP	*adjective* drunk
FAR	*adverb* at, to, or from a great distance; *adjective* remote in space or time; *verb* go far
FAS	inflected form of fa
FAT	*adjective* having excess flesh on the body; *noun* extra flesh on the body
FAW	*noun* gypsy
FAX	*noun* electronic system; *verb* send (a document) by this system
FAY	*noun* fairy or sprite; *adjective* of or resembling a fay; *verb* fit or be fitted closely or tightly
FED	*noun* FBI agent
FEE	*noun* charge paid to be allowed to do something; *verb* pay a fee to
FEG	same as fig
FEH	expression of contempt or disgust
FEM	*noun* partner in a sexual or romantic relationship who adopts a traditionally feminine role
FEN	*noun* low-lying flat marshy land
FER	same as far
FES	inflected form of fe
FET	*verb* fetch
FEU	*noun* (in Scotland) type of rent
FEW	*adjective* not many; *noun* as in the few small number of people considered as a class
FEY	*adjective* whimsically strange; *verb* clean out
FEZ	*noun* brimless tasselled cap, originally from Turkey
FIB	*noun* trivial lie; *verb* tell a lie

FID   *noun* spike for separating strands of rope in splicing

FIE   same as fey

FIG   *noun* soft pear-shaped fruit; *verb* dress (up) or rig (out)

FIL   *noun* monetary unit of Bahrain, Iraq, Jordan, and Kuwait

FIN   *noun* any of the appendages of some aquatic animals; *verb* provide with fins

FIR   *noun* pyramid-shaped tree

FIT   *verb* be appropriate or suitable for; *adjective* appropriate; *noun* way in which something fits

FIX   *verb* make or become firm, stable, or secure; *noun* difficult situation

FIZ   fizz: *verb* make a hissing or bubbling noise; *noun* hissing or bubbling noise

FLU   *noun* any of various viral infections

FLY   *verb* move through the air on wings or in an aircraft; *noun* fastening at the front of trousers; *adjective* sharp and cunning

FOB   *noun* short watch chain; *verb* cheat

FOE   *noun* enemy, opponent

FOG   *noun* mass of condensed water vapour in the lower air; *verb* cover with steam

FOH   expression of disgust

FON   *verb* compel

FOO   *noun* temporary computer variable or file

FOP   *noun* man excessively concerned with fashion; *verb* act like a fop

FOR   *preposition* indicating a person intended to benefit from or receive something, span of time or distance, person or thing represented by someone, etc

FOU   *adjective* full; *noun* bushel

FOX	*noun* reddish-brown bushy-tailed animal of the dog family; *verb* perplex or deceive
FOY	*noun* loyalty
FRA	*noun* brother: a title given to an Italian monk or friar
FRO	*adverb* away; *noun* afro
FRY	*verb* cook or be cooked in fat or oil; *noun* dish of fried food
FUB	*verb* cheat
FUD	*noun* rabbit's tail
FUG	*noun* hot stale atmosphere; *verb* sit in a fug
FUM	*noun* phoenix, in Chinese mythology
FUN	*noun* enjoyment or amusement; *verb* trick
FUR	*noun* soft hair of a mammal; *verb* cover or become covered with fur
GAB	*verb* talk or chatter; *noun* mechanical device
GAD	*verb* go about in search of pleasure; *noun* carefree adventure
GAE	Scot word for go
GAG	*verb* choke or retch; *noun* cloth etc put into or tied across the mouth
GAK	*noun* (slang) cocaine
GAL	*noun* girl
GAM	*noun* school of whales; *verb* (of whales) form a school
GAN	*verb* go
GAP	*noun* break or opening
GAR	*noun* primitive freshwater bony fish
GAS	*noun* airlike substance that is not liquid or solid; *verb* poison or render unconscious with gas
GAT	*noun* pistol or revolver
GAU	*noun* district set up by the Nazi Party

GAW	*noun* as in weather gaw partial rainbow
GAY	*adjective* homosexual; *noun* homosexual
GED	*noun* (Scots) pike: large predatory freshwater fish
GEE	mild exclamation of surprise, admiration, etc; *verb* move (an animal, esp a horse) ahead
GEL	*noun* jelly-like substance; *verb* form a gel
GEM	*noun* precious stone or jewel; *verb* set or ornament with gems
GEN	*noun* information; *verb* gain information
GEO	*noun* (esp in Shetland) a small fjord or gully
GER	*noun* portable Mongolian dwelling
GET	*verb* obtain or receive
GEY	*adverb* extremely; *adjective* gallant
GHI	*noun* (in Indian cookery) clarified butter
GIB	*noun* metal wedge, pad, or thrust bearing; *verb* fasten or supply with a gib
GID	*noun* disease of sheep
GIE	Scot word for give
GIF	*noun* file held in GIF format (a compressed format for a series of pictures)
GIG	*noun* single performance by pop or jazz musicians; *verb* play a gig or gigs
GIN	*noun* spirit flavoured with juniper berries; *verb* free (cotton) of seeds with an engine; begin
GIO	same as geo
GIP	offensive same as gyp
GIS	inflected form of gi
GIT	*noun* contemptible person; *verb* dialect version of get
GJU	*noun* type of violin used in Shetland
GNU	*noun* ox-like S African antelope

GOA	*noun* Tibetan gazelle
GOB	*noun* lump of a soft substance; *verb* spit
GOD	*noun* spirit or being worshipped as having supernatural power; *verb* deify
GOE	same as go
GON	*noun* geometrical grade
GOO	*noun* sticky substance
GOR	interjection God!; *noun* seagull
GOS	inflected form of go
GOT	inflected form of get
GOV	*noun* boss
GOX	*noun* gaseous oxygen
GOY	*noun* offensive Jewish word for a non-Jew
GRR	interjection expressing anger or annoyance
GUB	*noun* offensive name for a white man; *verb* hit or defeat
GUE	same as gju
GUL	*noun* design used in oriental carpets
GUM	*noun* any of various sticky subtances; *verb* stick with gum
GUN	*noun* weapon with a tube from which missiles are fired; *verb* cause (an engine) to run at high speed
GUP	*noun* gossip
GUR	*noun* unrefined cane sugar
GUS	inflected form of gu
GUT	*noun* intestine; *verb* remove the guts from; *adjective* basic or instinctive
GUV	informal name for governor
GUY	*noun* man or boy; *verb* make fun of
GYM	*noun* gymnasium

GYP	*verb* offensive meaning to swindle, cheat, or defraud; *noun* offensive word meaning an act or instance of cheating
HAD	*verb* Scots form of hold
HAE	Scot variant of have
HAG	*noun* ugly old woman; *verb* hack
HAH	same as ha
HAJ	*noun* pilgrimage a Muslim makes to Mecca
HAM	*noun* smoked or salted meat from a pig's thigh; *verb* overact
HAN	archaic inflected form of have
HAO	*noun* monetary unit of Vietnam
HAP	*noun* luck; *verb* cover up
HAS	third person singular present tense of have
HAT	*noun* covering for the head, often with a brim; *verb* supply (a person) with a hat or put a hat on (someone)
HAW	*noun* hawthorn berry; *verb* make an inarticulate utterance
HAY	*noun* grass cut and dried as fodder; *verb* cut, dry, and store (grass, clover, etc) as fodder
HEH	exclamation of surprise or inquiry
HEM	*noun* bottom edge of a garment; *verb* provide with a hem
HEN	*noun* female domestic fowl; *verb* lose one's courage
HEP	*adjective* aware of or following the latest trends
HER	*pronoun* refers to anything personified as feminine; *adjective* belonging to her; *determiner* of, belonging to, or associated with her
HES	inflected form of he
HET	short for heterosexual; *adjective* Scot word for hot

HEW	*verb* cut with an axe
HEX	*adjective* of or relating to hexadecimal notation; *noun* evil spell; *verb* bewitch
HEY	expression of surprise or for catching attention; *verb* perform a country dance
HIC	representation of the sound of a hiccup
HID	inflected form of hide
HIE	*verb* hurry
HIM	*pronoun* refers to a male person or animal; *noun* male person
HIN	*noun* Hebrew unit of capacity
HIP	*noun* either side of the body between the pelvis and the thigh; *adjective* aware of or following the latest trends; exclamation used to introduce cheers
HIS	*adjective* belonging to him
HIT	*verb* strike, touch forcefully; *noun* hitting
HMM	same as hm
HOA	offensive same as ho
HOB	*noun* flat top part of a cooker; *verb* cut or form with a hob
HOC	*adjective* Latin for this
HOD	*noun* open wooden box attached to a pole; *verb* bob up and down
HOE	*noun* long-handled tool used for loosening soil or weeding; *verb* scrape or weed with a hoe
HOG	*noun* castrated male pig; *verb* take more than one's share of
HOH	offensive same as ho
HOI	same as hoy
HOM	*noun* sacred plant of the Parsees and ancient Persians

HON	short for honey
HOO	expression of joy, excitement, etc
HOP	*verb* jump on one foot; *noun* instance of hopping
HOS	offensive inflected form of ho
HOT	*adjective* having a high temperature
HOW	*adverb* in what way, by what means; *noun* the way a thing is done; sentence substitute supposed Native American greeting
HOX	*verb* hamstring
HOY	cry used to attract someone's attention; *noun* freight barge; *verb* drive animal with cry
HUB	*noun* centre of a wheel, through which the axle passes
HUE	*noun* colour, shade
HUG	*verb* clasp tightly in the arms, usually with affection; *noun* tight or fond embrace
HUH	exclamation of derision or inquiry
HUI	*noun* meeting of Māori people
HUM	*verb* make a low continuous vibrating sound; *noun* humming sound
HUN	*noun* member of any of several nomadic peoples
HUP	*verb* cry hup to get a horse to move
HUT	*noun* small house, shelter, or shed
HYE	same as hie
HYP	short for hypotenuse
ICE	*noun* water in the solid state, formed by freezing liquid water; *verb* form or cause to form ice
ICH	archaic form of eke
ICK	expression of disgust
ICY	*adjective* very cold
IDE	*noun* silver orfe fish

IDS	inflected form of id
IFF	conjunction in logic, a shortened form of if and only if
IFS	inflected form of if
IGG	*verb* antagonize
ILK	*noun* type; *determiner* each
ILL	*adjective* not in good health; *noun* evil, harm; *adverb* badly
IMP	*noun* (in folklore) creature with magical powers; *verb* method of repairing the wing of a hawk or falcon
ING	*noun* meadow near a river
INK	*noun* coloured liquid used for writing or printing; *verb* mark in ink (something already marked in pencil)
INN	*noun* pub or small hotel, esp in the country; *verb* stay at an inn
INS	inflected form of *in*
ION	*noun* electrically charged atom
IOS	inflected form of *io*
IRE	*verb* anger; *noun* anger
IRK	*verb* irritate, annoy
ISH	*noun* issue
ISM	*noun* doctrine, system, or practice
ISO	*noun* short segment of film that can be replayed easily
ITA	*noun* type of palm
ITS	*determiner* belonging to it; *adjective* of or belonging to it
IVY	*noun* evergreen climbing plant
IWI	*noun* Māori tribe
JAB	*verb* poke sharply; *noun* quick punch or poke

JAG	*noun* period of uncontrolled indulgence in an activity; *verb* cut unevenly
JAI	*interjection* victory (to)
JAK	same as *jack*
JAM	*verb* pack tightly into a place; *noun* fruit preserve; hold-up of traffic
JAP	*verb* splash
JAR	*noun* wide-mouthed container; *verb* have a disturbing or unpleasant effect
JAW	*noun* one of the bones in which the teeth are set; *verb* talk lengthily
JAY	*noun* type of bird
JEE	variant of *gee*
JET	*noun* aircraft driven by jet propulsion; *verb* fly by jet aircraft
JEU	*noun* game
JEW	*verb* obsolete offensive meaning to haggle; *noun* obsolete offensive word for a haggler
JIB	same as *jibe*
JIG	*noun* type of lively dance; *verb* dance a jig
JIN	*noun* Chinese unit of weight
JIZ	*noun* wig
JOB	*noun* occupation or paid employment; *verb* work at casual jobs
JOE	same as *jo*
JOG	*verb* run at a gentle pace, esp for exercise; *noun* slow run
JOL	*noun* party; *verb* have a good time
JOR	*noun* movement in Indian music
JOT	*verb* write briefly; *noun* very small amount
JOW	*verb* ring (a bell)

JOY	*noun* feeling of great delight or pleasure; *verb* feel joy
JUD	*noun* large block of coal
JUG	*noun* container for liquids; *verb* stew or boil (meat, esp hare) in an earthenware container
JUN	*noun* North and South Korean monetary unit
JUS	*noun* right, power, or authority
JUT	*verb* project or stick out; *noun* something that juts out
KAB	variant spelling of *cab*
KAE	*noun* dialect word for jackdaw or jay; *verb* (in archaic usage) help
KAF	*noun* letter of the Hebrew alphabet
KAI	*noun* food
KAK	*noun* offensive South African slang word for *faeces*
KAM	Shakespearean word for *crooked*
KAS	inflected form of *ka*
KAT	*noun* white-flowered evergreen shrub
KAW	variant spelling of *caw*
KAY	*noun* name of the letter K
KEA	*noun* large brownish-green parrot of NZ
KEB	*verb* Scots word meaning miscarry or reject a lamb
KED	*noun* as in *sheep ked* sheep tick
KEF	same as *kif*
KEG	*noun* small metal beer barrel; *verb* put in kegs
KEN	*verb* know; *noun* range of knowledge or perception
KEP	*verb* catch
KET	*noun* dialect word for *carrion*
KEX	*noun* any of several hollow-stemmed umbelliferous plants

KEY	*noun* device for operating a lock by moving a bolt; *adjective* of great importance; *verb* enter (text) using a keyboard
KHI	*noun* letter of the Greek alphabet
KID	*noun* child; *verb* tease or deceive (someone); *adjective* younger
KIF	*noun* type of drug
KIN	*noun* person's relatives collectively; *adjective* related by blood
KIP	*verb* sleep; *noun* sleep or slumber
KIR	*noun* drink made from dry white wine and cassis
KIS	inflected form of *ki*
KIT	*noun* outfit or equipment for a specific purpose; *verb* fit or provide
KOA	*noun* Hawaiian leguminous tree
KOB	*noun* any of several species of antelope
KOI	*noun* any of various ornamental forms of the common carp
KON	old word for *know*
KOP	*noun* prominent isolated hill or mountain in southern Africa
KOR	*noun* ancient Hebrew unit of capacity
KOS	*noun* Indian unit of distance
KOW	old variant of *cow*
KUE	*noun* name of the letter Q
KYE	*noun* Korean fundraising meeting
KYU	*noun* (in judo) one of the five student grades
LAB	*noun* laboratory
LAC	*noun* (in India) 100 000, esp referring to this sum of rupees
LAD	*noun* boy or young man

LAG	*verb* go too slowly, fall behind; *noun* delay between events
LAH	*noun* (in tonic sol-fa) sixth degree of any major scale
LAM	*verb* attack vigorously
LAP	*noun* part between the waist and knees when sitting; *verb* overtake so as to be one or more circuits ahead
LAR	*noun* boy or young man
LAS	inflected form of *la*
LAT	*noun* former coin of Latvia
LAV	short for *lavatory*
LAW	*noun* rule binding on a community; *verb* prosecute; *adjective* (in archaic usage) low
LAX	*adjective* not strict; *noun* laxative
LAY	inflected form of *lie*
LEA	*noun* meadow
LED	inflected form of *lead*
LEE	*noun* sheltered side; *verb* (Scots) lie
LEG	*noun* limb on which a person or animal walks, runs, or stands
LEI	inflected form of *leu*
LEK	*noun* bird display area; *verb* gather at lek
LEP	dialect word for *leap*
LES	offensive word for *lesbian*
LET	*noun* act of letting property; *verb* obstruct
LEU	*noun* monetary unit of Romania
LEV	*noun* monetary unit of Bulgaria
LEW	*adjective* tepid
LEX	*noun* system or body of laws
LEY	*noun* land under grass

LEZ	offensive word for *lesbian*
LIB	*noun* informal word for liberation; *verb* geld
LID	*noun* movable cover
LIE	*verb* make a false statement; *noun* falsehood
LIG	*noun* function with free entertainment and refreshments; *verb* attend such a function
LIN	*verb* cease
LIP	*noun* either of the fleshy edges of the mouth; *verb* touch with the lips
LIS	*noun* fleur-de-lis
LIT	*noun* (archaic) dye or colouring
LOB	*noun* ball struck in a high arc; *verb* strike in a high arc
LOD	*noun* type of logarithm
LOG	*noun* portion of a felled tree stripped of branches; *verb* saw logs from a tree
LOO	*noun* toilet; *verb* Scots word meaning love
LOP	*verb* cut away; *noun* part(s) lopped off
LOR	exclamation of surprise or dismay
LOS	*noun* approval
LOT	*pronoun* great number; *noun* collection of people or things; *verb* draw lots for
LOU	Scot word for *love*
LOW	*adjective* not high; *adverb* in a low position; *noun* low position; *verb* moo
LOX	*verb* load fuel tanks of spacecraft with liquid oxygen; *noun* kind of smoked salmon
LOY	*noun* narrow spade with a single footrest
LUD	*noun* lord; exclamation of dismay or surprise
LUG	*verb* carry with great effort; *noun* projection serving as a handle

LUM	*noun* chimney
LUN	*noun* sheltered spot
LUR	*noun* large bronze musical horn
LUV	*noun* love; *verb* love
LUX	*noun* unit of illumination; *verb* clean with a vacuum cleaner
LUZ	*noun* supposedly indestructible bone of the human body
LYE	*noun* caustic solution
LYM	*noun* lyam: leash
MAA	*verb* (of goats) bleat
MAC	*noun* macintosh
MAD	*adjective* mentally deranged, insane; *verb* make mad
MAE	*adjective* more
MAG	*verb* talk; *noun* talk
MAK	Scot word for *make*
MAL	*noun* illness
MAM	same as *mother*
MAN	*noun* adult male; *verb* supply with sufficient people for operation or defence
MAP	*noun* representation of the earth's surface or some part of it; *verb* make a map of
MAR	*verb* spoil or impair; *noun* disfiguring mark
MAS	inflected form of *ma*
MAT	*noun* piece of fabric used as a floor covering or to protect a surface; *verb* tangle or become tangled into a dense mass; *adjective* having a dull, lustreless, or roughened surface
MAW	*noun* animal's mouth, throat, or stomach; *verb* eat or bite
MAX	*verb* reach the full extent

MAY	*verb* used as an auxiliary to express possibility, permission, opportunity, etc
MED	*noun* doctor
MEE	*noun* Malaysian noodle dish
MEG	*noun* megabyte: 220 or 1 048 576 bytes
MEH	expression of indifference or boredom
MEL	*noun* pure form of honey
MEM	*noun* thirteenth letter in the Hebrew alphabet, transliterated as *m*
MEN	inflected form of *man*
MES	inflected form of *me*
MET	*noun* meteorology
MEU	*noun* European umbelliferous plant
MEW	*noun* cry of a cat; *verb* utter this cry
MHO	*noun* SI unit of electrical conductance
MIB	*noun* marble used in games
MIC	*noun* microphone
MID	*adjective* intermediate, middle; *noun* middle; *preposition* amid
MIG	*noun* marble used in games
MIL	*noun* unit of length equal to one thousandth of an inch
MIM	*adjective* prim, modest, or demure
MIR	*noun* peasant commune in prerevolutionary Russia
MIS	inflected form of *mi*
MIX	*verb* combine or blend into one mass; *noun* mixture
MIZ	shortened form of *misery*
MMM	*interjection* expressing agreement or enjoyment
MNA	*noun* ancient unit of weight and money, used in Asia Minor

MOA	*noun* large extinct flightless New Zealand bird
MOB	*noun* disorderly crowd; *verb* surround in a mob
MOC	*noun* moccasin: soft leather shoe
MOD	*noun* member of a group of fashionable young people, originally in the 1960s; *verb* modify (a piece of software or hardware)
MOE	*adverb* more; *noun* wry face
MOG	*verb* go away
MOI	*pronoun* (used facetiously) me
MOL	*noun* the SI unit mole
MOM	same as *mother*
MON	dialect variant of *man*
MOO	*noun* long deep cry of a cow; *verb* make this noise; *interjection* instance or imitation of this sound
MOP	*noun* long stick with twists of cotton or a sponge on the end, used for cleaning; *verb* clean or soak up with or as if with a mop
MOR	*noun* layer of acidic humus formed in cool moist areas
MOS	inflected form of *mo*
MOT	*noun* girl or young woman, esp one's girlfriend
MOU	Scots word for *mouth*
MOW	*verb* cut (grass or crops); *noun* part of a barn where hay, straw, etc, is stored
MOY	*noun* coin
MOZ	*noun* hex
MUD	*noun* wet soft earth; *verb* cover in mud
MUG	*noun* large drinking cup; *verb* attack in order to rob
MUM	*noun* mother; *verb* act in a mummer's play
MUN	*verb* maun: dialect word for *must*

MUS	inflected form of *mu*
MUT	another word for *em*
MUX	*verb* spoil
MYC	*noun* oncogene that aids the growth of tumorous cells
NAB	*verb* arrest (someone)
NAE	Scot word for *no*
NAG	*verb* scold or find fault constantly; *noun* person who nags
NAH	same as *no*
NAM	*noun* distraint
NAN	*noun* grandmother
NAP	*noun* short sleep; *verb* have a short sleep
NAS	*verb* has not
NAT	*noun* supporter of nationalism
NAV	short for *navigation*
NAW	same as *no*
NAY	*interjection* no; *noun* person who votes against a motion; *adverb* used for emphasis; *sentence substitute* no
NEB	*noun* beak of a bird or the nose of an animal; *verb* look around nosily
NED	*noun* derogatory name for an adolescent considered to be a hooligan
NEE	*adjective/preposition* indicating the maiden name of a married woman
NEF	*noun* church nave
NEG	*noun* photographic negative
NEK	*noun* mountain pass
NEP	*noun* catmint

NET	*noun* fabric of meshes of string, thread, or wire with many openings; *verb* catch (a fish or animal) in a net; *adjective* left after all deductions
NEW	*adjective* not existing before; *adverb* recently; *verb* make new
NIB	*noun* writing point of a pen; *verb* provide with a nib
NID	*verb* nest
NIE	archaic spelling of *nigh* (near)
NIL	*noun* nothing, zero
NIM	*noun* game involving removing one or more small items from several rows or piles; *verb* steal
NIP	*verb* hurry; *noun* pinch or light bite
NIS	*noun* friendly goblin
NIT	*noun* egg or larva of a louse
NIX	*sentence substitute* be careful! watch out!; *noun* rejection or refusal; *verb* veto, deny, reject, or forbid (plans, suggestions, etc)
NOB	*noun* person of wealth or social distinction
NOD	*verb* lower and raise (one's head) briefly in agreement or greeting; *noun* act of nodding
NOG	*noun* short horizontal timber member
NOH	*noun* stylized classic drama of Japan
NOM	*noun* name
NON	*adverb* not: expressing negation, refusal, or denial
NOO	*noun* type of Japanese musical drama
NOR	*preposition* and not
NOS	inflected form of *no*
NOT	*adverb* expressing negation, refusal, or denial
NOW	*adverb* at or for the present time
NOX	*noun* nitrogen oxide
NOY	*verb* harass

NTH	*adjective* of an unspecified number
NUB	*noun* point or gist (of a story etc); *verb* hang from the gallows
NUG	*noun* lump of wood sawn from a log
NUN	*noun* female member of a religious order
NUR	*noun* wooden ball
NUS	inflected form of *nu*
NUT	*noun* fruit consisting of a hard shell and a kernel; *verb* gather nuts
NYE	*noun* flock of pheasants; *verb* near
NYM	*adjective* as in *nym war* dispute about publishing material online under a pseudonym
NYS	inflected form of *ny*
OAF	*noun* stupid or clumsy person
OAK	*noun* deciduous forest tree
OAR	*noun* pole with a broad blade, used for rowing a boat; *verb* propel with oars
OAT	*noun* hard cereal grown as food
OBA	*noun* (in W Africa) a Yoruba chief or ruler
OBE	*noun* ancient Laconian village
OBI	*noun* broad sash tied in a large flat bow at the back; *verb* bewitch
OBO	*noun* ship carrying oil and ore
OBS	inflected form of *ob*
OCA	*noun* any of various South American herbaceous plants
OCH	expression of surprise, annoyance, or disagreement
ODA	*noun* room in a harem
ODD	*adjective* unusual
ODE	*noun* lyric poem, usually addressed to a particular subject

ODS	inflected form of *od*
OES	inflected form of *oe*
OFF	*preposition* away from; *adverb* away; *adjective* not operating; *noun* side of the field to which the batsman's feet point; *verb* kill
OFT	*adverb* often
OHM	*noun* unit of electrical resistance
OHO	*noun* exclamation expressing surprise, exultation, or derision
OHS	inflected form of *oh*
OIK	*noun* offensive word for a person regarded as inferior because ignorant or lower-class
OIL	*noun* viscous liquid, insoluble in water and usually flammable; *verb* lubricate (a machine) with oil
OIS	inflected form of *oi*
OKA	*noun* unit of weight used in Turkey
OKE	same as *oka*
OLD	*adjective* having lived or existed for a long time; *noun* earlier or past time
OLE	exclamation of approval or encouragement customary at bullfights; *noun* cry of olé
OLM	*noun* pale blind eel-like salamander
OMA	*noun* grandmother
OMS	inflected form of *om*
ONE	*adjective* single, lone; *noun* number or figure 1; *pronoun* any person
ONO	*noun* Hawaiian fish
ONS	inflected form of *on*
ONY	Scots word for *any*
OOF	*noun* money

OOH	exclamation of surprise, pleasure, pain, etc; *verb* say ooh
OOM	*noun* title of respect used to refer to an elderly man
OON	Scots word for *oven*
OOP	*verb* Scots word meaning *bind*
OOR	Scots form of *our*
OOS	inflected form of *oo*
OOT	Scots word for *out*
OPA	*noun* grandfather
OPE	archaic or poetic word for *open*
OPS	inflected form of *op*
OPT	*verb* show a preference, choose
ORA	inflected form of *os*
ORB	*noun* ceremonial decorated sphere; *verb* make or become circular or spherical
ORC	*noun* any of various whales, such as the killer and grampus
ORD	*noun* pointed weapon
ORE	*noun* (rock containing) a mineral which yields metal
ORF	*noun* infectious disease of sheep
ORG	*noun* organization
ORS	inflected form of *or*
ORT	*noun* fragment
OSE	*noun* long ridge of gravel, sand, etc
OUD	*noun* Arabic stringed musical instrument
OUK	Scots word for *week*
OUP	same as *oop*
OUR	*adjective* belonging to us; *determiner* of, belonging to, or associated in some way with us
OUS	inflected form of *ou*

OUT *adjective* denoting movement or distance away from; *verb* name (a public figure) as being homosexual

OVA plural of *ovum* (unfertilized egg cell)

OWE *verb* be obliged to pay (a sum of money) to (a person)

OWL *noun* night bird of prey; *verb* act like an owl

OWN *adjective* used to emphasize possession; *pronoun* thing(s) belonging to a particular person; *verb* possess

OWT dialect word for *anything*

OXO *noun* as in *oxo acid* acid that contains oxygen

OXY inflected form of *ox*

OYE same as *oy*

OYS inflected form of *oy*

PAC *noun* soft shoe

PAD *noun* piece of soft material used for protection, support, absorption of liquid, etc; *verb* protect or fill with soft material

PAH same as *pa*

PAK *noun* pack

PAL *noun* friend; *verb* associate as friends

PAM *noun* knave of clubs

PAN *noun* wide long-handled metal container used in cooking; *verb* sift gravel from (a river) in a pan to search for gold

PAP *noun* soft food for babies or invalids; *verb* (of the paparazzi) to follow and photograph (a famous person); *verb* feed with pap

PAR *noun* usual or average condition; *verb* play (a golf hole) in par

PAS *noun* dance step or movement, esp in ballet

PAT	*verb* tap lightly; *noun* gentle tap or stroke; *adjective* quick, ready, or glib
PAV	*noun* pavlova: meringue cake topped with whipped cream and fruit
PAW	*noun* animal's foot with claws and pads; *verb* scrape with the paw or hoof
PAX	*noun* peace; *interjection* signalling a desire to end hostilities
PAY	*verb* give money etc in return for goods or services; *noun* wages or salary
PEA	*noun* climbing plant with seeds growing in pods
PEC	*noun* pectoral muscle
PED	*noun* pannier
PEE	*verb* vulgar word for *urinate*; *noun* vulgar word for *urine*
PEG	*noun* pin or clip for joining, fastening, marking, etc; *verb* fasten with pegs
PEH	inflected form of *pe*
PEL	*noun* pixel
PEN	*noun* instrument for writing in ink; *verb* write or compose
PEP	*noun* high spirits, energy, or enthusiasm; *verb* liven by imbuing with new vigour
PER	*preposition* for each
PES	*noun* animal part corresponding to the foot
PET	*noun* animal kept for pleasure and companionship; *adjective* kept as a pet; *verb* treat as a pet
PEW	*noun* fixed benchlike seat in a church
PHI	*noun* twenty-first letter in the Greek alphabet
PHO	*noun* Vietnamese noodle soup
PHT	*interjection* expressing irritation or reluctance

PIA	*noun* innermost of the three membranes that cover the brain and the spinal cord
PIC	*noun* photograph or illustration
PIE	*noun* dish of meat, fruit, etc baked in pastry
PIG	*noun* animal kept and killed for pork, ham, and bacon; *verb* eat greedily
PIN	*noun* short thin piece of stiff wire with a point and head, for fastening things; *verb* fasten with a pin
PIP	*noun* small seed in a fruit; *verb* chirp
PIR	*noun* Sufi master
PIS	inflected form of *pi*
PIT	*noun* deep hole in the ground; *verb* mark with small dents or scars
PIU	*adverb* more (quickly, softly, etc)
PIX	less common spelling of *pyx*
PLU	*noun* (formerly in Canada) beaver skin used as a standard unit of value in the fur trade
PLY	*verb* work at (a job or trade); *noun* thickness of wool, fabric, etc
POA	*noun* type of grass
POD	*noun* long narrow seed case of peas, beans, etc; *verb* remove the pod from
POH	exclamation expressing contempt or disgust; *verb* reject contemptuously
POI	*noun* ball of woven flax swung rhythmically by Māori women during poi dances
POL	*noun* political campaigner
POM	*noun* offensive Australian and New Zealand word for an English person
POO	*verb* a childish word for *defecate*
POP	*verb* make or cause to make a small explosive sound; *noun* small explosive sound; *adjective* popular

POS   inflected form of *po*

POT   *noun* round deep container; *verb* plant in a pot

POW   exclamation to indicate that a collision or explosion has taken place; *noun* head or a head of hair

POX   *noun* disease in which skin pustules form; *verb* infect with pox

POZ   *adjective* positive

PRE   *preposition* before

PRO   *preposition* in favour of; *noun* professional; *adverb* in favour of a motion etc

PRY   *verb* make an impertinent or uninvited inquiry into a private matter; *noun* act of prying

PSI   *noun* twenty-third letter of the Greek alphabet

PST   *interjection* sound made to attract someone's attention

PUB   *noun* building with a bar licensed to sell alcoholic drinks; *verb* visit a pub or pubs

PUD   short for *pudding*

PUG   *noun* small snub-nosed dog; *verb* mix or knead (clay) with water to form a malleable mass or paste

PUH   exclamation expressing contempt or disgust

PUL   *noun* Afghan monetary unit

PUN   *noun* use of words to exploit double meanings for humorous effect; *verb* make puns

PUP   *noun* young of certain animals, such as dogs and seals; *verb* (of dogs, seals, etc) to give birth to pups

PUR   same as *purr*

PUS   *noun* yellowish matter produced by infected tissue

PUT   *verb* cause to be (in a position, state, or place); *noun* throw in putting the shot

PUY   *noun* small volcanic cone

PWN *verb* defeat (an opponent) in conclusive and humiliating fashion

PYA *noun* monetary unit of Myanmar worth one hundredth of a kyat

PYE same as *pie*

PYX *noun* any receptacle for the Eucharistic Host; *verb* put (something) in a pyx

QAT variant spelling of *kat*

QIN *noun* Chinese stringed instrument related to the zither

QIS inflected form of *qi*

QUA *preposition* in the capacity of

RAD *noun* former unit of absorbed ionizing radiation dose; *verb* fear; *adjective* slang term for great

RAG *noun* fragment of cloth; *verb* tease; *adjective* (in British universities and colleges) of various events organized to raise money for charity

RAH informal US word for *cheer*

RAI *noun* type of Algerian popular music

RAJ *noun* (in India) government

RAM *noun* male sheep; *verb* strike against with force

RAN inflected form of *run*

RAP *verb* hit with a sharp quick blow; *noun* quick sharp blow

RAS *noun* headland

RAT *noun* small rodent; *verb* inform (on)

RAV *noun* Hebrew word for *rabbi*

RAW *noun* as in *in the raw* without clothes; *adjective* uncooked

RAX *verb* stretch or extend; *noun* act of stretching or straining

RAY	*noun* single line or narrow beam of light; *verb* (of an object) to emit (light) in rays or (of light) to issue in the form of rays
REB	*noun* Confederate soldier in the American Civil War
REC	short for *recreation*
RED	*adjective* of a colour varying from crimson to orange and seen in blood, fire, etc; *noun* red colour
REE	*noun* Scots word meaning a walled enclosure
REF	*noun* referee in sport; *verb* referee
REG	*noun* large expanse of stony desert terrain
REH	*noun* (in India) salty surface crust on the soil
REI	*noun* name for a former Portuguese coin
REM	*noun* dose of ionizing radiation
REN	archaic variant of *run*
REO	*noun* New Zealand language
REP	*noun* sales representative; *verb* work as a representative
RES	informal word for *residence*
RET	*verb* moisten or soak (flax, hemp, jute, etc) to facilitate separation of fibres
REV	*noun* revolution (of an engine); *verb* increase the speed of revolution of (an engine)
REW	archaic spelling of *rue*
REX	*noun* king
REZ	*noun* informal word for an instance of reserving; reservation
RHO	*noun* seventeenth letter in the Greek alphabet
RHY	archaic spelling of *rye*
RIA	*noun* long narrow inlet of the seacoast

RIB	*noun* one of the curved bones forming the framework of the upper part of the body; *verb* provide or mark with ribs
RID	*verb* clear or relieve (of)
RIF	*verb* lay off
RIG	*verb* arrange in a dishonest way; *noun* apparatus for drilling for oil and gas
RIM	*noun* edge or border; *verb* put a rim on (a pot, cup, wheel, etc)
RIN	Scots variant of *run*
RIP	*verb* tear violently; *noun* split or tear
RIT	*verb* Scots word meaning to cut or slit
RIZ	(in some dialects) past form of *rise*
ROB	*verb* steal from
ROC	*noun* monstrous bird of Arabian mythology
ROD	*noun* slender straight bar, stick; *verb* clear with a rod
ROE	*noun* mass of eggs in a fish, sometimes eaten as food
ROK	same as *roc*
ROM	*noun* male gypsy
ROO	*noun* kangaroo
ROT	*verb* decompose or decay; *noun* decay
ROW	*noun* straight line of people or things; *verb* propel (a boat) by oars
RUB	*verb* apply pressure with a circular or backwards-and-forwards movement; *noun* act of rubbing
RUC	same as *roc*
RUD	*noun* red or redness; *verb* redden
RUE	*verb* feel regret for; *noun* plant with evergreen bitter leaves
RUG	*noun* small carpet; *verb* (in dialect) tug

RUM	*noun* alcoholic drink distilled from sugar cane; *adjective* odd, strange
RUN	*verb* move with a more rapid gait than walking; *noun* act or spell of running
RUT	*noun* furrow made by wheels; *verb* be in a period of sexual excitability
RYA	*noun* type of rug originating in Scandinavia
RYE	*noun* kind of grain used for fodder and bread
RYU	*noun* school of Japanese martial arts
SAB	*noun* person engaged in direct action to prevent a targeted activity taking place; *verb* take part in such action
SAC	*noun* pouchlike structure in an animal or plant
SAD	*adjective* sorrowful, unhappy; *verb* New Zealand word meaning to express sadness or displeasure strongly
SAE	Scot word for *so*
SAG	*verb* sink in the middle; *noun* droop
SAI	*noun* South American monkey
SAL	pharmacological term for *salt*
SAM	*verb* collect
SAN	*noun* sanatorium
SAP	*noun* moisture that circulates in plants; *verb* undermine
SAR	*noun* marine fish; *verb* Scots word meaning to savour
SAT	inflected form of *sit*
SAU	archaic past tense of *see*
SAV	*noun* saveloy: spicy smoked sausage
SAW	*noun* hand tool for cutting wood and metal; *verb* cut with a saw
SAX	same as *saxophone*

SAY	*verb* speak or utter; *noun* right or chance to speak
SAZ	*noun* Middle Eastern stringed instrument
SEA	*noun* mass of salt water covering three quarters of the earth's surface
SEC	*noun* secant: (in trigonometry) the ratio of the length of the hypotenuse to the length of the adjacent side
SED	old spelling of *said*
SEE	*verb* perceive with the eyes or mind; *noun* diocese of a bishop
SEG	*noun* metal stud on shoe sole
SEI	*noun* type of rorqual
SEL	Scot word for *self*
SEN	*noun* monetary unit of Brunei, Cambodia, Indonesia, Malaysia, and formerly of Japan
SER	*noun* unit of weight used in India
SET	*verb* put in a specified position or state; *noun* setting or being set; *adjective* fixed or established beforehand
SEV	*noun* Indian snack of deep-fried noodles
SEW	*verb* join with thread repeatedly passed through with a needle
SEX	*noun* state of being male or female; *verb* find out the sex of; *adjective* of sexual matters
SEY	*noun* Scots word meaning part of cow carcase
SEZ	*verb* informal spelling of *says*
SHA	*interjection* be quiet
SHE	*pronoun* female person or animal previously mentioned; *noun* female person or animal
SHH	*interjection* sound made to ask for silence
SHO	*adjective* sure, as pronounced in southern US

SHY	*adjective* not at ease in company; *verb* start back in fear; *noun* throw
SIB	*noun* blood relative
SIC	*adverb* thus; *verb* attack
SIF	*adjective* (South African slang) disgusting
SIG	short for *signature*
SIK	*adjective* excellent
SIM	*noun* computer game that simulates an activity
SIN	*noun* offence or transgression; *verb* commit a sin
SIP	*verb* drink in small mouthfuls; *noun* amount sipped
SIR	*noun* polite term of address for a man; *verb* call someone "sir"
SIS	*noun* sister
SIT	*verb* rest one's body upright on the buttocks
SIX	*noun* one more than five
SKA	*noun* type of West Indian pop music of the 1960s
SKI	*noun* one of a pair of long runners fastened to boots for gliding over snow or water; *verb* travel on skis
SKY	*noun* upper atmosphere as seen from the earth; *verb* hit high in the air
SLY	*adjective* crafty
SMA	Scots word for *small*
SNY	*noun* side channel of a river
SOB	*verb* weep with convulsive gasps; *noun* act or sound of sobbing
SOC	*noun* feudal right to hold court
SOD	*noun* (piece of) turf; *verb* cover with sods
SOG	*verb* soak
SOH	*noun* (in tonic sol-fa) fifth degree of any major scale
SOL	*noun* liquid colloidal solution

SOM	*noun* currency of Kyrgyzstan and Uzbekistan
SON	*noun* male offspring
SOP	*noun* concession to pacify someone; *verb* mop up or absorb (liquid)
SOS	inflected form of *so*
SOT	*noun* habitual drunkard; *adverb* indeed: used to contradict a negative statement; *verb* be a drunkard
SOU	*noun* former French coin
SOV	shortening of *sovereign*
SOW	*verb* scatter or plant (seed) in or on (the ground); *noun* female adult pig
SOX	informal spelling of *socks*
SOY	*noun* as in *soy sauce* salty dark brown sauce made from soya beans
SOZ	*interjection* (slang) sorry
SPA	*noun* resort with a mineral-water spring; *verb* visit a spa
SPY	*noun* person employed to obtain secret information; *verb* act as a spy
SRI	*noun* title of respect used when addressing a Hindu
STY	*verb* climb
SUB	*noun* subeditor; *verb* act as a substitute
SUD	singular of *suds*
SUE	*verb* start legal proceedings against
SUG	*verb* sell a product while pretending to conduct market research
SUI	*adjective* of itself
SUK	*noun* souk: open-air marketplace
SUM	*noun* result of addition, total; *verb* add or form a total of (something)

SUN	*noun* star around which the earth and other planets revolve; *verb* expose (oneself) to the sun's rays
SUP	*verb* have supper
SUQ	same as *suk*
SUR	*preposition* above
SUS	suss: *verb* attempt to work out (a situation, etc), using one's intuition; *noun* sharpness of mind
SWY	*noun* Australian gambling game involving two coins
SYE	*verb* strain
SYN	Scots word for *since*
TAB	*noun* small flap or projecting label; *verb* supply with a tab
TAD	*noun* small bit or piece
TAE	*preposition* Scots form of *to*; *verb* Scots form of *toe*
TAG	*noun* label bearing information; *verb* attach a tag to
TAI	*noun* type of sea bream
TAJ	*noun* tall conical cap worn as a mark of distinction by Muslims
TAK	Scots variant spelling of *take*
TAM	*noun* type of hat
TAN	*noun* brown coloration of the skin from exposure to sunlight; *verb* (of skin) go brown from exposure to sunlight; *adjective* yellowish-brown
TAO	*noun* (in Confucian philosophy) the correct course of action
TAP	*verb* knock lightly and usually repeatedly; *noun* light knock
TAR	*noun* thick black liquid distilled from coal etc; *verb* coat with tar
TAS	tass: *noun* cup, goblet, or glass

TAT	*noun* tatty or tasteless article(s); *verb* make a type of lace by looping a thread with a hand shuttle
TAU	*noun* nineteenth letter in the Greek alphabet
TAV	*noun* twenty-third and last letter in the Hebrew alphabet
TAW	*verb* convert skins into leather
TAX	*noun* compulsory payment levied by a government on income, property, etc to raise revenue; *verb* levy a tax on
TAY	Irish dialect word for *tea*
TEA	*noun* drink made from infusing the dried leaves of an Asian bush in boiling water; *verb* take tea
TEC	short for *detective*
TED	*verb* shake out (hay), so as to dry it
TEE	*noun* small peg from which a golf ball can be played at the start of each hole; *verb* position (the ball) ready for striking, on or as if on a tee
TEF	*noun* annual grass, of NE Africa, grown for its grain
TEG	*noun* two-year-old sheep
TEL	same as *tell*
TEN	*noun* one more than nine; *adjective* amounting to ten
TES	inflected form of *te*
TET	*noun* ninth letter of the Hebrew alphabet
TEW	*verb* work hard
TEX	*noun* unit of weight used to measure yarn density
THE	*determiner* definite article, used before a noun
THO	short for *though*
THY	*adjective* of or associated with you (thou); *determiner* belonging to or associated in some way with you (thou)

TIC   *noun* spasmodic muscular twitch

TID   *noun* girl

TIE   *verb* fasten or be fastened with string, rope, etc; *noun* long narrow piece of material worn knotted round the neck

TIG   *noun* child's game

TIK   *noun* (South African slang) crystal meth

TIL   another name for *sesame*

TIN   *noun* soft metallic element; *verb* put (food) into tins

TIP   *noun* narrow or pointed end of anything; *verb* put a tip on

TIS   inflected form of *ti*

TIT   *noun* any of various small songbirds; *verb* jerk or tug

TIX   *plural noun* tickets

TIZ   *noun* state of confusion

TOC   *noun* in communications code, signal for letter T

TOD   *noun* unit of weight, used for wool, etc; *verb* produce a tod

TOE   *noun* digit of the foot; *verb* touch or kick with the toe

TOG   *noun* unit for measuring the insulating power of duvets; *verb* dress oneself

TOM   *noun* male cat; *adjective* (of an animal) male; *verb* (offensive) prostitute oneself

TON   *noun* unit of weight

TOO   *adverb* also, as well

TOP   *noun* highest point or part; *adjective* at or of the top; *verb* form a top on

TOR   *noun* high rocky hill

TOT   *noun* small child; *verb* total

TOW	*verb* drag, esp by means of a rope; *noun* towing
TOY	*noun* something designed to be played with; *adjective* designed to be played with; *verb* play, fiddle, or flirt
TRY	*verb* make an effort or attempt; *noun* attempt or effort
TSK	*verb* utter the sound "tsk", usually in disapproval
TUB	*noun* open, usually round container; *verb* wash (oneself or another) in a tub
TUG	*verb* pull hard; *noun* hard pull
TUI	*noun* New Zealand honeyeater that mimics human speech and the songs of other birds
TUM	informal or childish word for *stomach*
TUN	*noun* large beer cask; *verb* put into or keep in tuns
TUP	*noun* male sheep; *verb* cause (a ram) to mate with a ewe
TUT	exclamation of mild disapproval, or surprise; *verb* express disapproval by the exclamation of "tut-tut"; *noun* payment system based on measurable work done
TUX	*noun* tuxedo: dinner jacket
TWA	Scots word for *two*
TWO	*noun* one more than one
TWP	*adjective* stupid
TYE	*noun* trough used in mining to separate valuable material from dross; *verb* (in mining) isolate valuable material from dross using a tye
TYG	*noun* mug with two handles
UDO	*noun* stout perennial plant of Japan and China
UDS	*interjection* God's or God save
UEY	*noun* u-turn

UFO	*noun* flying saucer
UGH	exclamation of disgust; *noun* sound made to indicate disgust
UGS	inflected form of *ug*
UKE	short form of *ukulele*
ULE	*noun* rubber tree
ULU	*noun* type of knife
UMM	same as *um*
UMP	umpire: *noun* official who rules on the playing of a game; *verb* act as umpire in (a game)
UMS	inflected form of *um*
UMU	*noun* type of oven
UNI	*noun* (in informal English) university
UNS	inflected form of *un*
UPO	*preposition* upon
UPS	inflected form of *up*
URB	*noun* urban area
URD	*noun* type of plant with edible seeds
URE	*noun* recently extinct European wild ox
URN	*noun* vase used as a container for the ashes of the dead; *verb* put in an urn
URP	dialect word for *vomit*
USE	*verb* put into service or action; *noun* using or being used
UTA	*noun* side-blotched lizard
UTE	same as *utility*
UTS	inflected form of *ut*
UTU	*noun* reward
UVA	*noun* grape or fruit resembling this
VAC	*verb* clean with a vacuum cleaner

VAE	same as *voe*
VAG	*noun* vagrant
VAN	*noun* motor vehicle for transporting goods; *verb* send in a van
VAR	*noun* unit of reactive power of an alternating current
VAS	*noun* vessel or tube that carries a fluid
VAT	*noun* large container for liquids; *verb* place, store, or treat in a vat
VAU	same as *vav*
VAV	*noun* sixth letter of the Hebrew alphabet
VAW	*noun* Hebrew letter
VEE	*noun* letter V
VEG	*noun* vegetable or vegetables; *verb* relax
VET	*verb* check the suitability of; *noun* military veteran
VEX	*verb* frustrate, annoy
VIA	*preposition* by way of; *noun* road
VID	same as *video*
VIE	*verb* compete (with someone)
VIG	*noun* interest on a loan that is paid to a moneylender
VIM	*noun* force, energy
VIN	*noun* French wine
VIS	*noun* power, force, or strength
VLY	*noun* area of low marshy ground
VOE	*noun* (in Orkney and Shetland) a small bay or narrow creek
VOG	*noun* air pollution caused by volcanic dust
VOL	*noun* heraldic wings
VOM	*verb* vomit
VOR	*verb* (in dialect) warn

VOW	*noun* solemn and binding promise; *verb* promise solemnly
VOX	*noun* voice or sound
VUG	*noun* small cavity in a rock or vein, usually lined with crystals
VUM	*verb* swear
WAB	*noun* web
WAD	*noun* black earthy ore of manganese; *noun* small mass of soft material; *verb* form (something) into a wad
WAE	old form of *woe*
WAG	*verb* move rapidly from side to side; *noun* wagging movement
WAI	*noun* (in New Zealand) water
WAN	*adjective* pale and sickly looking; *verb* make or become wan
WAP	*verb* strike
WAR	*noun* fighting between nations; *adjective* of, like, or caused by war; *verb* conduct a war
WAS	past tense of *be*
WAT	*adjective* wet; drunken
WAW	another name for *vav*
WAX	*noun* solid shiny fatty or oily substance used for sealing, making candles, etc; *verb* coat or polish with wax
WAY	*noun* manner or method; *verb* travel
WAZ	*verb* urinate; *noun* act of urinating
WEB	*noun* net spun by a spider; *verb* cover with or as if with a web
WED	*verb* marry

WEE	*adjective* small or short; *noun* instance of urinating; *verb* urinate
WEM	*noun* belly, abdomen, or womb
WEN	*noun* cyst on the scalp
WET	*adjective* covered or soaked with water or another liquid; *noun* moisture or rain; *verb* make wet
WEX	obsolete form of *wax*
WEY	*noun* measurement of weight
WHA	Scots word for *who*
WHO	*pronoun* which person
WHY	*adverb* for what reason; *pronoun* because of which; *noun* reason, purpose, or cause of something
WIG	*noun* artificial head of hair; *verb* furnish with a wig
WIN	*verb* come first in (a competition, fight, etc); *noun* victory, esp in a game
WIS	*verb* know or suppose (something)
WIT	*verb* detect; *noun* ability to use words or ideas in a clever and amusing way
WIZ	shortened form of *wizard*
WOE	*noun* grief
WOF	*noun* fool
WOG	*noun* offensive and derogatory word for a foreigner, esp one who is not White
WOK	*noun* bowl-shaped Chinese cooking pan, used for stir-frying
WON	*noun* standard monetary unit of North Korea; *verb* live or dwell
WOO	*verb* seek the love or affection of (a woman)
WOP	*verb* strike, beat, or thrash; *noun* heavy blow or the sound made by such a blow

WOS	inflected form of *wo*
WOT	past tense of *wit*
WOW	exclamation of astonishment; *noun* astonishing person or thing; *verb* be a great success with
WOX	past tense of *wax*
WRY	*adjective* drily humorous; *verb* twist or contort
WUD	Scots form of *wood*
WUS	*noun* casual term of address
WUZ	*verb* nonstandard spelling of *was*
WYE	*noun* y-shaped pipe
WYN	*noun* rune equivalent to English w
XED	*verb* marked a cross against
XIS	inflected form of *xi*
YAD	*noun* hand-held pointer used for reading the sefer torah
YAE	same as *ae*
YAG	*noun* artificial crystal
YAH	exclamation of derision or disgust; *noun* affected upper-class person
YAK	*noun* Tibetan ox with long shaggy hair; *verb* talk continuously about unimportant matters
YAM	*noun* tropical root vegetable
YAP	*verb* bark with a high-pitched sound; *noun* high-pitched bark
YAR	*adjective* nimble
YAS	inflected form of *ya*
YAW	*verb* (of an aircraft or ship) turn to one side or from side to side while moving; *noun* act or movement of yawing
YAY	*noun* cry of approval

YEA	*interjection* yes; *adverb* indeed or truly; *sentence substitute* aye; *noun* cry of agreement
YEH	*noun* positive affirmation
YEN	*noun* monetary unit of Japan; *verb* have a longing
YEP	*noun* affirmative statement
YER	*adjective* (colloquial) your; you
YES	*interjection* expresses consent, agreement, or approval; *noun* answer or vote of yes, used to express acknowledgment, affirmation, consent, etc; *verb* reply in the affirmative
YET	*adverb* up until then or now
YEW	*noun* evergreen tree with needle-like leaves and red berries
YEX	*verb* hiccup
YEZ	*interjection* yes
YGO	archaic past participle of *go*
YID	*noun* offensive word for a Jew
YIN	Scots word for *one*
YIP	*noun* emit a high-pitched bark
YOB	*noun* bad-mannered aggressive youth
YOD	*noun* tenth letter in the Hebrew alphabet
YOK	*verb* chuckle
YOM	*noun* day
YON	*adjective* that or those over there; *adverb* yonder *pronoun* that person or thing
YOU	*pronoun* person or people addressed; *noun* personality of the person being addressed
YOW	*verb* howl
YUG	*noun* (in Hindu cosmology) one of the four ages of mankind

YUK	exclamation indicating contempt, dislike, or disgust; *verb* chuckle
YUM	expression of delight
YUP	*noun* informal affirmative statement
YUS	inflected form of *yu*
ZAG	*verb* change direction sharply
ZAP	*verb* kill (by shooting); *noun* energy, vigour, or pep; exclamation used to express sudden or swift action
ZAS	inflected form of *za*
ZAX	*noun* tool for cutting roofing slate
ZEA	*noun* corn silk
ZED	*noun* British and New Zealand spoken form of the letter Z
ZEE	the US word for *zed*
ZEK	*noun* Soviet prisoner
ZEL	*noun* Turkish cymbal
ZEP	*noun* type of long sandwich
ZEX	*noun* tool for cutting roofing slate
ZHO	same as *zo*
ZIG	same as *zag*
ZIN	*noun* zinfandel: type of Californian wine
ZIP	same as *zipper*
ZIT	*noun* spot or pimple
ZIZ	*noun* short sleep; *verb* take a short sleep, snooze
ZOA	plural of *zoon* (independent animal body)
ZOL	*noun* (South African slang) a cannabis cigarette
ZOO	*noun* place where live animals are kept for show
ZOS	inflected form of *zo*
ZUZ	*noun* ancient Hebrew silver coin
ZZZ	*noun* informal word for *sleep*